Italian
phrase book

Berlitz Publishing Company, Inc.

Princeton   Mexico City   Dublin   Eschborn   Singapore

Contents

Pronunciation

This section is designed to make you familiar with the sounds of Italian using our simplified phonetic transcription. You'll find the pronunciation of the Italian letters and sounds explained below, together with their "imitated" equivalents. This system is used throughout the phrase book: simply read the pronunciation as if it were English, noting any special rules below.

The Italian language

There are approximately 64 million speakers of Italian. These are the countries where you can expect to hear Italian spoken (figures are approximate):

Italia Italy

Italian is the national language, spoken by almost the entire population (59 million). Other languages: Sardinian in Sardinia (1.5 million); Rhaeto-Romanic in Friuli, near the border with Slovenia and Austria.

Svizzera Switzerland

Italian is one of the four official languages, spoken by about 800,000 people in the southern part of the country, particularly the canton of Ticino (capital: Bellinzona). Other languages: German in the north (5 milllion); French in the west (1.3 million), Romansch in the east (50,000).

Italian is also spoken amongst large Italian emigré communities, particularly in the United States (**Stati Uniti**), with almost 1.5 million speakers, and Canada (**Canada**), with over half a million speakers.

The Italian alphabet is the same as English, with the addition of accents which indicate stress only (see below). However, the letters **j**, **k**, **w**, **x** and **y** only appear in foreign words.

English has absorbed numerous Italian words, for example: **balcony**, **studio**, **umbrella**, **volcano** as well as many terms in the fields of food (e.g. **broccoli**, **macaroni**, **pizza**, **spaghetti**) and music (e.g. **concerto**, **piano**, **solo**, **trio**, **viola**).

Consonants

Letter	Approximate pronunciation	Symbol	Example	
b, d, f, k, l, l, m, n, p, q, t, v	as in English			
c	1) before **e** and **i**, like *ch* in *ch*ip	ch	cerco	*ch<u>ay</u>rko*
	2) elsewhere, like *c* in *c*at	k	conto	*konto*
ch	like *c* in *c*at	k	che	*kay*
g	1) before **e** and **i**, like *j* in *j*et	j	valigia	*val<u>ee</u>ja*
	2) elsewhere, like *g* in *g*o	g	grande	*gr<u>an</u>day*
gh	like *g* in *g*o	g	ghiaccio	*gee<u>a</u>cho*
gl	like *lli* in mi*lli*on	ly	gli	*lyee*
gn	like *ni* in o*ni*on	ñ	bagno	*baño*
h	always silent		ha	*ah*
r	trilled like a Scottish *r*	r	deriva	*deh<u>ree</u>va*
s	1) generally like *s* in *s*it	s	questo	*kw<u>ay</u>sto*
	2) sometimes like *z* in *z*oo	z	viso	*v<u>ee</u>zo*
sc	1) before **e** and **i**, like *sh* in *sh*ut	sh	uscita	*oosh<u>ee</u>ta*
	2) elsewhere, like *sk* in *sk*in	sk	scarpa	*sk<u>a</u>rpa*
z/zz	1) generally like *ts* in hi*ts*	ts	grazie	*gr<u>aa</u>tseeay*
	2) sometimes like *ds* in roa*ds*	dz	romanzo	*rom<u>an</u>dzo*

Vowels

a	1) short. like *a* in c*a*t	a	gatto	*gatto*
	2) long, like *a* in f*a*ther	aa	casa	*k<u>aa</u>sa*
e	1) can always be pronounced like *ay* in w*ay*, but without moving tongue or lips	ay	sera	*s<u>ay</u>ra*
	2) in correct speech, it is sometimes pronounced like *e* in g*e*t or, when long, more like *ai* in h*ai*r	eh	bello	*beh<u>llo</u>*

Vowels

i	like *ee* in m*ee*t	ee	**vini**	v<u>ee</u>nee
o	can always be pronounced like *o* in g*o*,	o	**sole**	s<u>o</u>lay
u	1. like *oo* in f*oo*t	oo	**fumo**	f<u>oo</u>mo
	2. like *w* in *w*ell	w	**buono**	bw<u>o</u>no

Two or more vowels

In groups of vowels **a**, **e** and **o** are strong, and **i** and **u** are weak vowels. The following combinations occur:

two strong vowels	pronounced as two separate syllables	**beato**	bay-<u>aa</u>to
a stong vowel and a weak vowel	1) the weak one is pronounced more quickly and with less stress than the strong one; such sounds are diphthongs and constitute only one syllable:	**piede**	pee<u>ay</u>day
	2) if the weak vowel is stressed, then it is pronounced as a separate syllable	**due**	d<u>oo</u>-ay
two weak vowels	pronounced as a dipthong; it is generally the second one that is more strongly stressed	**guida**	gw<u>ee</u>da

Stress

Stress has been indicated in the phonetic transcription by underlining the letters that should be pronounced louder than the others.

Generally, the vowel of the next to last syllable is stressed.

When a final vowel is stressed, it has an accent written over it (**caffè**).

Normally, when the stress falls on the syllable before the next to last one, it is not indicated by an accent.

Pronunciation of the Italian alphabet

A	*ah*	**N**	*ehnnay*
B	*bee*	**O**	*o*
C	*chee*	**P**	*pee*
D	*dee*	**Q**	*koo*
E	*ay*	**R**	*ehrray*
F	*ehffay*	**S**	*ehssay*
G	*jee*	**T**	*tee*
H	*aaka*	**U**	*oo*
I	*ee*	**V**	*voo*
J	*ee loongga*	**W**	*voo doppeea*
K	*kaappa*	**X**	*eeks*
L	*ehllay*	**Y**	*ee grayka*
M	*ehmmay*	**Z**	*dzaytah*

Basic Expressions

ESSENTIAL

Yes.	**Sì.** *see*
No.	**No.** *no*
Okay.	**D'accordo./Va bene.** *daakordo/va baynay*
Please.	**Per piacere./Per favore.** *pehr peeachayray/pehr favoray*
Thank you (very much).	**(Mille) grazie.** *(meellay) graatseeay*

Greetings/apologies   Saluti e scuse

Hello/Hi!	**Salve./Ciao!** *saalvay/chaao*
Good morning.	**Buongiorno.** *bwon jorno*
Good afternoon (from 1 p.m.).	**Buonasera.** *bwona sayra*
Good evening.	**Buonasera.** *bwona sayra*
Good night.	**Buonanotte.** *bwona nottay*
Good-bye.	**Arrivederci.** *arreevaydehrchee*
Excuse me! (getting attention)	**Scusi!** *skoozee*
Excuse me. (may I get past?)	**Permesso?** *pehrmehsso*
Excuse me!/Sorry!	**Scusi!/Sono spiacente!** *skoozee/sono speeachehntay*
It was an accident.	**È stato un incidente.** *eh staato oon eencheedehntay*
Don't mention it.	**Prego.** *praygo*
Never mind.	**Non importa.** *non eemporta*

Communication difficulties
Difficoltà di comunicazione

Do you speak English? **Parla inglese?**
parla eengglaysay

Does anyone here speak English? **C'è qualcuno qui che parla inglese?**
cheh kwalkoono kwee kay parla eengglaysay

I don't speak (very well) Italian. **Non parlo italiano (molto bene).**
non parlo eetaleeaano (molto baynay)

Could you speak more slowly? **Può parlare più lentamente?**
pwo parlaaray peeoo layntamayntay

Could you repeat that? **Può ripetere?** *pwo reepehtayray*

Pardon?/What was that? **Prego?/Cosa ha detto?**
praygo/kosa ah daytto

Could you spell it? **Come si scrive?**
komay see skreevay

Please write it down. **Lo scriva, per piacere.**
lo skreeva pehr peeachayray

Can you translate this for me? **Può tradurre questo?**
pwo tradoorray kwaysto

What does this/that mean? **Cosa significa questo/quello?**
kosa seeñeefeeka kwaysto/kwayllo

Please point to the phrase in the book. **Per piacere, indichi la frase nel libro.**
pehr peeachayray eendeekee la fraazay nel leebro

I understand. **Capisco.** *kapeesko*

I don't understand. **Non capisco.** *non kapeesko*

Do you understand? **Capisce?** *kapeeshay*

– *Fa tredicimila cinquecento lire.*
– Non capisco.
– *Fa tredicimila cinquecento lire.*
– Lo scriva, per piacere …
Ah. "13,500 lire" … Ecco.

11

Questions Domande

GRAMMAR

Questions can be formed in Italian:
1. by a questioning intonation
   (note that the personal pronoun is rarely used):

Parlo italiano.	I speak Italian.
Parla italiano?	Do you speak Italian?

2. by using a question word (➤12-17) + the inverted order:

Quando apre il museo?	When does the museum open?

Where? Dove?

Where is it?	**Dov'è?** *doveh*
Where are you going?	**Dove va?** *dovay va*
at the meeting place/point	**al punto d'incontro** *al poonto deenkontro*
away from me	**lontano da me** *lontaano da meh*
downstairs	**al piano inferiore** *al peeaano eenfayreeoray*
from the U.S.	**dagli Stati Uniti** *daalyee staatee ooneetee*
here (to here)	**(da) qui** *(da) kwee*
in the car	**in automobile** *een owtomobeelay*
in Italy	**in Italia** *een eetaaleea*
inside	**dentro** *dayntro*
near the bank	**vicino alla banca** *veecheeno alla banka*
next to the apples	**accanto alle mele** *akkanto allay maylay*
opposite the market	**di fronte al mercato** *dee frontay al mayrkaato*
on the left/right	**a sinistra/a destra** *ah seeneestra/ah daystra*
there (to there)	**là** *la*
to the hotel	**all'albergo** *allalbehrgo*
toward Florence	**verso Firenze** *vehrso feerehnzay*
outside the café	**fuori del bar** *fworee dayl baar*
upstairs	**al piano superiore** *al peeaano soopayreeoray*

When? Quando?

When does the museum open?	**Quando apre il museo?** _kwando_ apray eel _moozeho_
When does the train arrive?	**Quando arriva il treno?** _kwando_ arreeva eel _trayno_
10 minutes ago	**Dieci minuti fa** dee-_ehchee_ meenootee fa
after lunch	**dopo pranzo** _dopo prandzo_
always	**sempre** _sehmpray_
around midnight	**verso mezzanotte** _vehrso mehdzanottay_
at 7 o'clock	**alle sette** _allay sehttay_
before Friday	**prima di venerdì** _preema dee vaynayrdee_
by tomorrow	**entro domani** _ayntro domaanee_
early	**di buon'ora** dee bwonora
every week	**ogni settimana/tutte le settimane** _oñee saytteemaana/toottay lay saytteemaanay_
for 2 hours	**per due ore** pehr _doo-ay_ oray
from 9 a.m. to 6 p.m.	**dalle nove alle diciotto** _dallay novay allay deechotto_
immediately	**immediatamente** eemaydeeatamayntay
in 20 minutes	**in venti minuti** een _vayntee_ meenootee
never	**non mai** non _maee_
not yet	**non ancora** non _ankora_
now	**ora/adesso** _ora/adehsso_
often	**sovente/spesso** so_vayntay/spehsso_
on March 8	**l'otto marzo** _lotto martso_
on weekdays	**nei giorni feriali** _nayee jornee fehreeaalee_
sometimes	**qualche volta** _kwalkay volta_
soon	**presto/fra poco** _prehsto/fra poko_
then	**poi** _poee_
within 2 days	**entro due giorni** _ayntro doo-ay jornee_

What sort of …? Che tipo di …?

I'd like something … **Vorrei qualcosa …** *vorrehee kwalkosa*

It's … **È** *eh*

beautiful/ugly	**bellissimo(-a)/brutto(-a)** *behlleesseemo(-a)/brootto(-a)*
better/worse	**migliore/peggiore** *meelyoray/paydjoray*
big/small	**grande/piccolo(-a)** *granday/peekkolo(-a)*
cheap/expensive	**a buon prezzo/caro(-a)** *a bwon pretso/kaaro(-a)*
clean/dirty	**pulito(-a)/sporco(-a)** *pooleeto(-a)/sporko(-a)*
dark/light	**scuro(-a)/chiaro(-a)** *skooro(-a)/keeahro(-a)*
delicious/revolting	**delizioso(-a)/disgustoso(-a)** *dehleetzeeozo(-a)/deesgoostozo(-a)*
easy/difficult	**facile/difficile** *faacheelay/deeffeecheelay*
empty/full	**vuoto(-a)/pieno(-a)** *vwoto(-a)/peeayno(-a)*
good/bad	**buono(-a)/cattivo(-a)** *bwono(-a)/katteevo(-a)*
heavy/light	**pesante/leggero(-a)** *paysantay/laydjehro(-a)*
hot/warm/cold	**molto caldo(-a)/caldo(-a)/freddo(-a)** *molto kaldo(-a)/kaldo(-a)/frayddo(-a)*
modern/old-fashioned	**moderno(-a)/antiquato(-a)** *modayrno(-a)/anteekwato(-a)*
narrow/wide	**stretto(-a)/largo(-a)** *straytto(-a)/lahrgo(-a)*
old/new	**vecchio(-a)/nuovo(-a)** *vehkkeeao(-a)/nwovo(-a)*
open/shut	**aperto(-a)/chiuso(-a)** *apehrto(-a)/keeooso(-a)*
pleasant, nice/unpleasant	**gradevole/bello(-a)/sgradevole** *grahdayvolay/behllo(-a)/zgradayvolay*
quick/slow	**veloce/lento(-a)** *vaylochay/laynto(-a)*
right/wrong	**guisto(-a)/sbaglaito(-a)** *joosto(-a) zbalyaato(-a)*
tall/short	**alto(-a)/basso(-a)** *alto(-a)/basso(-a)*
vacant/occupied	**libero(-a)/occupato(-a)** *leebayro(-a)/okoopaato(-a)*

How much/many? Quanto/quanti?

GRAMMAR

> Nouns in Italian are either masculine or feminine and the adjectival endings change accordingly. See page 169 for more explanation.

How much is that?	**Quanto costa?** _kwanto kosta_
How many are there?	**Quanti ce ne sono?** _kwantee cheh neh sono_
1/2/3	**uno(-a)/due/tre** _oono(-a)/doo-ay/tray_
4/5	**quattro/cinque** _kwattro/cheenkway_
none	**nessuno(-a)** _nayssoono(-a)_
about 10,000 lira	**circa diecimila lire** _cheerka dee-ehcheemeela leeray_
a little	**un poco** _oon poko_
a lot of traffic	**molto traffico** _molto traffeeko_
enough (adv/adj)	**abbastanza/sufficiente** _abbastantsa/soofeecheeayntay_
few/a few of them	**alcuni(-e)/alcuni(-e) di loro** _alkoonee(-ay)/alkoonee(-ay) dee loro_
more than that	**più di quello(-a)** _peeoo dee kwayllo(-a)_
less than that	**meno di quello(-a)** _mayno dee kwayllo(-a)_
much more	**molto di più** _molto dee peeoo_
nothing else	**nient'altro** _neeayntaltro_
too much	**troppo(-a)** _troppo(-a)_

Why? Perchè?

Why is that?	**Perchè?** _pehrkay_
Why not?	**Perchè no?** _pehrkay no_
because of the weather	**a causa del tempo** _a kowsa dayl tehmpo_
because I'm in a hurry	**perchè ho fretta** _pehrkay o fraytta_
I don't know why	**non so perchè** _non so pehrkay_

NUMBERS ➤ 216

Who?/Which? Chi?/Quale?

Who's there	**Chi è?** *kee eh*
It's me!	**Sono io!** *sono eeo*
It's us!	**Siamo noi!** *seeamo noee*
someone	**qualcuno** *kwalkoono*
no one	**nessuno** *nayssoono*
Which one do you want?	**Quale vuole?** *kwalay vwolay*
one like that	**uno(-a) come quello(-a)** *oono(-a) komay kwayllo(-a)*
that one/this one	**quello(-a)/questo(-a)** *kwayllo(-a)/kwaysto(-a)*
not that one	**non quello(-a)** *non kwayllo(-a)*
something	**qualcosa** *kwalkosa*
nothing	**nulla** *noolla*
none	**nessuno(-a)** *nayssoono(-a)*

Whose? Di chi?

Whose is that?	**Di chi è quello(-a)?** *dee kee eh kwayllo(-a)*
It's …	**È …** *eh*
mine/ours	**mio(-a)/nostro(-a)** *meeo(-a)/nostro(-a)*
yours (formal)/yours (fam)	**Suo(-a)/tuo(-a)** *soo-o(-a)/too-o(-a)*
his/hers/theirs	**suo(-a)/di lui (di lei)/loro** *soo-o(-a)/dee looee(di layee)/loro*

GRAMMAR

Possessive adjectives and pronouns

	masculine singular	masculine plural	feminine singular	feminine plural
my, mine	il mio	i miei	la mia	le mie
your, yours	il tuo	i tuoi	la tua	le tue
his, her, hers, its	il suo	i suoi	la sua	le sue
our, ours	il nostro	i nostri	la nostra	le nostre
your, yours	il vostro	i vostri	la vostra	le vostre
their, theirs,	il loro	i loro	la loro	le loro
*your, yours (sing.)	il suo	i suoi	la sua	le sue
*your, yours (plur.)	il loro	i loro	la loro	le loro

*These are the formal forms – used when addressing people you do not know well.

16

How? Come?

How would you like to pay?	**Come desidera pagare?** *komay dayzeedayra pagaaray*
How are you getting here?	**Come arriva qui?** *komay arreeva kwee*
by car	**in automobile/in macchina** *een owtomobeelay/een makkeena*
by credit card	**con carta di credito** *kon karta dee kraydeeto*
by chance	**per caso** *pehr kazo*
(fairly, justly) equally	**equamente** *aykwamayntay*
extremely	**estremamente** *aystraymamayntay*
on foot	**a piedi** *a peeaydee*
quickly	**presto** *prehsto*
slowly	**lentamente** *lehntamayntay*
too fast	**troppo veloce** *troppo vehlochay*
totally	**totalmente** *totalmayntay*
very	**molto** *molto*
with a friend	**con un amico/un'amica** *kon oon ameeko/ameeka*

Is it ...?/Are there ...? È ...?/Ci sono ...?

Is it ...?	**È ...?** *eh*
Is it free (unoccupied)?	**È libero(-a)?** *eh leebayro(-a)*
It isn't ready.	**Non è pronto(-a).** *non eh pronto(-a)*
Is there ...?	**C'è ...?** *cheh*
Are there ...?	**Ci sono ...?** *chee sono*
Is there a bus into town?	**C'è un autobus per il centro?** *cheh oon owtobooss pehr eel chayntro*
Are there buses to the airport?	**Ci sono autobus per l'aeroporto?** *chee sono owtobooss pehr la-ayroporto*
Here it is/they are.	**Eccolo(-a)/eccoli(-e).** *ehkkolo/ehkkolee*
There it is/they are.	**È là/sono là** *eh la/sono la*

17

Can/May? Potere?

Can I have …?	**Posso avere …?** *posso avayray*
Can we have …?	**Possiamo avere …?** *posseeamo avayray*
Can you tell me?	**Può dirmi …?** *pwo deermee*
Can you help me?	**Può aiutarmi?** *pwo aeeootaarmee*
Can I help you?	**Posso aiutare?** *posso aeeootaaray*
Can you direct me to …?	**Può indicarmi la via per …?** *pwo eendeekaarmee la veea pehr*
I can't.	**Non posso.** *non posso*

What do you want? Cosa desidera?/vuole?

I'd like …	**Vorrei…..** *vorrehee*
Do you have …?	**Ha…….?** *ah*
We'd like …	**Vorremmo …** *vorrehmmo*
Give me …	**Mi dia …** *mee deea*
I'm looking for …	**Cerco …** *chayrko*
I need to …	**Ho bisogno di …** *o beezoño dee*
go …	**andare …** *andaaray*
find …	**trovare…..** *trovaaray*
see …	**vedere …** *vaydayray*
speak to …	**parlare a …** *parlaaray ah*

– Scusi.
– Sì?
– Può aiutarmi?
– Sì, certamente.
– Ho bisogno di parlare al Signor Gambetti.
– Un momento, per favore.

Other useful words
Altre parole utili

fortunately	**fortunatamente** *fortoonatamayntay*
hopefully	**con (la) speranza di** *kon (la) spayrantsa dee*
of course	**naturalmente** *natooralmayntay*
perhaps/possibly	**forse/possibilmente** *forsay/posseebeelmayntay*
probably	**probabilmente** *probabeelmayntay*
unfortunately	**sfortunatamente** *sfortoonatamayntay*

Exclamations   Esclamazioni

At last!	**Finalmente!** *feenalmayntay*
Damn!	**Maledizione!** *malaydeetseeonay*
Go on.	**Continui.** *konteenooee*
Good Heavens!	**Santo Cielo!** *santo cheeaylo*
I can't believe it!	**Incredibile!** *eenkraydeebeelay*
I don't mind.	**Mi è indifferente.** *mee eh eendeeffayrayntay*
No way!	**Assolutamente no.** *assolootamayntay no*
Really?	**Davvero?** *davvayro*
Rubbish.	**Stupidaggini.** *stoopeedadjeenee*
That's enough!	**Basta!** *basta*
That's true.	**É vero.** *eh vayro*
How are things?	**Come vanno le cose?** *komay vanno lay kosay*
Fine, thanks.	**Bene, grazie.** *baynay graatseeay*
great/brilliant	**magnificamente** *mañeefeekamayntay*
great	**benissimo** *bayneesseemo*
fine	**bene** *baynay*
not bad	**non male** *non malay*
okay	**abbastanza bene** *abbastantza baynay*
not good	**non bene** *non baynay*

Accommodations

Early reservation is essential in most major tourist centers, especially during high season or special events. If you haven't booked, most towns and arrival points have a tourist information office (**azienda di promozione turistica** or **ufficio turistico**).

The Italian tourist organization **E.N.I.T.** publishes an annual directory of all the 37,000 hotels in Italy, with details of minimum and maximum prices and facilities.

There is a wide range of accommodation options available, from **locande** (country inns), **rifugi alpini** (mountain huts) to converted historic buildings, and the following:

albergo/hotel al<u>bay</u>rgo/o<u>teh</u>l
Hotels in Italy are classified as **di lusso** (international luxury class), or **prima**, **seconda**, **terza**, **quarta categoria** (first, second, third, fourth class).

Note: especially near railway stations, one often finds **alberghi diurni** ("daytime hotels"). These have no sleeping accommodations, but provide bathrooms, rest rooms, hairdressers, and other similar services. Most close at midnight.

motel mo<u>teh</u>l
Increasing in number and improving in service; the Automobile Association of Italy has a list of recommended motels.

pensióne paynsee<u>o</u>nay
Corresponds to a boardinghouse; it usually offers **pensióne completa** (full board) or **mezza pensióne** (half board). Meals are likely to be from a set menu. **Pensioni** are classified first, second or third class.

ostello della gioventù os<u>teh</u>llo <u>day</u>lla jovayn<u>too</u>
Youth hostel. They are open to holders of membership cards issued by the International Youth Hostel Association. The Italian Association of Youth Hostels (**AIG**) publishes a complete guide of youth hostels in Italy (head office: Via Cavour 44 ☎ 06/4871152); information can also be obtained from any **CTS** (**Centro Turistico Studentesco**). Reservations are advisable.

Reservations/Booking Prenotazioni

In advance In anticipo

Can you recommend a
hotel in …?
**Può consigliarmi
un albergo a …?**
*pwo konsilyarmee oon
albayrgo ah*

Is it near the center
of town?
È vicino al centro città? *eh veecheeno
al chayntro cheetta*

How much is it per night?
Quanto costa per notte?
kwanto kosta pehr nottay

Is there anything cheaper?
C'è qualcosa di più economico? *cheh
kwalkosa dee peeoo aykonomeeko*

Could you reserve me
a room there, please?
**Può prenotarmi una camera lì, per
piacere?** *pwo prehnotaarmee oona
kamayra lee pehr peeachayray*

How do I get there?
Come ci arrivo? *komay chee arreevo*

At the hotel All'albergo

Do you have any vacancies?
Ha camere libere? *ah kamayray leebayray*

I'm sorry, we're full.
Mi dispiace, siamo al completo. *mee
deespeeachay seeamo al komplayto*

Is there another hotel nearby?
C'è un altro albergo qui vicino?
cheh oon altro kwee veecheeno

I'd like a single/double room.
Vorrei una camera singola/doppia.
*vorrehee oona kamayra seengola/
doppeea*

A room with …
Una camera con … *oona kamayra kon*

twin beds
due letti *doo-ay lehttee*

a double bed
il letto matrimoniale
eel lehtto matreemoneeaalay

a bath/shower
il bagno/la doccia
eel baaño/la dotcha

– Ha camere libere? Vorrei una camera doppia.
– *Mi dispiace, siamo al completo.*
– C'è un altro albergo qui vicino?
– *Sì. Albergo "La Giara" è vicino.*

Reception Ricezione

I have a reservation. My name is …	**Ho una prenotazione. Il nome è …** o oona praynotatseeonay. eel nomay eh
We've reserved a double and a single room.	**Abbiamo prenotato una camera doppia e una camera singola.** abbeeaamo praynotaato oona kamayra doppeea ay oona kamayra seengola
I confirmed my reservation by mail.	**Ho confermato la prenotazione per lettera.** o konfehrmaato la praynotatseeonay pehr lehttayra
Could we have adjoining rooms?	**Possiamo avere camere adiacenti?** posseeamo avayray kamayray adjachehntee

Amenities and facilities Amenità e servizi

Is there … in the room?	**C'è … nella camera?** cheh naylla kamayra
air conditioning	**l'aria condizionata** lareea kondeetseeonaata
TV/telephone	**la televisione/il telefono** la taylayveezeeonay/ eel taylayfono
Does the hotel have a(n)…?	**L'albergo ha …** lalbayrgo ah
laundry service	**il servizio di lavanderia** eel sayrveetseeo dee lavandayreea
satellite TV	**la televisione via satellite** la taylayveezeeonay veea sataylleetay
solarium	**il solarium** eel solareeoom
swimming pool	**la piscina** la peesheena
Could you put … in the room?	**Può mettere … nella camera?** pwo mayttehrray … naylla kamayra
an extra bed	**un letto supplementare** oon lehtto soopplaymayntaray
a crib	**una culla** oona koolla
Do you have facilities for children/the disabled?	**È attrezzato per i bambini/i clienti disabili?** eh attraytsaato pehr ee bambeenee/ ee kleeehntee deesabeelee

How long? Quanto si ferma?

We'll be staying …   **Ci fermeremo …**
                     chee fehrmay<u>ray</u>mo

overnight only   **solo per una notte**
                     <u>so</u>lo pehr <u>oo</u>na <u>not</u>tay

a few days   **per alcuni giorni**
                     pehr al<u>koo</u>nee <u>jor</u>nee

a week (at least)   **una settimana (minimo)**
                     <u>oo</u>na saytee<u>maa</u>na (<u>mee</u>neemo)

I don't know yet.   **Non so ancora.** non so an<u>ko</u>ra

I'd like to stay an extra night.   **Vorrei fermarmi per un'altra notte.** vor<u>reh</u>ee
                                    fehr<u>maar</u>mee pehr oon<u>aal</u>tra <u>not</u>tay

---

– Buona sera. Il nome è Philippa Newton.
  – *Ah, buona sera, Signora Newton.*
– Vorrei fermarmi per due giorni.
  – *Ah sì. Firmi qui, per piacere …*
  ecco la chiave della sua camera.

Posso vedere il suo passaporto, per piacere?   May I see your passport, please?

Per piacere compili questo modulo/firmi qui.   Please fill in this form/ sign here.

Qual'è il suo nomero di targa?   What is your car registration number?

SOLO CAMERE LIRE …	room only … lira
COLAZIONE COMPRESA	breakfast included
RISTORANTE	meals available
IL COGNOME/IL NOME	name/first name
L'INDIRIZZO/IL DOMICILIO/ LA VIA/IL NUMERO	home address/street/ number
LA NAZIONALITÀ/ LA PROFESSIONE	nationality/profession
LA DATA/IL LUOGO DI NASCITA	date/place of birth
IL NUMERO DI PASSAPORTO	passport number
IL NUMERO DI TARGA DEL VEICOLO	car registration number
IL LUOGO/LA DATA	place /date
LA FIRMA	signature

Price Il prezzo

How much is it ...?	**Quant'è...?** *kwanteh*
per night/week	**per notte/per settimana** *pehr <u>not</u>tay/pehr saytteemaana*
for bed and breakfast	**per il pernottamento e la colazione** *pehr eel pehrnotta<u>mayn</u>to ay la kolatsee<u>o</u>nay*
excluding meals	**pasti esclusi** *paastee ays<u>kloo</u>zee*
for full board (American Plan [A.P.])	**per la pensione completa** *pehr la paynsee<u>o</u>nay kom<u>play</u>ta*
for half board (Modified American Plan [A.P.])	**per la mezza pensione** *pehr la <u>mehd</u>za paynsee<u>o</u>nay*
Does the price include ...?	**Il prezzo include ...?** *eel <u>preh</u>tso eeng<u>kloo</u>day*
breakfast	**la colazione** *la kolatsee<u>o</u>nay*
VAT (sales tax)	**l'IVA (Imposta Valore Aggiunto)** *<u>lee</u>va (eem<u>po</u>sta va<u>lo</u>ray ad<u>joon</u>to)*
Do I have to pay a deposit?	**Devo pagare un anticipo?** *<u>day</u>vo pa<u>gaa</u>ray oon an<u>tee</u>cheepo*
Is there a discount for children?	**Ci sono sconti per i bambini?** *chee <u>so</u>no <u>skon</u>tee pehr ee bam<u>bee</u>nee*

Decision Decisioni

May I see the room?	**Posso vedere la camera?** *<u>pos</u>so vay<u>day</u>ray la <u>ka</u>mayra*
That's fine. I'll take it.	**Va bene. La prendo.** *va <u>bay</u>nay. la <u>prayn</u>do*
It's too ...	**È troppo ...** *eh <u>trop</u>po*
dark/small	**buia/piccola** *<u>boo</u>eea/<u>peek</u>ola*
noisy	**rumorosa** *roomo<u>ro</u>za*
Do you have anything ...?	**Ha qualcosa di ...?** *ah kwal<u>ko</u>za dee*
bigger/cheaper	**più grande/più economico** *pee<u>oo</u> <u>gran</u>day/pee<u>oo</u> aykon<u>o</u>meeko*
quieter/warmer	**più tranquillo/più caldo** *pee<u>oo</u> trank<u>wee</u>llo/pee<u>oo</u> <u>kal</u>do*
No, I won't take it.	**No, non la prendo.** *no non la <u>prehn</u>do*

24

Problems Problemi

The ... doesn't work.	**... non funziona.** *non foontseeona*
air conditioning	**L'aria condizionata** *laareea kondeetseeonaata*
fan	**Il ventilatore** *eel vaynteelatoray*
heating	**Il riscaldamento** *eel reeskaldamaynto*
light	**La luce** *la loochay*
I can't turn the heat (heating) on/off.	**Non posso accendere/spegnere il riscaldamento.** *non posso atchayndehray/spayñehray eel reeskaldamaynto*
There is no hot water/ toilet paper.	**Non c'è acqua calda/carta igienica.** *non cheh akwa kalda/karta eejayneeka*
The faucet/tap is dripping.	**Il rubinetto perde.** *eel roobeenehto pehrday*
The sink/toilet is blocked.	**Il lavello/gabinetto è bloccato.** *eel lavehllo/ga-bee-nay-to eh blokaato*
The window/door is jammed.	**La finestra/porta è bloccata.** *la feenaystra/porta eh blokaata*
My room has not been made up.	**La mia camera non è stata rifatta.** *la meea kamayra non eh staata reefatta*
The ... is broken.	**... è rotto(-a).** *eh rotto(-a)*
blind	**La tapparella** *la tapparehlla*
lock	**La serratura** *la sehrratoora*
There are insects in our room.	**Ci sono insetti nella nostra camera.** *chee sono eensehtee naylla nostra kamayra*

Action Azione

Could you have that seen to?	**Può farlo(-a) controllare?** *pwo farlo(-a) kontrollaaray*
I'd like to move to another room.	**Vorrei cambiare camera.** *vorrehee kambeeaaray kamayra*
I'd like to speak to the manager.	**Vorrei parlare con il direttore.** *vorrehee parlaaray kon eel deeraytoray*

Requirements Richieste

In the hotel In albergo

Where's the …?	**Dov'è …?** *doveh*
bar	**il bar** *eel baar*
bathroom	**la toeletta** *la toehlehta*
parking lot	**il parcheggio** *eel parkaydjo*
dining room	**la sala da pranzo** *la sala da pranzdo*
elevator	**l'ascensore** *lashaynsoray*
shower	**la doccia** *la dotchay*
swimming pool	**la piscina** *la peesheena*
tour operator's bulletin board	**la bacheca dell'agente di viaggio** *la bakayka dayllajayntay dee veeadjo*
Does the hotel have a garage?	**L'albergo ha un garage?** *lalbayrgo ah oon garazh*
What time is the front door locked?	**A che ora chiude la porta d'ingresso?** *ah kay ora keeooday la porta deegngrehsso*
What time is breakfast served?	**A che ora è servita la colazione?** *a kay ora eh sayrveeta la kolatseeonay*
Is there room service?	**C'è servizio camera?** *cheh sayrveetseeo kamayra*

SOLO PER RASOI	shavers only
USCITA D'EMERGENZA	emergency exit
PORTA ANTINCENDIO	fire door
NON DISTURBARE	do not disturb
FARE … PER OTTENERE LA LINEA ESTERNA	dial … for an outside line

Personal needs Richieste personali

The key to room …, please.	**La chiave della camera …, per piacere.** *la keeaavay daylla kamayra … pehr peeaachayray*
I've lost my key.	**Ho perso la mia chiave.** *o pehrso la meeaa keeaavay*
I've locked myself out of my room.	**Mi sono chiuso(-a) fuori della camera.** *mee sono keeooso(-a) fworee daylla kamayra*
Could you wake me at …?	**Può svegliarmi alle …?** *pwo zvaylyaarmee allay*
I'd like breakfast in my room.	**Vorrei la colazione in camera.** *vorrehee la kolatseeonay een kamayra*
Can I leave this in the safe?	**Vorrei mettere questo in cassaforte.** *vorrehee mayttehray kwaysto een kassafortay*
Could I have my things from the safe?	**Vorrei ritirare le mie cose dalla cassaforte.** *vorrehee reeteeraaray lay meeay kosay daylla kassafortay*
Where is our tour representative?	**Dove il nostro rappresentante?** *dovay eel nostro rappraysayntaantay*
maid	**una cameriera** *oona kamareeehra*
porter	**un portiere** *oon porteeayray*
May I have …?	**Ha …?** *ah*
bath towel	**un asciugamano** *oon ashoogamaano*
blanket	**una coperta** *oona kopehrta*
hangers	**grucce portabiti** *grootchay portabeetee*
(extra) pillow	**un cuscino** *oon koosheeno*
soap	**del sapone** *dayl saponay*
Is there any mail for me?	**C'è posta per me?** *cheh posta pehr meh*
Are there any messages for me?	**Ci sono messaggi per me?** *chee sono mayssadjee pehr meh*

BREAKFAST ➤ 43; CHANGING MONEY ➤ 138

Renting In affitto

We've reserved (booked) an apartment/cottage in the name of...	**Abbiamo prenotato un appartamento/una villa a nome di ...** *abbeeamo praynotato oon appartamaynto/ oona veella ah nomay dee*
Where do we pick up the keys?	**Dove passiamo a prendere le chiavi?** *dovay passeeamo a prayndehray lay keeaavee*
Where is the ...?	**Dov'è ...?** *doveh*
electricity meter	**il contatore dell'elettricità** *eel kontatoray dayll aylehttreecheeta*
fuse box	**i fusibili** *ee foozeebeelee*
faucet valve	**il rubinetto di arresto** *eel roobeenehtto dee arraysto*
water heater	**lo scaldaacqua** *low skalda-akwa*
Are there any spare ...?	**Ci sono ... di ricambio?** *chee sono ... dee reekambeeo*
fuses	**fusibili** *foozeebeelee*
gas bottles	**bombole di gas** *bombolay dee gaz*
sheets	**lenzuola** *layntsoo-ola*
On which day does the cleaner come?	**In che giorno viene la cameriera?** *een kay jorno veeaynay la kamareeayra*
Where/When do I put out the trash?	**Dove/Quando si mettono fuori i rifiuti?** *dovay/kwando see mehttono fworee ee reefeeootee*

Problems? Problemi?

Where can I contact you?	**Dove posso contattarla?** *dovay posso kontattaarla*
How does the stove/ water heater work?	**Come funziona la stufa/lo scaldaacqua?** *komay foontseeona la stoofa/ lo skalda-akwa*
The ... is dirty.	**Il ... è sporco.** *eel ... eh sporko*
The ... has broken down.	**La ... non funziona.** *la ... non foontseeona*
We have accidentally broken/lost ...	**Abbiamo accidentalmente rotto/perso ...** *abbeeamo acheedayntalmayntay rotto/pehrso*

HOUSEHOLD ARTICLES, CLEANING ITEMS ➤ 148

Useful terms Espressioni utili

water heater	**lo scaldaacqua** *lo skalda-akwa*
stove (gas/electric)	**la cucina a gas/elettrica** *la koocheena a gaz/ aylehttreeka*
crockery	**le stoviglie** *lay stoveelyay*
cutlery	**le posate** *lay posatay*
freezer	**il congelatore** *eel konjaylatoray*
refrigerator	**il frigorifero** *eel freegoreefayro*
frying pan	**la padella** *la padehlla*
kettle	**il bollitore** *eel bolleetoray*
lamp	**la lampada** *la lampada*
saucepan	**la pentola** *la payntola*
toilet paper	**la carta igienica** *la karta eejaayneeka*
washing machine	**la lavatrice** *la lavatreechay*

Rooms Camere

balcony	**il balcone** *eel balkonay*
bathroom	**il bagno** *eel baaño*
bedroom	**la camera da letto** *la kamayra da lehtto*
dining room	**la sala da pranzo/il tinello** *la saala da prandzo/eel teenehllo*
kitchen	**la cucina** *la koocheena*
living room	**il soggiorno** *eel sodjorno*
toilet	**la toeletta/il gabinetto** *la toaylehtta/eel gabeenehtto*

Youth hostel L'ostello della gioventù

Do you have any places left for tonight?	**Avete posti liberi per questa notte?** *avaytay postee leebayree pehr kwaysta nottay*
Do you rent bedding?	**Noleggiate la biancheria da letto?** *nolehdjatay la beeankayreea da lehtto*
What time are the doors locked?	**A che ora chiudete?** *a kay ora keeoodaytay*

REQUIREMENTS ➤ *26; CAMPING* ➤ *30*

Camping Il campeggio
Reservations Prenotazioni

Is there a camp site near here?	**C'è un campeggio qui vicino?** *cheh oon kampaydjo kwee veecheeno*
Do you have space for a tent/trailer?	**Avete un posto per una tenda/una roulotte?** *avaytay oon posto pehr oona tehnda/oona roolot*
What is the charge …?	**Quanto costa …?** *kwanto kosta*
per day/week	**al giorno/alla settimana** *al jorno/alla saytteemaana*
for a tent/a car	**per una tenda/un'auto(mobile)** *pehr oona tehnda/oonowto (oon owtomobeelay)*
for a trailer/caravan	**per una roulotte** *pehr oona roolot*

Facilities Attrezzature

Are there cooking facilities on site?	**Ci sono attrezzature per cucinare?** *chee sono attraytsatooray pehr koocheenaaray*
Are there any electric outlets?	**Ci sono delle prese di corrente?** *chee sono dayllay prayzay dee korrayntay*
Where is/are the …?	**Dov'è/Dove sono …?** *doveh/dovay sono*
drinking water	**l'acqua potabile** *lakwa potabeelay*
trash cans	**i cassettoni per i rifiuti** *ee kassayttonee pehr ee reefeeootee*
laundry facilities	**la lavanderia (sing.)** *la lavandayreea*
showers	**le docce** *lay dotchay*
Where can I get some butane gas?	**Dove si compra il campingaz?** *dovay see kompra eel campingaz*

CAMPEGGIO VIETATO	no camping
ACQUA POTABILE	drinking water
VIETATO ACCENDERE FUOCHI/ CUCINARE ALL'APERTO	no fires/barbeques

Complaints Reclami

It's too sunny/shady/ crowded here.	**È troppo esposto al sole/ombreggiato/affollato.** *eh troppo aysposto al solay/ombraydjaato/affollaato*
The ground's too hard/uneven.	**Il terreno è troppo duro/in dislivello.** *eel tayrrayno eh troppo dooro/een deesleevehllo*
Do you have a more level spot?	**C'è uno spazio su terreno più livellato?** *cheh oono spatseeo soo tayrrayno peeoo leevehllaato*
You can't camp here.	**Qui non può campeggiare.** *kwee non pwo kampaydjaaray*

Camping equipment Attrezzatura per campeggio

butane gas	**il campingaz** *eel campingaz*
campbed	**il lettino da campeggio** *eel lehtteeno da kampaydjo*
charcoal	**il carbone** *eel karbonay*
flashlight	**la torcia** *la torcheea*
hammer	**il martello** *eel martehllo*
knapsack	**lo zaino** *lo dzaaeeno*
mallet	**il maglio** *eel malyo*
matches	**i fiammiferi** *ee feeammeefayree*
(air) mattress	**materasso di gomma** *eel matayrasso dee gomma*
paraffin	**la paraffina** *la paraffeena*
primus stove	**il fornello da campeggio** *eel fornayllo da kampaydjo*
sleeping bag	**il sacco a pelo** *eel sakko a paylo*
tarpaulin	**il telo per il terreno** *eel taylo pehr eel tayrrayno*
tent	**la tenda** *la taynda*
tent pegs	**i picchetti** *ee peekkehttee*
tent pole	**il palo della tenda** *eel palo daylla taynda*

Checking out Partenza

Customers are required by law to have a receipt (**ricevuta fiscale**) for any services or goods purchased on leaving hotels, shops and restaurants.

Tipping: a service charge is generally included in hotel and restaurant bills. However, if the service has been particularly good, you may want to leave an extra tip.

What time do we need to vacate the room?	**A che ora dobbiamo lasciare libere le camere?** *a kay ora dobbeeaamo lashaaray leebayray lay kamayray*
Could we leave our baggage/luggage here until … p.m.?	**Possiamo lasciare i nostri bagagli qui fino alle …?** *posseeaamo lashaaray ee nostree bagalyee kwee feeno allay …*
I'm leaving now.	**Parto ora.** *parto ora*
Could you order me a taxi, please?	**Può chiamarmi un tassì, per piacere?** *pwo keeamaarmee oon tassee pehr peeachayray*
It's been a very enjoyable stay.	**È stato un soggiorno molto piacevole.** *eh staato oon sodjorno molto peeachayvolay*

Paying Pagare

May I have my bill, please?	**Vorrei il conto, per favore.** *vorrehee eel konto pehr favoray*
I think there's a mistake in this bill.	**Penso che ci sia un errore in questo conto.** *paynso kay chee seea oon ayrroray een kwaysto konto*
I've made … telephone calls.	**Ho fatto … telefonate.** *oh fatto … taylayfonatay*
I've taken … from the minibar.	**Ho preso … dal minibar.** *oh prayzo … dal minibar*
Can I have an itemized bill?	**Vorrei un conto dettagliato, per favore.** *vorrehee oon konto dayttalyaato pehr favoray*

Porter	Hotel maid, per week	Waiter
L.1,500	L.1,000–2,000	5–10%

Eating Out

Restaurants Ristoranti

Autogrill _owtogreel_

A large restaurant on an expressway (motorway); usually table and cafe-
teria service available.

Bar _bar_

Bar; can be found on virtually every street corner; coffee and drinks
served. In most of them you first have to get a ticket from the cashier.
Then you go to the counter and order what you want.

Caffè _kaffeh_

Coffee shop; generally food isn't served there except for breakfast. If it
offers **panini** (sandwiches) or toasts you'll be able to get a snack. Coffee
shops always serve alcoholic beverages.

Gelateria _jaylatayreea_

Ice-cream parlor; Italian ice cream is very tasty, rich and creamy, often
reminiscent of old-fashioned, homemade ice cream. Ice cream and pastries can also be bought and consumed in a **sala da tè.**

Locanda _lokanda_

Simple restaurant serving local dishes.

Osteria _ostayreea_

Inn; wine and simple food are served.

Paninoteca _paneenotayka_

A sort of coffee shop where you can find a great variety
of sandwiches (**panini**) served hot or cold.

33

Ristorante *reestorantay*

You'll encounter restaurants classified by stars or forks and knives and endorsed by everyone including travel agencies, automobile associations and gastronomic guilds. Bear in mind that any form of classification is relative. Some restaurants are judged according to their fancy décor while others – linen and chandeliers aside – are rated merely by the quality of their cooking.

Trattoria *trattoreea*

a medium-priced restaurant serving meals and drinks. The food is simple but can be surprisingly good if you happen to hit upon the right place. A more modest type of **trattoria** is the **taverna.** Bear in mind that some very expensive restaurants may call themselves **Osteria, Trattoria** or **Taverna.**

Most restaurants display a menu in the window. Many offer a tourist menu (**menù turistico**), a fixed-price three- or four-course meal with limited choice, or the specialty of the day (**piatto del giorno**).

All restaurants, no matter how modest, must issue a formal bill (**la ricevuta fiscale**) with VAT, or sales tax (**I.V.A.**). A customer may actually be stopped outside the premises and fined if he or she cannot produce this receipt. The bill usually includes cover (**il coperto**) and service (**il servizio**) charges as well.

You may have difficulty finding a restaurant with a non-smoking area.

Meal times Orari dei pasti

la colazione *la kolatseeonay*

Breakfast is usually served at the hotel from 7 to 10 a.m. Hotels usually offer coffee or tea, bread, butter and jam. Italians usually have just a cappuccino and a brioche for breakfast.

il pranzo *eel prandzo*

Lunch is served from 12.30 to 2 p.m.

la cena *la chayna*

Dinner begins at 7 or 8 p.m., but hotels tend to open their dining rooms earlier for foreign tourists. The names of meals can be confusing. Lunch is sometimes called **colazione** and dinner **pranzo**, especially in towns. If you are invited out, make sure of the time, so you don't turn up at the wrong meal.

Italian cuisine Cucina italiana

Italian cuisine consists of a lot more than just pasta. You will be amazed at the rich variety available: tasty hors d'œuvres, long-simmered soups, traditional meat dishes, fresh fish and shellfish, high-quality poultry, an incredible number of cheeses, not to mention the magnificent cakes and ice cream.

Each of Italy's 18 regions has its own specialty, never lacking in flavor or originality, inspired by sun-drenched fruit and vegetables. Italian cooking is like the country itself: colorful, happy, generous, exuberant.

A table for …	**Un tavolo per …** *oon tavolo pehr*
1/2/3/4	**uno(-a)/due/tre/quattro** *oono(-a)/doo-ay/tray/kwattro*
Thank you.	**Grazie.** *graatseeay*
The bill, please.	**Il conto, per piacere.** *eel konto pehr peeachayray*

Finding a place to eat Trovare un ristorante

Can you recommend a good restaurant?	**Può consigliare un buon ristorante?** *pwo konseelyaaray oon bwon reestorantay*
Is there a … near here?	**C'è … qui vicino?** *cheh … kwee veecheeno*
traditional local restaurant	**un ristorante con cucina tradizionale** *oon reestorantay kon koocheena tradeetseeonaalay*
Chinese/Greek restaurant	**un ristorante cinese/greco** *oon reestorantay cheenaysay/grayko*
inexpensive restaurant	**una trattoria** *oona trattoreea*
Turkish restaurant	**un ristorante turco** *oon reestorantay toorko*
vegetarian restaurant	**un ristorante vegetariano** *oon reestorantay vayjaytareeaano*
Where can I find …?	**Dove si trova …?** *dovay see trova*
burger stand	**un chiosco dove vendono hamburger** *oon keeosko dovay vayndono hamburger*
café	**un bar** *oon bar*
café with terrace/garden	**un bar con terrazza/giardino** *oon bar kon tayrratsa/jardeeno*
fast-food restaurant	**una tavola calda (un self-service)** *oona tavola kalda (oon self-service)*
ice cream parlor	**una gelateria** *oona jaylatayreea*
pizzeria	**una pizzeria** *oona peettsayreea*
steak house	**ristorante specializzato in bistecche** *reestorantay spaychaleedzato een beestaykkay*

DIRECTIONS ➤ 94

35

Reservations Prenotare

I'd like to reserve a table for 2.	**Vorrei prenotare un tavolo per due.** *vorrehee praynotaaray oon tavolo pehr doo-ay*
For this evening/ tomorrow at ...	**Per questa sera/domani alle ...** *pehr kwasta sayra/domanee allay*
We'll come at 8:00.	**Arriveremo alle ore venti.** *arreevayraymo allay oray vayntee*
A table for 2, please.	**Un tavolo per due, per piacere.** *oon tavolo pehr doo-ay pehr peeachayray*
We have a reservation.	**Abbiamo una prenotazione.** *abbeeamo oona praynotatseeonay*

A che nome, prego?	What's the name, please?
Mi dispiace. Siamo al completo.	I'm sorry. We're very busy/full up.
Avremo un tavolo libero fra ... minuti.	We'll have a free table in ... minutes.
Dovrà ritornare fra ... minuti.	You'll have to come back in ... minutes.

Where to sit Dove sedersi

Could we sit ...?	**Vorremmo sederci...** *vorrehmmo saydayrchee*
over there	**là** *la*
outside	**fuori** *fworee*
in a non-smoking area	**in una zona per non fumatori** *een oona dzona pehr non foomatoree*
by the window	**vicino alla finestra** *veecheeno alla feenaystra*

– Vorrei prenotare un tavolo per questa sera.
  – *Per quante persone?*
  – Per quattro.
  – *A che ora arriva?*
– Arriveremo alle ore venti.
  – *E il nome, per favore?*
  – Evans. E-V-A-N-S.
  – *Bene. A questa sera.*

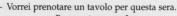

TIME ➤ 220; NUMBERS ➤ 216

Ordering Ordinare

Waiter!/Waitress!

Cameriere!/Cameriera!
*kamayree**eh**ray/
kamayree**eh**ra*

Could you bring
the wine list, please?

**Può portare la lista dei vini, per
piacere?** *pwo port**aa**ray la l**ee**sta
d**eh**ee v**ee**nee pehr pee**a**chayray*

Do you have a set menu?

Ha un menù fisso?
*ah oon may**noo** f**ee**sso*

Can you recommend some
typical local dishes?

**Può consigliare dei piatti tipici della
regione?** *pwo konseely**aar**mee d**eh**ee
pee**a**ttee teep**ee**chee d**ay**lla ray**jo**nay*

Could you tell me what … is?

Cos'è …? *k**o**zay*

What is in it?

Cosa c'è dentro? *k**o**sa cheh d**ay**ntro*

What kind of … do you have?

Che tipo di … ha? *kay t**ee**po dee ah*

I'd like some …

Vorrei … *vor**re**hee*

I'll have …

Prendo … *pr**ay**ndo*

a bottle/glass/carafe of …

una bottiglia/un bicchiere/una caraffa di …
*oona bott**ee**lya/oon beekkee**ee**hray/oona
kar**a**ffa dee*

E' pronto(-a) per ordinare?	Are you ready to order?
Cosa prende/desidera?	What would you like?
Vuole ordinare prima le bibete?	Would you like to order drinks first?
Consiglio …	I recommend …
Non abbiamo …	We haven't got …
Ci vogliono … minuti.	That will take … minutes.
Buon appetito!	Enjoy your meal.

> – *E' pronto(-a) per ordinare?*
> – Può consigliare qualcosa di tipicamente italiano?
>   – *Sì, consiglio il saltimbocca alla romana.*
>   – D'accordo, prendo quello e insalata
>   di contorno, per piacere.
>   – *Benissimo. E cosa vuole bere?*
> – Una caraffa di vino rosso, per piacere.

WHAT SORT OF … ? ➤ 14; DRINKS ➤ 49

Side dishes Contorni

I prefer … without the …	**Preferisco … senza …** *prayfay<u>ree</u>sko … <u>sayn</u>tsa*
With a side order of …	**Con un contorno di …** *kon oon kon<u>tor</u>no dee*
Could I have salad instead of vegetables, please?	**Si può avere insalata al posto dei legumi?** *see pwo a<u>vay</u>ray eensa<u>laa</u>ta al <u>pos</u>to <u>de</u>hee lay<u>goo</u>mee*
Does the meal come with vegetables/potatoes?	**Il piatto include legumi/patate?** *eel pee<u>a</u>tto een<u>kloo</u>day lay<u>goo</u>mee/ pa<u>ta</u>tay*
Do you have any sauces?	**Ha delle salse?** *ah <u>day</u>llay <u>sal</u>say*
Would you like … with your dish?	**Vuole … con il Suo piatto?** *<u>vwo</u>lay kon eel <u>soo</u>-o pee<u>a</u>tto*
vegetables	**legumi/verdure** *lay<u>goo</u>mee/vayr<u>doo</u>ray*
mixed salad	**insalata mista** *eensa<u>laa</u>ta <u>mees</u>ta*
potatoes/French fries	**patate/patatine fritte** *pa<u>ta</u>tay/pata<u>tee</u>nay <u>free</u>ttay*
sauce	**la salsa** *la <u>sal</u>sa*
ice	**il ghiaccio** *eel gee<u>a</u>tcho*
May I have some …?	**Mi può dare …?** *mee pwo <u>da</u>ray*
bread	**del pane** *dayl <u>pa</u>nay*
butter	**del burro** *dayl <u>boor</u>ro*
lemon	**del limone** *dayl lee<u>mo</u>nay*
mustard	**della senape** *<u>day</u>lla <u>say</u>napay*
pepper	**del pepe** *dayl <u>pay</u>pay*
salt	**del sale** *dayl <u>sa</u>lay*
seasoning (oil/vinegar)	**dei condimenti (olio/aceto)** *<u>de</u>hee kondee<u>mayn</u>tee (<u>o</u>lyo/a<u>cha</u>yto)*
sugar	**dello zucchero** *<u>day</u>llo <u>tsook</u>kayro*
(artificial) sweetener	**dello zucchero dietetico** *<u>day</u>llo <u>tsook</u>kayro deeay<u>tay</u>teeko*

General requests Richieste generali

Could you bring a(n) (clean) ..., please?	**Può portare ... (pulito), per piacere?** *pwo portaaray (pooleeto) pehr peeachayray*
ashtray	**un posacenere** *oon posachaynayray*
cup/glass	**una tazza/un bicchiere** *oona tattsa/oon beekkeeeehray*
fork/knife	**una forchetta/un coltello** *oona forkehtta/oon koltehllo*
napkin	**un tovagliolo** *oon tovalyolo*
plate/spoon/little spoon	**un piatto/un cucchiaio/un cucchiaino** *oon peeatto/oon kookkeeaeeo/oon kookkeeaeeno*
I'd like some more ..., please.	**Vorrei ancora un pò di ..., per piacere.** *vorrehee ankora oon poh dee ... pehr peeachayray*
Nothing more, thanks.	**Nient'altro, grazie.** *neeehntaltro gratseeay*
Where are the bathrooms?	**Dove sono le toelette?** *dovay sono lay toylayttay*

Special requirements Richieste particolari

I mustn't eat food containing ...	**Non devo mangiare piatti che contengono ...** *non dayvo manjaaray peeattee kay kontayngono*
salt/sugar	**sale/zucchero** *salay/tsookkayro*
Do you have meals/drinks for diabetics?	**Ha piatti/bevande per diabetici?** *ah peeattee/bayvanday pehr deeabayteechee*
Do you have vegetarian dishes?	**Ha piatti vegetariani?** *ah peeattee vayjaytareeanee*

For the children Per i bambini

Do you serve children's portions?	**Fate porzioni per bambini?** *fatay portseeonee pehr bambeenee*
Could you bring a child's seat, please?	**Può portare una seggiola per bambini, per piacere?** *pwo portaaray oona saydjola pehr bambeenee pehr peeachayray*

CHILDREN ➤ 113

Fast food/Café Bar/Tavola calda

Bars and cafés play an important part in Italian life; there is one on almost every corner. They are an ideal place to meet people, revive weary feet, write postcards, study maps, or just watch the world go by while sipping a cappuccino or beer. Bar staff are usually friendly and a mine of local information.

Something to drink Qualcosa da bere

I'd like …	**Vorrei …** _vorrehee_
a beer	**una birra** _oona beerra_
coffee	**un caffè/un espresso** _oon kaffeh/oon ehspraysso_
tea	**un tè** _oon teh_
red/white wine	**del vino rosso/bianco** _dayl veeno rosso/beeanko_

And to eat … E da mangiare …

A piece/slice of …, please.	**Un pezzo/una fetta di … , per piacere** _oon pehtso/oona fehtta dee … pehr peeachayray_
I'd like two of those.	**Vorrei due di quelli(e).** _vorrehee doo-ay dee kwehllee (ay)_
burger/French fries	**un hamburger/delle patatine fritte** _oon hamburger/dayllay patateenay freettay_
cake/sandwich	**una torta/un panino** _oona torta/oon paneeno_
bun/pastry	**una pasta** _oona pasta_

un gelato _oon jaylaato_
Ice cream; flavors/flavours include: **alla vaniglia** or **alla crema** (vanilla), **al cioccolato** (chocolate), **alla fragola** (strawberry), **al limone** (lemon), **misto** (mixed).

un panino imbottito _oon paneeno eembotteeto_
Sandwich; you may want yours **al formaggio** (cheese), **al prosciutto cotto** (ham), **al prosciutto crudo** (Parma ham) or **al salame** (salami).

A … portion, please.	**Una porzione … , per piacere.** _oona portseeonay … pehr peeachayray_
small	**piccola** _peekkola_
medium/regular	**regolare** _raygolaaray_
large	**grande** _granday_

OTHER DRINKS ➤ 49–51

– Cosa prende ?
– Due caffè, per piacere.
– Espresso, cappuccino?
– No, caffè lunghi con latte, per piacere.
– Nient'altro?
– No, nient'altro, grazie.

Complaints Reclami

I have no knife/fork/spoon.
Non ho il coltello/la forchetta/il cucchiaio.
non oh eel koltayllo/la forkaytta/eel kookeeaeeo

There must be some mistake.
Deve esserci un errore.
dayvay ehssayrchee oon ehrroray

That's not what I ordered.
Non ho ordinato questo.
non oh ordeenaato kwaysto

I asked for …
Ho ordinato … *oh ordeenaato*

I asked for …
Ho chiesto … *oh kee-ehsto …*

I can't eat this.
Non posso mangiare questo.
non posso manjaaray kwaysto

The meat is …
La carne è … *la karnay eh*

overdone
troppo cotta *troppo kotta*

underdone
non abbastanza cotta *non abbastantsa kotta*

too tough
troppo dura *troppo doora*

This is too …
Questo è troppo … *kwaysto eh troppo*

bitter/sour
amaro/acido *amaaro/acheedo*

This … is cold.
Questo … è freddo. *kwaysto … eh frehddo*

This isn't fresh.
Questo non è fresco. *kwaysto non eh fraysko*

How much longer will our food be?
Quanto dobbiamo aspettare ancora?
kwanto dobbeeaamo aspayttaray ankora

We can't wait any longer. We're leaving.
Non possiamo più aspettare. Andiamo via. *non posseeaamo peeoo aspehttaaray andeeaamo veea*

This isn't clean.
Questo non é pulito.
kwaysto non eh pooleeto

I'd like to speak to the head waiter/manager.
Vorrei parlare con il capocamieriere/il direttore. *Vorrehee parlaaray kon eel kapokamayree-ehray/eel deeraytoray*

Paying Pagare

Service charge (**il servizio**) is generally included in restaurant bills, but if the service has been especially good, an extra tip (**la mancia**) is appropriate and appreciated: 5–10%. You may also find the following items added to your bill: **coperto** (cover charge), **supplemento** (surcharge).

I'd like to pay.	**Vorrei pagare.** vor<u>reh</u>ee pag<u>aa</u>ray
The check, please.	**Il conto, per piacere.** eel <u>kon</u>to pehr peea<u>chay</u>ray
We'd like to pay separately.	**Vorremmo pagare separatamente.** vor<u>rehm</u>mo pag<u>aa</u>ray sayparata<u>mayn</u>tay
It's all together, please.	**Un conto unico, per piacere.** oon <u>kon</u>to <u>oo</u>neeko pehr peea<u>chay</u>ray
I think there's a mistake in this check.	**Penso che ci si un errore in questo conto.** <u>payn</u>so chee see oon ehr<u>ro</u>ray een kwaysto <u>kon</u>to
What is this amount for?	**Per cosa è questa cifra?** pehr <u>ko</u>sa eh k<u>way</u>sta <u>chee</u>fra
I didn't order that. I had ...	**Non ho ordinato questo. Ho preso ...** non oh ordee<u>naa</u>to k<u>way</u>sto. oh <u>pray</u>zo
Is service included?	**È compreso il servizio?** eh kom<u>pray</u>zo eel sayr<u>veet</u>seeo
I would like to pay with this credit card.	**Vorrei pagare con questa carta di credito.** vor<u>reh</u>ee pag<u>aa</u>ray kon k<u>way</u>sta <u>kar</u>ta dee <u>kray</u>deeto
I've forgotten my wallet.	**Ho dimenticato il portafoglio.** oh deemayntee<u>kaa</u>to eel porta<u>fol</u>yo
I haven't got enough cash.	**Non ho abbastanza contanti.** non oh abba<u>stan</u>tsa kon<u>tan</u>tee
Could I have a VAT receipt?	**Vorrei una Recevuta Fiscale.** vor<u>reh</u>ee <u>oo</u>na reechayv<u>oo</u>ota fees<u>kaa</u>lay

– Cameriere! Il conto, per piacere.
– *Certamente. Ecco a Lei.*
– È compreso il servizio?
– *Sì, il servizio è incluso.*
– Vorrei pagare con questa carta di credito.
– *Naturalmente.*
– Grazie. Che pranzo eccellente!

Course by course Portate

Breakfast Colazione

I'd like …	**Desidero …** *dayzeedayro*
bread	**del pane** *dayl paanay*
butter	**del burro** *dayl boorro*
eggs	**delle uova** *dayllay wova*
fried/scrambled	**fritte/strapazzate** *freettay/strapattsaatay*
fruit juice	**un succo di frutta** *oon sookko dee frootta*
grapefruit/orange	**un pompelmo/un'arancia** *oon pompaylmo/oon arancheea*
milk	**del latte** *dayl lattay*
jam	**della marmellata** *daylla marmayllaata*
marmalade	**della marmellata d'arance** *daylla marmayllaata daranchay*
honey	**del miele** *dayl mee-aylay*
rolls	**dei panini** *dehee paneenee*
toast	**del pane tostato** *dayl paanay tostaato*

Appetizers/Starters Antipasti

anchovies	**acciughe** *achoogay*
assorted appetizer	**antipasto assortito** *anteepasto assorteeto*
artichoke hearts in olive oil	**carciofini sottolio** *karchofeenee sottolyo*
cured pork shoulder	**coppa** *koppa*
Bologna sausage	**mortadella** *mortadehlla*
cured ham from Parma	**prosciutto crudo di Parma** *proshootto kroodo dee parma*
pickled vegetables	**sottaceti** *sottachaytee*

bagna cauda *baaña kaooda*
raw vegetables accompanied by a hot sauce made from anchovies, garlic, oil, butter and sometimes truffles (Northern Italy)

Pizza Pizza

Pizza (plural **pizze**) is one of Italy's best-known culinary exports. The variety of toppings is endless. A **calzone** has basically the same ingredients, but the pastry forms a sealed sandwich, with the filling inside.

ai funghi	*ai foonggee*	with mushrooms
capricciosa	*kapreetchosa*	the cook's specialty
siciliana	*seecheeleeaana*	with black olives, capers and cheese

màrgherita *margayreeta*
named after Italy's first queen, the pizza ingredients, tomato, cheese and basil, reflect the national colors

napoletana *napolaytaana*
the classic pizza with anchovies, ham, capers, tomatoes, cheese and oregano

quattro formaggi *kwattro formadjee*
pizza with four different types of cheese, usually including **gorgonzola** and **caciotta**

quattro stagioni *kwattro stajonee*
"four seasons", containing a variety of vegetables: tomatoes, artichoke, mushrooms, olives; plus cheese, ham and bacon

Soups Minestre, zuppe

An Italian meal always includes a **pastasciutta** or a soup; some of them are sufficient for a main course.

brodo di manzo	*brodo dee manzo*	meat broth
busecca	*boozaykka*	thick tripe, vegetable and bean soup
cacciucco	*kachookko*	spicy seafood chowder/stew
crema di legumi	*krehma dee laygoomee*	vegetable cream soup
minestrone	*meenehstronay*	vegetable soup (sometimes with noodles) sprinkled with parmesan cheese
passato di verdura	*passaato dee vehrdoora*	mashed vegetable soup, generally with croutons
zuppa alla pavese	*tsooppa alla pavayzay*	consommé with poached egg, croutons and grated cheese
zuppa di vongole	*tsooppa dee vonggolay*	clams and white wine soup

Pasta Pasta

Pasta (or **pastasciutta**), constitutes the traditional Italian first course. In addition to the well-known **spaghetti**, pasta comes in a bewildering variety of sizes and shapes– **penne** (quills), **tagliatelle** (flat noodles), and the following examples:

cannelloni *kanaylonee*
tubular dough stuffed with meat, cheese or vegetables, covered with a white sauce and baked

cappelletti *kapaylayttee*
small ravioli filled with meat, herbs, ham, cheese and eggs

fettuccine *faytoocheenay*
narrow flat noodles

lasagne *lazaañay*
thin layers of white or green (**lasagne verdi**) dough alternating with tomato sauce and sausage meat, white sauce and grated cheese; baked in the oven

tortellini *tortehlleenee*
rings of dough filled with seasoned minced meat and served in broth or with a sauce

Fish and seafood Pesci e frutti di mare

acciughe	*atchoogay*	anchovies
anguilla	*anggooeella*	eel
bianchetti	*beeangkayttee*	herring/whitebait
gamberi	*gambayree*	prawns
granchi	*grangkee*	crabs
merluzzo	*mayrloottso*	cod
orata	*oraata*	type of sea bream
polpo	*polpo*	octopus
sogliola	*solyola*	sole

Fish specialties Specialità di pesce

anguilla alla veneziana *anggooeella alla vaynaytseeaana*
eel cooked in sauce made from tuna and lemon

fritto misto *freetto meesto*
fry of small fish and shellfish

lumache alle milanese *loomaakay allay meelanaysay*
snails with anchovy, fennel and wine sauce

stoccafisso *stokkafeesso*
dried cod cooked with tomatoes, olives and artichoke

Meat Carne

Among small fowl considered gourmet dishes in Italy are lark (**allodola**), thrush (**tordo**) and ortolan (**ortolano**). They are usually grilled or roasted.

Vorrei ...	vorrehee	I'd like some ...
della pancetta	_dayl_la panchehtta	bacon
del manzo	dayl _mandzo_	beef
del pollo	dayl _pollo_	chicken
dell'anatra	dayl_laa_natra	duck
dell'oca	dayl_lo_ka	goose
del prosciutto	dayl proshootto	ham
dell'agnello	dayl_lañehllo_	lamb
del maiale	dayl maee_aa_lay	pork
della salsicce	_dayl_la sal_see_tchay	sausages
della bistecca	_dayl_la bee_stay_kka	steak
del vitello	dayl veetehllo	veal

Meat dishes Piatti di carne

bistecca alla fiorentina bee_stay_kka _a_lla feeorayn_tee_na
grilled steak flavored with pepper, lemon juice and parsley

cima alla genovese _cheema alla_ jayno_vay_say
rolled veal stuffed with eggs, sausage and mushrooms

cotoletta alla milanese kosto_lay_tta _a_lla meela_nay_say
breaded veal cutlet, flavored with cheese

fegato alla veneziana _fay_gato _a_lla vaynayt_seeaa_na
thin slices of calf's liver fried with onions

filetto al pepe verde feelaytto al paypay vehrday
filet steak in a creamy sauce with green peppercorns

galletto amburghese gal_lay_tto amboor_gay_say
young tender chicken, oven-roasted

involtini eenvol_tee_nee
thin slices of meat rolled and stuffed

polenta e coniglio po_leh_nta ay ko_nee_lyo
rabbit stew with cornmeal mush

pollo alla romana _pollo_ _a_lla ro_maa_na
diced chicken with tomato sauce and sweet peppers

saltimbocca alla romana salteem_bo_kah _a_lla ro_maa_na
veal escalope braised in marsala wine with ham and sage

Vegetables/Salads Verdure/Insalate

You'll recognize: **asparagi, broccoli, carote, patate, spinaci, zucchini**.

cavolo	_kaavolo_	cabbage
cipolle	_cheepollay_	onions
funghi	_foonggee_	mushrooms
insalata mista	_eensalaata meesta_	mixed salad
lattuga	_lattooga_	lettuce
piselli	_peesehllee_	peas
pomodoro	_pomodoro_	tomatoes
radicchio	_radeekeeo_	bitter red and white lettuce
verdura mista	_vehrdoora meesta_	mixed vegetables

carciofi alla giudea _karchofee alla jeeoodeea_
a delicious, crispy, deep-fried artichoke, originally a specialty of the old Jewish quarter in the heart of Rome

carciofi alla romana _karchofee alla romaana_
whole lightly stewed artichockes stuffed with garlic, salt, olive oil, wild mint (**mentuccia**) and parsley

fagioli alla toscana _fajolee alla toskana_
Tuscan-style beans, simmered for hours and seasoned with salt, black pepper and crude olive oil

fagioli in umido _fajolee een oomeedo_
all types of haricot beans cooked in tomato sauce and spices

funghi porcini arrosti _foonggee arrosto_
boletus mushrooms roasted or grilled with garlic, parsley and chili peppers

peperoni ripieni _paypayronee reepeeaynee_
stuffed sweet peppers (usually containing mince meat); similarly, zucchini is also served this way (**zucchini ripieni**)

Sauces Salse

Italian cooks are masters at making the sauces that make spaghetti and macaroni taste so delicious.

al burro	_al boorro_	butter, grated parmesan
bolognese	_boloñayzay_	tomatoes, minced meat, onions, herbs
carbonara	_karbonaara_	smoked ham, cheese, eggs, olive oil
pesto	_paysto_	basil leaves, garlic, cheese
pommarola	_pommarola_	tomatoes, garlic, basil

Cheese Formaggio

Bel Paese	smooth cheese with delicate taste
caciotta	firm, usually mild cheese; some sharper varieties can be found
caciocavallo	firm, slightly sweet cheese from cow's or sheep's milk
gorgonzola	most famous of the Italian blue-veined cheese, rich with a tangy flavor
grana	a grained cheese similar to parmesan originating from Padova usually grated on pasta dishes
mascarpone	a thick, full-fat creamy cheese mostly used for desserts; similar to clotted cream
mozzarella	soft, unripened cheese with a bland, slightly sweet flavor, made from buffalo's milk in southern Italy, elsewhere with cow's milk
parmigiano (-reggiano)	parmesan (also called **grana**), a hard cheese generally grated for use in hot dishes and pasta but also eaten alone
pecorino	a hard cheese with a strong flavor made from sheep's milk usually grated on certain pasta dishes such as **Pasta all'amatriciana** and **Trippa alla romana**
provolone	a firm, tasty cheese
ricotta	soft cow's or sheep's milk cheese

Fruit Frutta

You'll recognize: **banana, datteri, limone, melone, pera**.

ciliege	*cheelee-ehjay*	cherries
uva	*oova*	grapes
bianca/nera	*beeanka/nayra*	white/black
arancia	*arancha*	orange
pesca	*pehska*	peach
prugna	*prooña*	plum
lamponi	*lamponee*	raspberries
fragole	*fraagolay*	strawberries
anguria	*angoorreea*	watermelon (northern Italy)
cocomero	*kokomayro*	watermelon (Rome & southern Italy)

Dessert Dolce

cassata siciliana *kassaata seecheeleeaana*
sponge cake garnished with sweet cream cheese, chocolate and candied fruit

tiramisù *teerameesoo*
mascarpone, eggs and lady fingers

Drinks Bevande

Aperitifs Aperitivi

Often bittersweet, some aperitifs have a wine and brandy base
with herbs and bitters, while others may have a vegetable base.

Americano *amayreekaano*: vermouth with bitters, brandy and lemon peel
Aperol *apayrol*: a non-alcoholic bitters
bitter analcolico *beettehr analkoleeko*: a non-alcoholic aperitif
Campari *kampaaree*: reddish-brown bitters with orange peel and herbs
Campari soda *kampaaree soda*: Campari diluted with soda
Cynar *cheenaar*: produced from artichoke
Gingerino *jeenjehreeno*: ginger-flavored aperitif
Martini *marhteenee*: brand-name vermouth, sweet or dry

neat/straight	**liscio** *leesho*
on the rocks	**con ghiaccio** *kon geeacho*
with (seltzer or soda) water	**con acqua (di seltz)**
	kon akwa (dee sehltz)

Beer Birra

Do you have … beer?	**Avete della birra …?** *avayta daylla beerra*
bottled/draft/draught	**in bottiglia/alla spina**
	een botteelya/alla speena

Wine Vino

Italy is one of the most important wine producers in Europe, with
vineyards found all over the Italian peninsula and islands. Some of the
country's best come from northwestern Italy (like *Barbaresco*, *Barbera* and
Barolo). Italy's best-known wine abroad is Chianti, particularly **classico** and
riserva (superior quality); the best is produced between Florence and Siena.

More sophisticated restaurants have wine lists, while others list their
wines in a corner of the menu or have them marked up on the wall. Good
quality bottled wine from the various regions is now easily available all
over Italy in restaurants and specialized wine shops (*enoteche*).

Don't expect a trattoria to offer more than a few types of wine. In smaller
places you may find **vino sfuso** (unbottled wine usually served as house wine)
at a moderate price, served in one-quarter, one-half or one-liter carafes.

I'd like a bottle of white/ red wine.	**Vorrei una bottiglia di vino bianco/ rosso.** *vorrehee oona botteelya dee veeno beeanko/rosso*
I'd like the house wine, please.	**Desidero il vino della casa, per favore.** *dayzeedayro eel veeno dayllya kassa pehr favoray*

There is no standard labeling of Italian wines, which may be named by place (e.g. *Chianti, Orvieto, Frascati, Asti*), descriptive term (e.g. **classico, dolce, liquoroso, riserva, superiore**), grape (e.g. **Barbera, Dolcetto, Moscato, Pinot nero**), proprietary name or a combination of these elements. However, the table below will help you with some important terms.

Reading the Label

abboccato semi-dry	**imbottigliato dal produttore all'origine** bottled by producers at source
amabile slightly sweet	**leggero** light
bianco white	**pieno** full-bodied
DOC guarantee of origin (240 regions)	**rosato/rosatello** rosé
DOCG highest quality wine complying with most stringent regulations (13 wines)	**rosso** red
	secco dry
dolce sweet	**spumante** sparkling
IGT higher quality than "**vino tipico**"	**vino del paese** local wine

Type of wine	Examples
sweet white wine	Aleatico, Vino Santo (Tuscany); Marsala and Malvasia (Sicily), Moscato, Passito di Pantelleria
dry white wine	Frascati (Latium), Verdicchio dei Castelli di Jesi (Adriatic Marches), Orvieto (Umbria), Vermentino (Sardinia), Corvo bianco, Colombo Platino (Sicily); Cortese di Gavi (Liguria) Gavi dei Gavi (Piedmont) Chardonnay, Pino bianco, Pino grigio (Friuli); local white wine generally falls into this category
rosé	Lagrein (Trentino-Alto Adige)
light-bodied red wine	Bardolino, Valpolicella (Lake Garda); Vino Novello (in the Autumn, mostly from Tuscany); local red wine, including Italian-Swiss Merlot, usually fits into this category
full-bodied red wine	Barolo, Barbera, Barbaresco, Dolcetto, Gattinara, Nebbiolo (Piedmont); Amarone (Veneto); Brunello di Montalcino (one of the most famous wines in Italy), Chianti Classico, Vino Nobile di Montepulciano (Tuscany); Corvo Rosso (Sicily).
sparkling sweet white wine	Asti Spumante
sparkling dry white wine	Prosecco, Ferrari Brut Spumante; metodo champenoise in general
sparkling sweet red wine	Braghetto d'Acqui (Piedmont); Fragolino (made from "uva fragola" with a distinct strawberry flavour, Veneto region)

Other drinks Altre bevande

You'll certainly want to take the opportunity to sip an after-dinner drink. If you'd like something that approaches French cognac try **Vecchia Romagna etichetta nera** or **Carpene Malvolta Stravecchio**.

If you feel like a digestive (**un digestivo**), why not try the following:

amaro *amaaro*
Bitter; three of the most popular being *Amaro Averna*, *Amaro Lucano* or *Amaro Montenegro* (bittersweet), or a glass of *Fernet-Branca* (very bitter) should fit the bill.

liquore *leekworay*
Popular liqueurs include *Strega* (sweet herb), *Sambuca* (aniseed-flavored), *Amaretto* (almond), *Millefiore* (herb and alpine flower), *Silvestro* (herb and nut).

You'll recognize: **un brandy**, **un cognac**, **un gin e tonico**, **un porto**, **un rum**, **una vodka**.

Non-alcoholic drinks Bevande analcoliche

I'd like …	**Vorrei …** *vorrehee*
hot chocolate	**una cioccolata calda** *oona chokkolaata kalda*
lemonade	**una limonata** *oona leemonaata*
milk shake	**un frullato di latte** *oon froollaato dee lattay*
mineral water	**dell'acqua minerale** *dayllakwa meenayraalay*
carbonated/non-carbonated	**gassata/naturale** *gassaata/natooraalay*
tonic water	**dell'acqua tonica** *dayllakwa toneeka*

un caffè *oon kaffeh*
Any coffee drinker will be spoiled in Italy; try un (**caffè**) espresso, strong and dark with a rich aroma, served in demi-tasses, or **un ristretto** (concentrated espresso); alternatively, ask for a **un caffè lungo** (weaker coffee), which can be **con panna** (with cream), or **con latte** (with milk). **Un cappuccino** (coffee and hot milk, dusted with cocoa) is also a must; while in summer, **un caffè freddo** (iced coffee) is popular.

un succo di frutta *oon sookko dee frootta*
Common fruit juices include: **un succo di limone** (lemon), **di pompelmo** (grapefruit), **di pomodoro** (tomato) and **d'arancia** (orange); for a freshly squeezed fruit juice ask for **una spremuta**.

Menu Reader

Italian cooking is essentially regional. Although there are many well-known dishes that are common to the whole of Italy, the terminology may vary from place to place. (There are at least half a dozen names for octopus or squid!) So, be prepared for regional variations to the terms appearing in this Menu Reader.

How it is cooked

baked	**al forno**	*al forno*
breaded	**impanato(-a)**	*eempanaato(-a)*
boiled	**bollito(-a)**	*bolleeto(-a)*
braised	**stufato(-a)**	*stoofaato(-a)*
diced	**tagliato(-a) a cubetti**	*talyaato(-a) a koobayttee*
fried	**fritto(-a)**	*freetto(-a)*
grilled	**alla griglia**	*alla greelya*
roasted	**arrosto(-a)**	*arrosto(-a)*
poached	**in camicia**	*een kameecha*
marinated	**marinato(-a)**	*mareenaato(-a)*
sautéed	**saltato(-a)**	*saltaato(-a)*
smoked	**affumicato(-a)**	*affoomeekaato(-a)*
spicy	**speziato(-a)/piccante**	*spaytsaato(-a)/peekkantay*
steamed	**al vapore**	*al vaporay*
stewed	**in umido**	*een oomeedo*
stuffed	**ripieno(-a)**	*reepeeayno(-a)*
creamed	**in purè**	*een pooreh*

very rare	**quasi crudo(-a)**	*kwasee kroodo(-a)*
rare/underdone	**al sangue**	*al sanway*
medium	**a puntino**	*a poonteeno*
well done	**ben cotto(-a)**	*behn kotto (a)*

A **a puntino** medium
a scelta choice
abbacchio roast lamb; ~ **al forno con patate** with potatoes; ~ **alla cacciatora** "hunting style": diced and cooked with white wine, garlic, rosemary, anchovy paste and hot peppers

abbacchio alla scottadita tender grilled lamb cutlets
(all')abruzzese Abruzzi style; with red peppers and sometimes ham
acciughe anchovies
aceto vinegar
acetosella sorrel
acqua water ~ **calda** hot water; ~ **minerale** mineral water; ~ **tonica** tonic water

acquacotta soup of bread and vegetables, sometimes with egg and cheese

affettati cold cuts; **~ misti** ~ of pork

affogato poached

affumicato smoked

aglio garlic; **~ olio, peperoncino** sauce of garlic, olive oil, sweet peppers, anchovies and parmesan

agnello lamb; **~ abbacchio** very young lamb

agnolotti round-filled pasta

(all')agro dressing of lemon juice and oil

agrodolce sweet-sour dressing of caramelized sugar, vinegar and flour

aguglie garfish

ai ferri grilled

ai funghi (pizza) with mushrooms

ai funghi porcini sauce of boletus mushrooms

al burro with butter and grated parmesan

al forno baked

al sangue rare/underdone

al sugo with tomato sauce and grated parmesan

al tartufo sauce of grated truffle

al, all', alla in the style of; with

ala wing

albicocca apricot

alfredo dairy sauce

alice anchovy

alici al limone baked anchovies with lemon juice

all'Amatriciana with **pancetta**, tomatoes and hot pepper

alla boscaiola with eggplant, mushrooms and tomato sauce

alla carrettiera "cart driver style"; with hot peppers and pork

alla graticola barbequed

alla griglia grilled

alla milanese with marrow, white wine, saffron and parmesan (risotto)

alla Norma with spices and tomato sauce *(Sicily)*

alla pescatora with tomatoes and seafood

alla rustica with garlic, anchovies and oregano

alla spina draft/draught (beer)

alle vongole sauce of clams, garlic, parsley, pepper, olive oil, sometimes tomatoes

allo spiedo broiled; spit-roasted

allodola lark

alloro bay leaf

amaro after-dinner drink/ digestive ➤ 51

amatriciana sauce of tomatoes, red peppers, bacon, onions, garlic and white wine (Latium)

Americano a vermouth ➤ 49

ananas pineapple

anatra duck

anelli small egg-pasta rings

anguilla eel; **~ alla veneziana** cooked in sauce made from tuna and lemon

anguria watermelon *(northern Italy)*

animelle di vitello calf's sweetbreads fried in butter and Marsala

anitra duck; **~ selvatica** wild duck

annegati slices of meat in white wine or Marsala

antipasti appetizers, hors d'oeuvres ➤ 43; **~ a scelta** of one's choice; **~ assortiti** assorted; **~ di mare** seafood

aperitivi aperitifs ➤ 49

Aperol a non-alcoholic bitters

arachidi peanuts

aragosta lobster
arancia orange
aranciata orangeade
arancini very popular and tasty Italian rice snack specialties
aringa herring
arista loin of pork; **~ alla fiorentina** roast with garlic, cloves and rosemary
arrosto roast(ed)
arselle scallops
asparagi asparagus; **~ alla Fiorentina** with fried eggs and cheese
assortito assorted
astice lobster
attesa: 15 minuti waiting time: 15 minutes

B **baccalà** dried salt cod; **~ alla romana** cooked with tomato sauce, garlic and parsley; **~ alla vicentina** cooked in milk
bagna cauda raw vegetables with a hot sauce (*northern Italy*)
barbabietola beet
basilico basil
bavette type of spaghetti
beccaccia woodcock
beccaccino snipe
Bel Paese smooth cheese with delicate taste
ben cotto well done
ben fritto deep fried
bevande drinks ➤ 49; **~ analcoliche** non-alcoholic drinks
bianchetti herring/whitebait
bianco white (wine)
bibita soft drink
bicchiere glass
bieta swiss chard
bionda light (beer)

birra beer; **~ rossa** stout (dark beer)
biscotti cookies/biscuits
bistecca steak; **~ di cinghiale** wild boar in a sweet-sour sauce; **~ alla fiorentina** grilled and flavored with pepper, lemon juice and parsley; **~ di filetto** rib steak
bitter analcolico a non-alcoholic aperitif
bollito boiled
bollito misto sausages with other boiled meats
bologna smooth, mild, slightly smoked sausage, usually of pork or beef, occasionally of veal or chicken
bolognese sauce of tomatoes, minced meat, onions and herbs
bottiglia bottle
braciola chop or cutlet
branzino (sea) bass
brasato braised
briciolata olive oil, black pepper and crisp breadcrumb sauce
broccoli broccoli; **~ al burro e formaggio** with butter and cheese; **~ alla romana** sauteed in olice oil and braised in wine
brodo bouillon, broth, soup
bruidda fish soup
bucatini thick spaghetti; **~ con le sarde alla Palermitana** with fresh sardines
budino pudding; **~ di ricotta** souffle with ricotta cheese and candied fruits
burrida fish stew with dogfish and skate (*Sardinia*)
burro butter; **~ e salvia** butter and sage sauce
busecca thick tripe, vegetable and bean soup

C **cacciagione** game

cacciucco spicy seafood chowder/stew

cachi persimmon

caciocavallo firm, slightly sweet cheese ➤ 48

caciotta firm, mild cheese ➤ 48

caffè coffee ➤ 51

caffè freddo iced coffee

calamaretti baby squid

calamari squid

caldo hot

camoscio chamois

Campari reddish-brown bitters, flavored with orange peel and herbs; has a quinine taste; **~ soda** *campari* diluted with soda, one of the most common Italian apertifis

canederli bread, ham and salami dumplings

cannariculi fried honey biscuits

cannella cinnamon

cannelloni stuffed tubular pasta baked with a white sauce ➤ 45 **alla partenopea** with ricotta, mozzarella and ham

cannoli sweetened ricotta cheese stuffed in deep-fried pastry shells

canoe di mele canoe-shaped pastry boats with rum pastry cream and glazed apples

canoe salate savory canoes

capellini type of spaghetti

caponata olives, eggplants and anchovies *(Sicily)*

capone apparecchiate mahi mahi fish fried with tomatoes, capers, olives *(Sicily)*

cappelletti "little hats" filled pasta ➤ 45; **~ di Romagna** with cheese

capperi capers

cappone capon

capretto kid goat; **~ ripieno al forno** stuffed with herbs and oven-roasted

capricciosa the cook's specialty (pizza)

capriolo roebuck

carbonara sauce of smoked ham, cheese, eggs and olive oil

carciofi artichokes; **~ alla giudea** deep-fried ➤ 47; **~ alla romana** lightly stewed and stuffed

carciofini sottolio artichoke hearts in olive oil

carne meat ➤ 46; **~ ai ferri** grilled

carota carrot; **~ rossa** beet

carpa carp

carrettiera sauce of tuna, mushrooms, tomato purée, freshly ground pepper

cassata ice cream with candied fruit (spumoni); **~ siciliana** garnished sponge cake ➤ 48

castagna chestnut

castagnaccio chestnut cake with sultanas and pine nuts *(Tuscany)*

caviale caviar

cavolfiore cauliflower; **~ stracciato** boiled and fried in olive oil and garlic

cavolini di Bruxelles Brussels sprouts

cavolo cabbage

ceci chickpeas

cedro citron

cereali cereal

cervello brains

cervo deer

cetriolini pickles/gherkins

cetriolo cucumber

chiodi di garofano cloves

cicoria chicory

ciliege cherries

55

cima alla genovese rolled veal stuffed with eggs, sausage and mushrooms

cima genovese cold veal stuffed with onions, herbs and calf's brains

cinghiale wild boar

cioccolata (calda) (hot) chocolate

cipolle onions

cipollina spring onion

clementino seedless mandarin orange

cocomero watermelon (*Rome, southern Italy*)

colazione breakfast ➤ 43

con with

con acqua (di seltz) with (seltzer or soda) water

con briciolata with toasted breadcrumbs

con funghi with mushrooms

con ghiaccio on the rocks (with ice)

con il sugo di melanze e peperoni with peppers and eggplant

con latte with milk

con le lumache with snails and parsley

con limone with lemon

con panna with cream

con polpettine with tiny meatballs

con porchetta with tasty cold pork (sandwich)

con salsa di noci with walnut sauce

conchiglie conch shell-shaped pasta

coniglio rabbit; **~ ai capperi** cooked with capers

contorno a scelta choice of vegetables

coppa cured pork shoulder

cosciotto leg

costata al prosciutto filled chop

costola rib

costolette di maiale al finocchio braised pork chops with white wine and fennel seed

cotechino con lenticchie sausage-like spicy pork mix

cotogna quince

cotoletta cutlet; **~ alla milanese** breaded veal cutlet, flavored with cheese

cotto cooked; **~ a vapore** steamed

cozze mussels

crema custard; **~ di legumi** vegetable cream soup; **~ di pomodori** tomato cream soup

crespelle di farina dolce chestnut-flour crepes with ricotta and rum

crostacei shellfish

crostata pie; **~ di mele** apple pie; **~ di ricotta** cheesecake with raisins and Marsala

crudo di Parma cured ham from Parma

cumino cumin

cuscus couscous

Cynar aperitif produced from artichoke

D **d', di** of, with

datteri dates

decaffeinato decaffeinated

dentice type of sea bream

digestivo after-dinner drink/digestive

ditali pasta thimbles

dolce cake; dessert ➤ 48; mild (cheese); sweet (wine)

doppio double (a double shot)

E **elicoidali** short, twisted pasta tubes

eperlano smelt

F **fagiano** pheasant; ~ **al tartufo** stuffed with truffles

fagioli (haricot) beans; ~ **all'uccelletto** cooked in tomatoes and black olives; ~ **in umido** cooked in tomato sauce

fagioli alla toscana Tuscan-style beans, simmered for hours and garnished with salt, black pepper and crude olive oil

fagiolini French (green) beans

faraona guinea fowl

farcito stuffed

farfalle butterfly-shaped pasta

farfallini small bow-shaped egg-pasta

favata beans and port stew *(Sardinia)*

fave broad beans

fazzoletti salati savory turnovers

fegato liver; ~ **alla veneziana** thin slices fried with onions; ~ **alla salvia** with tomatoes, garlic and sage

fesa round cut from the rump

fetta di pizza slice of pizza

fettuccine egg-pasta ribbons ➤ 45; ~ **Alfredo** with parmesan and cream

fico fig

filetto fillet; ~ **al pepe verde** fillet steak served in a creamy sauce with green peppercorns

finocchio fennel

focaccia savory flatbread; ~ **alla salvia** sage bread; ~ **alla salsiccia** sausage bread; ~ **alle noci** walnut bread; ~ **genovese** savory bread with sage and olive oil

focaccia al Gorgonzola warm yeast flatbread topped with cheese

fonduta hot dip of Fontina cheese, egg yolks and truffles

formaggio cheese ➤ 48

fragole strawberries

fragoline di bosco wild strawberries

freddo cold

frittata omelet; ~ **campagnola** with onion, grated cheese, milk and cream; ~ **primaverile** with vegetables

frite al buro nero brains with black butter

frite alla fiorentina marinated, breadcrumbed, fried brains served with spinach

fritto fried

fritto misto a fry of various small fish and shellfish

frullato di latte milk-shake

frustenga cornmeal fruit cake

frutta fruit ➤ 48

frutti di mare seafood

funghi mushrooms; ~ **alla parmigiani** stuffed with breadcrumbs, Parmesan, garlic, herbs; ~ **porcini arrosti** roasted or grilled with chili peppers

fusilli pasta twists

G **galletto amburghese** young tender chicken, oven-roasted

gallina stewing fowl

gallo cedrone grouse

gamberetti shrimps

gamberi prawns

gassata carbonated/fizzy (water)

gelato ice cream

gianduia cold chocolate pudding

gin e tonico gin and tonic

gingerino ginger-flavored aperitif (also sold in small bottles)

gnocchi alla genovese dumplings with pesto sauce

gnocchi di patate potato dumplings

gorgonzola blue-veined cheese ➤ 48

granchi crabs

granita coarse sorbet ice cream

gronghi conger eel

i nostri piatti di carne sono serviti con contorno our meat dishes are accompanied by vegetables

in bianco without tomato sauce

in bottiglia bottled (beer)

in casseruola casseroled

in umido stewed

indivia endive

insalata salad

insalata di frutti di mare prawns and squid with lemon, pickles and olives

insalata di pollo chicken salad with green salad, lemon and cream

insalata mista mixed salad

insalata russa diced boiled vegetables in mayonnaise

involtini thin slices of meat (beef, veal or pork) rolled and stuffed

lamponi raspberries

lamprede lampreys

lasagne thin layers of pasta lined with meat and tomato sauce ➤ 45; **~ al forno** with Bel Paese and Mozzarella cheeses; **~ con anitra** with duck; **~ con le verdure** vegetable lasagna

lasagnette del lucchese lasagna with sauce of spinach, ricotta, chicken livers

lattaiolo cinnamon custard

latte milk

lattuga lettuce

lauro bay

leggero light (wine)

lenticchie lentils

lepre hare; **~ in agrodolce** with pine kernels, sultanas and chocolate; **~ piemontese** cooked in Barbera wine, sprinkled with herbs and bitter chocolate

lesso boiled

limonata lemonade

limone lemon

lingua tongue

linguine type of thick spaghetti

liquore liqueur ➤ 51

liscio straight/neat

lo chef consiglia the chef recommends …

lombata/lombo loin

lombo di maiale al forno garlic-roasted pork loin

lombo di maiale al prosciutto grilled pork loin with prosciutto

luccio pike

luganeghe fresh pork sausages sold by the length

lumache snails; snail shell-shaped pasta

lumache alle milanese snails with anchovy, fennel and wine sauce

lumache di mare sea snails

lunette half-moon-shaped stuffed pasta

maccheroni alla chitarra handmade pasta cut into strips

macchiato with milk

maggiorana marjoram

maiale pork

malfade thin pasta strips

mandarino tangerine
mandorle almonds
manzo beef
margherita tomato, cheese and basil pizza ➤ 44
marinara sauce of tomatoes, olives, garlic, clams and mussels
marinato marinated
marmellata jam; **~ d'arance** marmalade
mascarpone a thick, full-fat creamy cheese mostly used for desserts similar to clotted cream
Martini a brand-name vermouth, sweet or dry; not to be confused with a martini cocktail
medaglioni round fillet
mela apple
melanzane eggplant/aubergine
mele apples
melone melon
menta mint
menù a prezzo fisso set menu
merlano whiting
merluzzo cod
metà pollo arrosto half a roasted chicken
midollo marrow
miele honey
minestra soup ➤ 44; **~ di funghi** cream of mushroom soup; **~ di sedano e riso** celery and rice; **~ in brodo** with noodles or rice
minestrone a thick vegetable soup (sometimes with noodles) sprinkled with parmesan cheese
mirtilli blueberries
misto mixed
molle soft (egg)
montone mutton
more blackberries
mortadella Bologna sausage
mostaccioli chocolate biscuits

mozzarella soft, unripened cheese ➤ 48; **~ con pomodori** with tomatoes

N **napoletana** anchovies, ham, tomatoes, cheese (pizza topping) ➤ 44
nasello coal-fish
naturale still (water)
nero black (coffee)
nocciole hazelnuts
noce di cocco coconut
noce moscata nutmeg
noci walnuts
nodini veal chops

O **oca** goose
odori herbs
olio (d'oliva) (olive) oil
olive olives
orata type of sea bream
orecchiette ear-shaped pasta
origano oregano
ortolano ortolan
osso buco braised veal knuckles and shins
ostriche oysters

P **palombacce allo spiedo** wood pigeon, spit-roasted
pan di Spagna honey and rum sponge
pancetta affumicata bacon
pandorato alla crema di formaggio fried bread with cream cheese
pandoro large, sponge cake served with powdered vanilla on top
pane bread; **~ al latte** milk bread: **~ all'olio** olive oil white bread: **~ tostato** toast
pane, grissini e coperto L. ... bread, **grissini** and cover L....

panettone butter-enriched Christmas bread with candied fruit, sultanas and raisins

panforte similar to **pangiallo**

pangiallo fairly hard nut and honey cake

panini rolls

panino imbottito sandwich

panna cotta delicious Italian adaptation of blancmange and creme brulé

panpepato very spicy nut cake

pansotti con salsa di noci alla ligure triangles stuffed with greens in walnut sauce

pappardelle fat ribbons of egg-pasta; **~ alla lepre** with hare sauce

papriot thick spinach soup

parmigiana breaded veal escalopes with tomato sauce and mozzarella

parmigiano (-reggiano) parmesan ➤ 48

passato di verdura mashed vegetable soup, generally with croutons

pasta pasta, noodles ➤ 45; **~ e ceci** with chickpeas; **~ e fagioli** with beans

pasta Maddalena plain génoise cake

pastasciutta pasta

pasticcini pastries

pasticcio macaroni, white sauce, meat and tomato

pastiera ricotta cake with wheat berries

pastina small pasta pieces; **~ in brodo** in broth

patate potatoes

patatine fritte French fries, chips

pecorino hard cheese ➤ 48

penne pasta quills

peperonata peppers sauteed with tomato and onion

peperoni peppers; **~ ripieni** stuffed ➤ 47

pera pear

pernice partridge

pesca peach

pescanoce nectarine

pesce all'acqua pazza fish cooked in seawater

pesce persico perch

pesce spada swordfish

pescespada grilled swordfish stuffed with Mozzarella, brandy and herbs

pesche peaches

pesci fish ➤ 45; **~ al cartoccio** baked in a parchment envelope; **~ in carpione** boiled and cooked in vinegar, served cold with lemon

pestingolo rich fruit cake with figs and honey

pesto sauce of basil leaves, garlic, cheese and sometimes pine kernels *(Liguria)* and marjoram

piatti di carne meat dishes

piatti freddi cold dishes

piatto del giorno dish of the day

piccante sharp (cheese)

piccata al marsala thin veal escalope braised in marsala sauce

piccione pigeon

pieno full-bodied (wine)

pinoli pine nuts

piselli peas; **~ al prosciutto** cooked slowly with Parma ham and bacon

piviere plover

pizelle thin waffle cones with cream or ice cream

pizza pizza ➤ 44

polenta mush made from cornmeal; **~ alla piemontese** layered with meat; **~ e coniglio**

with rabbit stew; **~ e uccelli** with roasted small birds *(northern Italy)*
pollame poultry
pollo chicken; **~ all'abruzzese** with sweet peppers; **~ alla romana** diced and served with tomato sauce and sweet peppers; **~ alla diavola** highly spiced and grilled chicken; **~ novello** spring chicken
polpette meatballs
polpettone meat loaf of seasoned beef or veal
polpo octopus
pommarola sauce of tomatoes, garlic, basil *(Campania)*
pomodori tomatoes
pomodori e capperi salad with capers
pompelmo grapefruit
porcellino da latte suckling pig
porcetto arrosto suckling spit-roasted pig *(Sardinia)*
porchetta roasted whole pig with fennels and sausages
porchetta very spicy cooked pork served cold
porcini boletus mushrooms
porrata pancetta and leeks in yeast dough crust
porro leek
porto port
prezzemolo parsley
primo piatto first course
prosciutto ham
prosciutto crudo con melone/con fichi sliced melon or figs with cured ham from Parma
provolone firm cheese ➤ 48
prugna plum
prugna secca prune
puttanesca sauce of capers, black olives, parsley, garlic, olive oil, black pepper

Q **quaglia** quail
quattro formaggi four types of cheese (pizza topping) ➤ 44
quattro stagioni vegetables, cheese, ham and bacon (pizza topping) ➤ 44

R **radicchio** a kind of bitter red and white lettuce
ragù sauce like bolognese
ravanelli radishes
ravioli alla piemontese ravioli with beef and vegetable stuffing
razza ray
ribes red currants
ribes nero black currants
ricci sea urchins
ricciarelli delicate honey and almond biscuit *(Tuscany)*
ricotta soft cow's or sheep's milk cheese
rigatoni short, wide pasta tubes; **~ alla pagliata** with veal guts
risi e bisi rice with peas and bacon
riso rice ➤ 44
riso con le seppie cattlefish risotto
riso in bianco boiled rice with butter and grated parmesan
risotto rice casserole; **~ con fegatini** with chicken livers; **~ con gamberetti in bianco** with prawns and red wine
rognoncini trifolati kidneys sauteed with Marsala
rognoni kidneys
rombo turbot
rosato rosé (wine)
rosbif roast beef
rosmarino rosemary
rosso red (wine)

ruoti wheel-shaped pasta

S salame salami
salami spicy sausages made with uncooked beef or pork, often flavored with pepper and garlic
salciccia small sausage, country-style pork mixture
sale salt
salmone salmon
salse sauces ➤ 47
salsicce sausages
saltimbocca veal escalopes with prosciutto ham; ~ **alla romana** braised in marsala wine with sage
salumi assorted pork products
salvia sage
sardine sardines; ~ **all'olio** in oil
sauersuppe sour tripe soup marinated in white wine vinegar
scalogno shallot
scaloppina veal escalope; ~ **alla Valdostana** filled with cheese and ham; ~ **al Marsala** with Marsala wine
scampi prawns
sciule pieuno onions stuffed with macaroons, breadcrumbs, cheese, spices and sultanas
scorfano sea-scorpion, sculpin
scura dark (beer)
secco dry (wine)
secondo piatto second (main) course
sedano celery
selvaggina venison
semi-freddo ice cream cake
senape mustard
seppia cuttlefish
seppie con piselli baby squid and peas
sfogliatelle sweet Ricotta cheese turnovers

sgombri in umido stewed mackerel in white wine with green peas
sgombro mackerel
siciliana with black olives, capers and cheese (pizza)
sodo hard (egg)
sogliola sole
sogliole alla mugnaia sole sautéed in butter, garnished with parsley and lemon
solubile instant (coffee)
sottaceti pickled vegetables
spaghetti all'amatriciana spaghetti with tomato, bacon and Pecorino cheese sauce
spalla shoulder
specialità della casa specialties of the house
specialità di pesce fish specialties
specialità locali local specialties
spezie spices
spezzatino meat or poultry stew
spezzatino di cinghiale alla cacciatora diced wild boar stewed in white wine with garlic and bay leaves
spezzato di tacchino turkey casserole with olives (*Umbria*)
spiedino pieces of meat grilled or roasted on a skewer
spigola sea bass
spinaci spinach
spremuta di ... freshly squeezed (juice)
spumante sparkling (wine)
stecca di cioccolato chocolate bar
stelline small pasta stars
stoccafisso dried cod cooked with tomatoes, olives and artichoke
storione sturgeon
stracciatella clear egg and cheese soup
stracotto meat stew with sausages, beef and vegetables in white wine,

slowly cooked for several hours *(Tuscany)*

strangola-preti bread and spinach dumpling

straniera foreign (beer)

su ordinazione made to order

succo di frutta fruit juice ➤ 51

supplemento extra charge

supplì very popular and tasty Italian rice croquettes with Mozzarella cheese and minced meat, breadcrumbed and fried

susina plum (yellow) or greengage

T tacchino turkey

tagliatelle egg-pasta ribbons

tartufi truffles

tartufi di cioccolata chocolate truffles

timballo con le sarde macaroni, sardines, pine nuts, fennel, raisins

timo thyme

tiramisù sponge cake, custard, cream and chocolate dessert ➤ 48

tisana herb tea

tonno tuna

tonno alla livornese fried tuna in slices, stewed in garlic and tomato

tordo thrush

Torrone delicious Italian nougat which can be found hard and crispy or soft, also chocolate flavored.

torta cake; pie

torta di cioccolata chocolate cake

torta di frutta fruit cake

torta di mandorle almond pie

torta di mele apple pie

torta di ricotta delicious pie made with ricotta cheese (roughly similar to cheese cake)

torta manfreda liver pate with Marsala and Parmesan

torta Margherita layered cake with meringue, fresh fruit and whipped cream

tortelli di zucca tortellini with pumpkin stuffing

tortellini stuffed egg-pasta rings ➤ 45; **~ alla panna con tartufi** with cream and truffles; **~ di piccioncello** with pigeon stuffing

tortino di zucchine zucchini with white sauce

triglie red mullet; **~ alla livornese** baked; **~ alla siciliana** grilled with orange peel and white wine

trippa tripe; **~ alla fiorentina** and beef braised in a tomato sauce and served with cheese *(Tuscany)*; **~ verde** in green sauce

trota trout; **~ alla brace** grilled

tutto mare seafood sauce

tè tea; **~ freddo** iced tea

U uova eggs

uova alla Romana omelet with beans, onions and herbs

uova e pancetta bacon and eggs

uova e prosciutto ham and eggs

uova fritte fried eggs

uova strapazzate scrambled eggs

uovo alla coque boiled egg

uva bianca/nera white/black grapes

uva passa raisins

uva spina gooseberries

V vaniglia vanilla

veneziana sweet bread with whole almonds

verde with creamed green vegetables

verdura mista mixed vegetables

verdure vegetables ➤ 47; **~ di stagione** vegetables in season
vermicelli thin spaghetti
verza green cabbage
vincigrassi cooked pasta with cream sauce and gravy
vino wine ➤ 49-50
vitello veal; **~ alla bolognese** cutlet cooked with Parma ham and cheese; **~ tonnato** cold with tuna fish sauce; **~ valdostana** stuffed with soft cheese
vongole clams

WX Y Z
whisky (e soda/con seltz) whisky (and soda)
Würstel frankfurters
zabaglione egg yolks, sugar and Marsala wine
zafferano saffron
zampone pig's foot/trotter filled with seasoned pork, boiled and served in slices
zenzero ginger
ziti long, solid eggless-pasta tubes
zucca pumpkin, gourd; **~ gialla al forno** baked and served with parmesan cheese (winter only)
zucchero sugar
zucchini ripieni stuffed zucchini (usually containing mince meat)
zuppa soup ➤ 44; **~ alla cacciatora** meat soup with mushrooms; **~ alla marinara** spicy fish chowder/stew; **~ alla pavese** consommé with poached egg, croutons and grated cheese; **~ alla senese** sausages with lentils; **~ alla veneta** vegetable soup with white wine and noodles; **~ di bue con spaghettini** spaghetti in beef soup;

~ di cipolle onion soup with brandy; **~ di cozze** mussels soup; **~ di datteri di mare** sea dates (kind of mussel) soup; **~ di frutti di mare** seafood soup; **~ di pesce** spicy fish chowder/stew; **~ di vongole** clams and white wine soup
zuppa inglese sponge cake steeped in rum with candied fruit and custard or whipped cream

Travel

ESSENTIAL

1/2/3 for ...	**Uno/due/tre per ...** *oono/doo-ay/tray pehr*
A ticket to ...	**Un biglietto per ...** *oon beelyaytto pehr*
one-way/single	**Solo andata** *solo andaata*
round-trip/return	**andata e ritorno** *andaata ay reetorno*
How much ...?	**Quanto ... ?** *kwanto*

Safety Sicurezza

Would you accompany me ...?	**Le spiace accompagnarmi?** *lay speeachay akkompañaarmee*
to the bus stop	**alla fermata dell'autobus** *alla fayrmaata dayllowtobooss*
to my hotel	**al mio albergo** *al meeo albayrgo*
I don't want to ... on my own.	**Non voglio ... da solo(-a).** *non volyo ... da solo(-a)*
stay here	**rimanere qui** *reemanayray kwee*
walk home	**rientrare a piedi** *reeayntraaray ah peeaydee*
I don't feel safe here.	**Non mi sento sicuro(-a) qui.** *non me saynto seekooro(-a) kwee*

Arrival Arrivo

Most visitors, including citizens of all EU{European Union} countries, the US, Canada, Eire, Australia and New Zealand, require only a valid passport for entry to Italy.

Import restrictions between EU countries have been relaxed on items for personal use or consumption which are bought duty-paid within the EU. Suggested maximum: 90L. wine or 60L. sparkling wine, 20L. fortified wine, 10L. spirits and 110L. beer.

There are duty-free shops at the following airports: Bologna, Genova, Milan, Naples, Pisa, Rimini, Rome Ciampino, Rome Fiumicino, Turin, and Venice.

Passport control Il controllo passaporti

We have a joint passport.	**Abbiamo un passaporto congiunto.** *abbeeamo oon passaporto konjoonto*
The children are on this passport.	**I bambini sono su questo passaporto.** *ee bambeenee sono soo kwaysto passaporto*
I'm here on vacation/ business.	**Sono qui per vacanza/per lavoro.** *sono kwee pehr vakantsa/pehr lavoro*
I'm just passing through.	**Sono solo di passaggio.** *sono solo dee passadjo*
I'm going to …	**Vado a …** *vado a*
I'm …	**Sono …** *sono*
on my own	**da solo(-a)** *da solo(-a)*
with my family	**con la mia famiglia** *kon la meea fameelya*
with a group	**con un gruppo** *kon oon groopo*

FAMILY ➤ 120

Customs Dogana

I have only the
normal allowances.

**Ho solo beni in esenzione
fiscale.** *oh solo baynee
een ayzentseeonay feeskalay*

It's a gift.

È un regalo.
eh oon raygaalo

It's for my personal use.

È per mio uso personale.
eh pehr meeo oozo pehrsonaalay

Ha qualcosa da dichiarare?	Do you have anything to declare?
Deve pagare il dazio per questo.	You must pay duty on this.
Dove l'ha comprato?	Where did you buy this?
Apra questa borsa, per favore.	Please open this bag.
Ha altri bagagli?	Do you have any more luggage?

I would like to declare …

Vorrei dichiarare ..
vorrehee deekeearaaray

I don't understand.

Non capisco. *non kapeesko*

Does anyone here speak English?

C'è qualcuno qui che parla inglese?
*cheh kwalkoono kwee kay parla
eengglaysay*

IL CONTROLLO PASSAPORTI	passport control
LA FRONTIERA	border crossing
LA DOGANA	customs
NULLA DA DICHIARARE	nothing to declare
MERCI DA DICHIARARE	goods to declare
ESENTE DA DAZIO	duty-free

Duty-free shopping Comprare al negozio duty-free

What currency is this in?

In che valuta è questo?
een kay valoota eh kwaysto

Can I pay in …

Posso pagare in …
posso pagaaray een

dollars

dollari *dollaree*

lira

lire *leeray*

pounds

sterline *stayrleenay*

COMMUNICATION DIFFICULTIES ➤ 11

Plane L'aereo

Italian cities and major islands are well connected by air. This includes a shuttle service (**Arcobaleno**) between Rome and Milan every 20 minutes. Domestic flights can be expensive. However, cheaper rates can be obtained off-peak, and special fares are generally available for family groups, young people/students and senior citizens.

Tickets and reservations Biglietti e prenotazioni

When is the ... flight to ...?	**Quando parte il volo ... per ...?** *kwando partay eel volo ... pehr*
first/next/last	**il primo/il prossimo/l'ultimo** *eel preemo/eel prosseemo/loolteemo*
I'd like 2 ... tickets to ...	**Vorrei due biglietti ... per ...** *vorrehee doo-ay beelyayttee ... pehr*
one-way/single	**di andata** *dee andaata*
round-trip/return	**di andata e ritorno** *dee andaata ay reetorno*
first class	**di prima classe** *dee preema klassay*
economy class	**in classe turistica** *een klassay tooreesteeka*
business class	**business class**
How much is a flight to ...?	**Quanto costa il volo per ...?** *kwanto kosta eel volo pehr*
I'd like to ... my reservation for flight number ...	**Vorrei ... la mia prenotazione per il volo numero ...** *vorrehee ... la meea praynotatseeonay pehr eel volo noomayro*
cancel	**annullare** *annoollaaray*
change	**cambiare** *kambeeaaray*
confirm	**confermare** *konfayrmaaray*

Inquiries about the flight Informazioni sul volo

How long is the flight?	**Quanto dura il volo?** *kwanto doora eel volo*
What time does the plane leave?	**A che ora decolla l'aereo?** *ah kay ora daykolla la-ayrayo*
What time will we arrive?	**A che ora arriveremo?** *ah kay ora arreevayraymo*
What time do I have to check in?	**A che ora devo registrare i bagagli?** *ah kay ora dayvo rayjeestraaray ee bagaalyee*

Checking in Accettazione

Where is the check-in desk for flight …?

Dov'è il banco accettazione per il volo …?
dovay ell banko achaytatseeonay pehr eel volo

I have …

Ho … *oh*

3 cases to check in

tre valige da registrare
treh valeejay da rayjeestraaray

2 pieces of hand luggage

due borse a mano
doo-ay borsay ah mano

Il suo biglietto/passaporto/ carta d'imbarco, per favore.	Your ticket/passport/ boarding card please.
Preferisce un posto vicino al finestrino o nel corridoio?	Would you like a window or an aisle seat?
Fumatori o non fumatori?	Smoking or non-smoking?
Si accomodi nella sala partenze.	Please go through to the departure lounge.
Quanti pezzi/quante valige ha?	How many pieces of luggage do you have?
Ha un eccesso di bagaglio.	You have excess luggage.
Deve pagare un supplemento di … lire per ogni chilo in più.	You'll have to pay a supplement of … Lira per kilo of excess luggage.
Questo bagaglio a mano è troppo pesante/grande.	That's too heavy/ large for hand luggage.
Ha fatto i bagagli personalmente?	Did you pack these bags yourself?
Ci sono articoli elettrici o taglienti?	Do they contain any sharp or electrical items?

ARRIVI	arrivals
PARTENZE	departures
I CONTROLLI DI SICUREZZA	security check
TENERE CON SÈ I BAGAGLI	do not leave luggage unattended

LUGGAGE/BAGGAGE ➤ 71

Information Informazioni

Is there any delay on flight ...?	**C'è un ritardo sul volo ...?** *cheh oon reetardo sool volo*
How late will it be?	**Di quanto ritarderà?** *dee kwanto reetardayra*
Has the flight from ... landed?	**È atterrato il volo da ...?** *eh attayrraato eel volo da*
Which gate does flight ... leave from?	**Da quale uscita parte il volo ...?** *da kwalay oosheeta partay eel volo*

Boarding/In-flight L'imbarco/In volo

Your boarding card, please.	**La sua carta d'imbarco, per favore.** *la sooa karta deembarko pehr favoray*
Could I have a drink/something to eat, please?	**Può portarmi qualcosa da bere/da mangiare, per favore?** *pwo portaarmee kwalkosa da bayray/da manjaaray pehr favoray*
Please wake me for the meal.	**Mi svegli per il pasto, per favore.** *mee svaylyee pehr eel pasto pehr favoray*
What time will we arrive?	**A che ora arriveremo?** *ah kay ora arreevayraymo*
A sick bag, quick, please.	**Un sacchetto di carta, presto, per favore.** *oon sakkaytto dee karta praysto pehr favoray*

Arrival L'arrivo

Where is/are ...?	**Dov'è/Dove sono ...?** *doveh/dovay sono*
currency exchange	**l'ufficio cambio** *looffeecho kambeeo*
buses	**gli autobus** *lyee owtobooss*
car rental	**il noleggio auto** *eel nolaydjo owto*
exit	**l'uscita** *loosheeta*
taxis	**i tassì** *ee tassee*
Is there a bus into town?	**C'è un autobus per il centro città?** *cheh oon owtobooss pehr eel chayntro cheetta*
How do I get to the ... Hotel?	**Come si arriva all' albergo ...?** *komay see arreeva allalbayrgo*

Luggage/Baggage Il bagaglio

Tipping: The suggested rate for the porter is Lit. 2,000-5,000 per bag; in railway stations, tariffs are generally displayed.

Porter! Excuse me!	**Facchino! Scusi!** *fakkeeno. skoozee*
Could you take my luggage to …?	**Può portarmi i bagagli fino …?** *pwo portaarmee ee bagalyee feeno*
a taxi/bus	**al tassì/alla fermata dell'autobus** *al tassee/ alla faymaata daylowtobooss*
Where is/are …?	**Dov'è/Dove sono …?** *doveh /dovay sono*
luggage carts/trolleys	**i carrelli portabagaglio** *ee karrayllee portabagaalyo*
luggage lockers	**il deposito bagagli automatico** *eel dayposeeto bagalyee owtomateeko*
luggage check/ left-luggage office	**il deposito bagagli** *eel dayposeeto bagalyee*
Where is the luggage from flight …?	**Dove sono i bagagli del volo …?** *dovay sono ee bagalyee dayl volo*

Loss, damage and theft Smarrimento, danni e furti

My luggage has been lost.	**Ho smarrito i bagagli.** *oh smarreeto ee bagalyee*
My luggage has been stolen.	**Il mio bagaglio è stato rubato.** *eel meeo bagaalyo eh staato roobaato*
My suitcase was damaged in transit.	**La mia valigia è stata danneggiata durante il viaggio.** *la meea valeeja eh staata dannaydjaata doorantay eel veeadjo*

Può descrivere i suoi bagagli?	What does your luggage look like?
Ha l'etichetta di ricupero bagagli?	Do you have the claim check/ reclaim tag?
I suoi bagagli …	Your luggage …
potrebbero essere stati mandati a …	may have been sent to …
potrebbero arrivare oggi più tardi	may arrive later today
Ritorni domani, per favore.	Please come back tomorrow.
Chiami questo numero per controllare se i suoi bagagli sono arrivati.	Call this number to check if your luggage has arrived.

POLICE ➤ 152; COLORS ➤ 143

Train Treno

EuroCity (EC) *ayoorosseetee*
International express connecting main European cities; first and second class. A supplement is payable and reservation is obligatory.

Pendolino-ETR 450 (P) *pehndoleeno*
High-speed train connecting major Italian cities. Luxury first class and second class; tickets include hostess service and a meal. Reservations are obligatory.

Rapido *raapeedo*
Long-distance express train stopping at major cities only; first and second class.

Intercity (IC) *"intercity"*
Intercity express with very few stops; luxury, international service with first and second class. Seat reservation is essential and a special supplement is charged.

Espresso (EXP) *aysprehsso*
Long-distance express train, stopping at major stations.

Diretto (D) *deerehtto*
Slower than the Espresso, it stops at most stations.

Interregionale (IR) *eentehrrayjeeonalay*
Train stopping at main stations within a region.

Regionale (R) *rayjeeonalay*
Local train stopping at many smaller locations. Not very fast, but an excellent means of visiting small hilltop towns that abound in Italy. Marked by a white "R" on a black background (to distinguish it from the **Rapido**).

carrozza ristorante *karrotsa reestorantay*
Dining car; attached to most international and long-distance trains. Some services include self-service restaurant cars. In addition, most trains have snacks and refreshments available.

vagone letto *vagonay lehtto*
Sleeping car with individual compartment and washing facilities. Sleeping cars containing berths with blankets and pillows (**carrozza cuccette**) are also available on some lines. First and second class are distinguished by the number of berths per compartment.

The National Railways (**Ferrovie dello Stato – FS**) publishes a free, easy-to-consult pocket timetable of the major trains running throughout Italy. Italy's trains can be crowded; if you haven't booked, it's wise to arrive at the station at least 30 minutes before departure to be sure of a seat.

Check out the various reductions and travel cards available. These include: **Biglietto turistico libera circolazione** (for extensive "travel-at-will," only available outside Italy); and **Chilometrico** (for groups of up to five people, valid for 2 months).

To the station Alla stazione ferroviaria

How do I get to the (main) rail station?	**Come si arriva alla stazione ferroviaria (principale)?** *komay see arreeva alla statseeonay fayrroveeaareea (preencheepaalay)*
Do trains to ... leave from ... Station?	**I treni per ... partono dalla stazione di ...?** *ee traynee pehr ... partono dalla statseeonay dee*
How far is it?	**Quanto distante?** *kwanto deestantay*
Can I leave my car here?	**Posso lasciare la mia macchina qui?** *posso lashaaray la meea makkeena kwee*

At the station Alla stazione ferroviaria

Where is/are ...?	**Dov'è/Dove sono ...?** *doveh /dovay sono*
currency-exchange office	**l'ufficio cambio** *looffeecho kambeeo*
information desk	**lo sportello informazioni** *lo sportayllo eenformatseeonay*
luggage check	**il deposito bagagli** *eel dayposeeto bagaalyee*
lost-and-found	**l'ufficio oggetti smarriti** *looffeecho odjayttee smarreetee*
luggage lockers	**il deposito bagagli automatico** *eel dayposeeto bagaalyee owtomaateeko*
platforms	**i binari** *ee beenaaree*
snack bar	**il bar** *eel bar*
ticket office	**la biglietteria** *la beelyayttayreea*
waiting room	**la sala d'aspetto** *la sala daspaytto*

ENTRATA	entrance
USCITA	exit
AI BINARI	to the platforms
INFORMAZIONI	information
PRENOTAZIONI	reservations
ARRIVI	arrivals
PARTENZE	departures

DIRECTIONS ➤ *94*

Tickets Biglietti

It is **very important** to validate tickets before commencing your journey by inserting them in machines (generally yellow) positioned on platforms, otherwise you will be liable for a fine.

I'd like a ... ticket to ...
Vorrei un biglietto ... per ...
vorrehee oon beelyayto ... pehr

one-way/single
di andata *dee andaata*

round-trip/return
di andata e ritorno
dee andaata ay reetorno

first/second class
di prima/di seconda classe
dee preema/dee saykonda klassay

I'd like to reserve a ...
Vorrei prenotare ...
vorrehee praynotaaray

window/aisle seat
un posto vicino al finestrino/al corridoio
oon posto veecheeno al feenaystreeno/al korreedoyo

Is there a sleeper/sleeping car?
C'è un vagone letto?
cheh oon vagonay laytto

I'd like a ... berth.
Vorrei una cuccetta ...
vorrehee oona koochaytta

upper/lower
superiore/inferiore
soopayreeoray/eenfayreeoray

Price Tariffe

How much is that?
Quant'è? *kwanteh*

Is there a discount for ...?
C'è una riduzione per ...?
cheh oon reedootseeonay pehr

children/families
bambini/famiglie
bambeenee/fameelyay

senior citizens
anziani *antseeanee*

students
studenti *stoodayntee*

Do you offer a cheap same-day round-trip?
Avete una tariffa economica per una andata e ritorno in giornata?
avaytay oona tareeffa aykonomeeka pehr oona andaata ay reetorno een jornaata

Queries Richieste d'informazione

Do I have to change trains?	**Devo cambiare treno?** *dayvo kambeeaaray trayno*
It's a direct train.	**È un treno diretto.** *eh oon trayno deeraytto*
You have to change at …	**Deve cambiare a …** *dayvay kambeeaaray ah*
How long is this ticket valid for?	**Per quanto tempo è valido questo biglietto?** *pehr kwanto taympo eh valeedo kwaysto beelyayto*
Can I return on the same ticket?	**Posso ritornare con lo stesso biglietto?** *posso reetornaaray kon lo staysso beelyaytto*
Which car/coach is my seat in?	**In quale carrozza è il mio posto?** *een kwalay karrotsa eh eel meeo posto*
Is there a dining car on the train?	**C'è un vagone ristorante sul treno?** *cheh oonh vagonay reestorantay sool trayno*

- Vorrei un biglietto per Siena, per favore.
  - *Andata o andata e ritorno?*
- Andata e ritorno, per favore.
  - *Fa 23.000 lire.*
- Devo cambiare treno?
  - *Sì, deve cambiare a Poggibonsi.*

Train times L'orario ferroviario

Could I have a timetable, please?	**Ha un orario ferroviario, per favore?** *ah oon orareeo fayrroveeaareeo pehr favoray*
When is the … train to … ?	**Quando parte … treno per** *kwando paartay … trayno pehr*
first/next/last	**il primo/il prossimo/l'ultimo** *eel preemo /eel prosseemo/ loolteemo*

How frequent are the trains to …?	**Che frequenza hanno i treni per …?**
	kay fray<u>kwayn</u>tsa <u>an</u>no ee <u>tray</u>nee pehr
once/twice a day	**una volta/due volte al giorno**
	<u>oo</u>na <u>vol</u>ta/<u>doo</u>-ay <u>vol</u>tay al <u>jor</u>no
5 times a day	**cinque volte al giorno**
	<u>cheen</u>kweh <u>vol</u>tay al <u>jor</u>no
every hour	**ogni ora**
	<u>on</u>ee <u>o</u>ra
What time do they leave?	**A che ora partono?**
	ah kay <u>o</u>ra <u>par</u>tono
on the hour	**ad ogni ora precisa**
	ad <u>on</u>ee <u>o</u>ra pray<u>chee</u>sa
What time does the train stop at …?	**A che ora si ferma il treno a …?**
	ah kay <u>o</u>ra see <u>fayr</u>ma eel <u>tray</u>no ah
What time does the train arrive in …?	**A che ora arriva il treno a …?**
	ah kay <u>o</u>ra ar<u>ree</u>va eel <u>tray</u>no ah
How long is the trip?	**Quanto dura il viaggio?**
	<u>kwan</u>to <u>doo</u>ra eel vee<u>ad</u>jo
Is the train on time?	**Il treno è in orario?**
	eel <u>tray</u>no eh een o<u>ra</u>reeo

Departures Partenze

Which platform does the train to … leave from?	**Da quale binario parte il treno per …?**
	da <u>kwa</u>lay been<u>aa</u>reeo <u>par</u>tay eel <u>tray</u>no pehr
Where is platform 4?	**Dov'è il binario quattro?**
	do<u>veh</u> eel been<u>aa</u>reeo <u>kwat</u>tro
over there	**laggiù**
	lad<u>joo</u>
on the left/right	**a sinistra/a destra**
	ah see<u>nee</u>stra/ah <u>day</u>stra
Where do I change for …?	**dove cambio per …?**
	<u>do</u>vay <u>kam</u>beeo pehr
How long will I have to wait for a connection?	**Quanto devo aspettare per la coincidenza?**
	<u>kwan</u>to <u>day</u>vo aspayt<u>taa</u>ray pehr la koeenchee<u>dayn</u>tsa

Boarding Salire a bordo

Is this the right platform for the train to …?	È questo il binario del treno diretto a …? *eh kwaysto eel beenaareeo dayl trayno deeraytto ah*
Is this the train to …?	È questo il treno diretto a …? *eh kwaysto eel trayno deeraytto ah*
Is this seat taken?	È occupato questo posto? *eh okoopaato kwaysto posto*
I think that's my seat.	Questo è il mio posto, credo. *kwaysto eh eel meeo posto kraydo*
Are there any seats/berths available?	Ci sono posti liberi/cuccette libere? *chee sono postee leebayree/koochayttay leebayray*
Do you mind …?	Le spiace …? *lay speeachay*
if I sit here	se mi siedo qui *say mee seeaydo kwee*
if I open the window	se apro la finestra *say apro la feenaystra*

On the journey Durante il viaggio

How long are we stopping here for?	Per quanto tempo ci fermiamo a …? *pehr kwanto taympo che fayrmeeaamo ah*
When do we get to …?	Quando arriviamo a …? *kwando arreeveeaamo ah*
Have we passed …?	Abbiamo passato …? *abbeeaamo passaato*
Where is the dining/sleeping car?	Dov'è la carrozza ristorante/il vagone letto? *doveh la karrotsa reestorantay/eel vagonay lehtto*
Where is my berth?	Dov'è la mia cuccetta? *doveh la meea koo\chaytta*
I've lost my ticket.	Ho perso il biglietto. *oh payrso eel beelyaytto*

FRENI D'EMERGENZA	emergency brake
PORTE AUTOMATICHE	automatic doors
SEGNALE D'ALLARME	alarm signal

TIME ➤ 220

Long-distance bus Corriera

Coach travel can be a convenient way of traveling to smaller towns and a cheaper way to reach major cities. You'll find information on destinations and timetables at coach terminals, usually situated near railway stations. Main companies include *A.M.T.* (Genoa), *Appian Line* (Rome), *Autostradale*, *Lazzi*, *Pesci*, *Sadem*, *Sita*.

Where is the bus station?	**Dov'è la stazione delle corriere/ dei pullman?** <u>doveh</u> la stats<u>ee</u>onay <u>day</u>llay korree<u>eh</u>ray/<u>day</u>ee <u>pull</u>man
When's the next bus to …?	**Quando parte la prossima corriera per …?** <u>kwan</u>do <u>par</u>tay la <u>pro</u>sseema korree<u>eh</u>ra pehr
Which terminal does it leave from?	**Da quale piazzola parte?** da <u>kwa</u>lay piats<u>o</u>la <u>par</u>tay
Where are the bus stops?	**Dove sono le piazzole di sosta?** <u>do</u>vay <u>so</u>no ley piats<u>o</u>lay dee <u>so</u>sta
Does this bus/coach stop at ‾…?	**Questa corriera ferma a …?** <u>kway</u>sta korree<u>eh</u>ra <u>fay</u>rma ah
How long does the trip/journey take?	**Quanto dura il viaggio?** <u>kwan</u>to <u>do</u>ora eel vee<u>ea</u>djo

Bus Autobus

Many cities have introduced an automatic system of fare-paying. Instructions are usually also given in English. Most machines now give change, though usually limited to L.2,000.

In most towns, bus or subway tickets are valid for 75 minutes and the fare is standard, irrespective of distance. If you're planning to travel extensively in one city, enquire about special runabout tickets, such as **biglietto giornaliero** (one-day ticket).

Deve andare a quella fermata lì	You need that stop over there.
Deve prendere quella strada.	You need to go down that road.
Deve prendere l'autobus numero …	You need bus number …
Deve cambiare autobus a …	You must change buses at …

LA FERMATA D'AUTOBUS	bus stop
LA FERMATA A RICHIESTA	request stop
VIETATO FUMARE	no smoking
USCITA (D'EMERGENZA)	(emergency) exit

DIRECTIONS ➤ 94; TIME ➤ 220

Buying tickets Comprare i biglietti

Where can I buy tickets?	**Dove si comprano i biglietti?** _dovay see komprano ee beelyaytee_
A ... ticket to ..., please.	**Un biglietto per ..., per favore.** _oon beelyaytto pehr ... pehr favoray_
one-way/single	**di corsa semplice** _dee korsa saympleechay_
round-trip/return	**circolare** _cheerkolaaray_
bus pass	**per corse multiple** _pehr korsay moolteeplay_
day/weekly/monthly	**giornaliero/settimanale/mensile** _jornaleeehro/saytteemanaalay/maynseelay_
A book of tickets, please.	**Un blocchetto di biglietti, per favore.** _oon blokkaytto dee beelyaytee pehr favoray_
How much is the fare to ...?	**Quant'è il biglietto per ...?** _kwanteh eel beelyaytto pehr_

Traveling In viaggio

Is this the right bus/tram to ...?	**È questo l'autobus/il tram per ...?** _eh kwaysto lowtobooss/eel tram pehr_
Could you tell me when to get off?	**Può dirmi quando devo scendere?** _pwo deermee kwando dayvo shayndayray_
Do I have to change buses?	**Devo cambiare autobus?** _dayvo kambeeaaray owtobooss_
How many stops are there to ...?	**Quante fermate ci sono per ...?** _kwantay fayrmaatay chee sono pehr_
Next stop, please!	**La prossima fermata, per favore!** _lah prosseema fayrmaata pehr favoray_

◎ **CONVALIDARE IL BIGLIETTO**   validate your ticket   ◎

– Scusi. E' questo l'autobus per il Municipio?
– No. Deve prendere l'autobus numero otto. Eccolo, laggiù.
– Dove si comprano i biglietti?
– In una edicola.
– Quando devo scendere?
– Fra quattro fermate.

BUYING TICKETS ➤ 74; _DIRECTIONS_ ➤ 94

Subway La metropolitana

The **metropolitana** in Rome and Milan provide big maps in
every station to make the system easy to use. The fare is
standard, irrespective of the distance traveled.

General Inquiries Richieste di informazioni generali

Where's the nearest subway/metro station?	**Dov'è la fermata della metropolitana più vicina?** _doveh la fayrmaata daylla maytropoleetaana peeoo veecheena_
Where do I buy a ticket?	**Dove si comprano i biglietti?** _do,vay see komprano ee beelyayttee_
Could I have a map of the subway/metro?	**Ha una carta/mappa della rete metropolitana?** _ah oona karta/mappa daylla raytay maytropoleetaana_

Traveling In viaggio

Which line should I take for …?	**Che linea devo prendere per …?** _kay leeneea dayvo prayndayray pehr_
Is this the right line for …?	**È questa la linea per …?** _eh kwaysta la leeneea pehr_
Which stop is it for …?	**Che fermata è per …?** _kay fayrmaata eh pehr_
How many stops is it to …?	**Quante fermate ci sono per arrivare a …?** _kwantay fayrmaatay chee sono pehr arreevaaray ah_
Is the next stop …?	**La prossima/fermata è …?** _la prosseema (fayrmaata) eh_
Where are we?	**Dove siamo?** _dovay seeaamo_
Where do I change for …?	**Dove devo cambiare per …?** _dovay dayvo kambeeaaray pehr_
What time is the last train to …?	**A che ora è l'ultimo treno per …?** _ah kay ora eh loolteemo trayno pehr_

PER ALTRE LINEE/ COINCIDENZE	to other lines/transfer

NUMBERS ➤ 216; BUYING TICKETS ➤ 79, 74

Ferry Il traghetto

Regular boat, ferry and hydrofoil services run to the Italian islands. In addition to the large state-owned services such as *Tirrenia* (esp. services to Sicily and Sardinia), there are many other operators that access islands such as Capri, Ischia, Ponza, Ventotene, the Tremiti Islands, Elba and Giglio.

Travelers to Venice can take tours on a myriad of canals, organized by the *Gondola Cooperative Service*. The price is usually quoted per gondola, which can seat 6 to 8 people, per 45 minutes—there may be scope for bargaining. A cheaper, but less romantic, way of getting around are the water bus services: **Vaporetti** (slow) and **Diretti** (express).

When is the … car ferry to …?	**Quando c'è … traghetto auto per …?** *kwando cheh tragaytto owto pehr*
first/next/last	**il primo/il prossimo/l'ultimo** *eel preemo/ eel prosseemo/ loolteemo*
hovercraft	**l'aliscafo** *laleeskaafo*
ship	**la nave** *la navay*
A round-trip/return ticket for …	**Un biglietto di andata e ritorno per …** *oon beelyaytto andaata ay reetorno pehr*
1 car and 1 trailer	**un'auto e una roulotte** *oonowto ay oona roolot*
2 adults and 3 children	**due adulti e tre bambini** *doo-ay adooltee ay tray bambeenee*
I want to reserve a … cabin.	**Vorrei prenotare una cabina …** *vorrehee praynotaaray oona kabeena*
single/double	**singola/doppia** *seenggola/ doppeea*

VIETATO L'ACCESSO AL PONTE AUTO	no access to car decks
LA SCIALUPPA DI SALVATAGGIO	life boat
LA CINTURA DI SALVATAGGIO	life preserver/life belt
PUNTO DI RACCOLTA	meeting point

Boat trips Gite in barca

Is there a …?	**C'è …?** *cheh*
boat trip	**una gita in barca** *oona jeeta een baarka*
Where can we buy tickets?	**Dove si comprano i biglietti?** *dovay see komprano*

NUMBERS ➤ 216; TIME ➤ 220

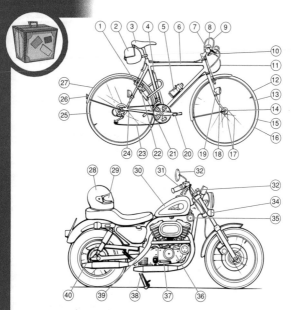

1 brake pad **il pattino/la pastiglia**
2 bicycle bag **il borsello**
3 saddle **il sellino**
4 pump **la pompa**
5 water bottle **la bottiglia dell'acqua**
6 frame **il telaio**
7 handlebars **il manubrio**
8 bell **il campanello**
9 brake cable **il cavo dei freni**
10 gear shift/lever
 la leva del cambio
11 gear/control cable **il cambio**
12 inner tube **la camera d'aria**
13 front/back wheel
 la ruota anteriore/posteriore
14 axle **l'asse**
15 tire **il pneumatico**
16 wheel **la ruota**
17 spokes **i raggi**
18 bulb **la lampadina**
19 headlamp **il fanalino anteriore**
20 pedal **il pedale**

21 lock **la serratura**
22 generator/dynamo **la dinamo**
23 chain **la catena**
24 rear light **il fanalino posteriore**
25 rim **il cerchione**
26 reflectors **il catarinfrangente**
27 fender/mudguard **il parafango**
28 helmet **il casco**
29 visor **l'antiabbagliante**
30 fuel tank **il serbatoio**
31 clutch lever **la leva della frizione**
32 mirror **lo specchietto**
33 ignition switch
 la leva dell'avviamento
34 turn signal/indicator
 l'indicatore di posizione
35 horn **il claxon**
36 engine **il motore**
37 gear shift **la leva del cambio**
38 kick/main stand **il cavalletto**
39 exhaust pipe **la marmitta**
40 chain guard **il paracatena**

CAR REPAIRS ➤ 89

Bicycle/Motorbike
Bicicletta/motocicletta

I'd like to rent a …	**Vorrei noleggiare …** *vorrehee nolaydjaaray*
3-/10-gear bicycle	**una bici(cletta) a tre/dieci marce** *oona beechee(beecheeklaytta) ah tray/deeaychee marchay*
moped	**un motorino** *oon motoreeno*
mountain bike	**una MTB** *oona ehmmayteebee*
motorbike	**una moto(cicletta)** *oona moto (motocheeklaytta)*
How much does it cost per day/week?	**Quanto costa al giorno/alla settimana?** *kwanto kosta al jorno/alla saytteemaana*
Do you require a deposit?	**Vuole una caparra?** *vwolay oona kaparra*
The brakes don't work.	**I freni non funzionano.** *ee fraynee non foontseeonano*
There are no lights.	**Non ci sono i fanalini.** *non chee sono ee fanaleenee*
The front/rear tire has a flat.	**il pneumatico anteriore/posteriore è bucato.** *eel pnayoomateeko antayreeoray/postayreeoray ay bookato*

Hitchhiking Fare l'autostop

Where are you heading?	**In che direzione va?** *een kay deeraytseeonay va*
I'm heading for …	**Vado verso …** *vado vayrsoh*
Is that on the way to …?	**È sulla strada per …?** *eh soolla straada pehr*
Could you drop me off …?	**Può farmi scendere …?** *pwo faarmee shayndayray*
here	**qui** *kwee*
at the … exit	**all'uscita** *alloosheeta*
in the town center	**in centro città** *een chayntro cheetta*
Thanks for the lift.	**Grazie per il passaggio.** *gratseeay pehr eel passadjeeo*

DIRECTIONS ➤ 94; NUMBERS ➤ 216

Taxi/Cab   Il tassì

All cabs must be metered by law, but it is still wise to ask the fare for longer journeys. All rates (including supplements for Sundays, holidays, night journeys [11 p.m. – 6 a.m.], airport journeys, baggage) are indicated on an official chart, which should be posted inside the taxi. Before getting into an argument with your driver when arriving at or from an airport, remember there is a return journey surcharge to be added to what you read on the meter.

Beware of unlicensed cabs ("**abusivi**") touting for business at airports and stations – they charge greatly over the normal tariffs.

Tipping suggestions: 10-15% for the taxi driver.

Where can I get a taxi?	**Dove si trovano i tassi?** *dovay see trovano ee tassee*
Do you have the number for a taxi?	**Ha il numero dei tassi?** *ah eel noomayro dayee tassee*
I'd like a taxi …	**Vorrei un tassì …** *vorrehee oon tassee*
now	**subito** *soobeeto*
in an hour	**fra un'ora** *fra oonora*
for tomorrow at 9:00 am	**per domani alle nove** *pehr domaanee allay novay*
The address is …, going to …	**L'indirizzo è … vado a …** *leendeereetzo eh … vado ah*
Please take me to …	**Per favore, mi porti …** *pehr favoray mee portee*

| ◎ | **LIBERO** | for hire | ◎ |

airport	**all'aeroporto** *allaayroporto*
train station	**alla stazione ferroviaria** *alla statseeonay fayrrooveeareea*
this address	**a questo indirizzo** *ah kwaysto eendeereetzo*
How much will it cost?	**Quanto costerà?** *kwanto kostayra*
On the meter it's …	**Sul tassametro è segnato …** *sool tasseemaytroa eh sayñaato*

– Può portarmi alla stazione, per favore?
– Certo.
– Quanto tempo impiegherà?
– Circa 10 minuti … Eccoci.
– Grazie. Quant'è?

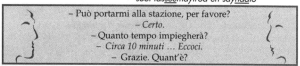

NUMBERS ➤ 216; DIRECTIONS ➤ 94

Car/Automobile   Automobile

While driving, the following documents must be carried at all times: valid full driver's license/licence, vehicle registration document and insurance documentation. If you don't hold an EC format license, a translation of the license is also required. Visitors must carry their vehicle registration book/logbook and, if it is not their car, written consent from the owner.

Insurance for minimum Third Party risks is compulsory in Europe. It is recommended that you take out International motor insurance (or a "Green Card") through your insurer.

The most common crime against tourists in Italy is theft from rental/hire cars. Always look for secure parking areas overnight and never leave valuables in your car at any time.

Essential equipment: warning triangle, nationality plate; wearing seat-belts is compulsory. Children under 13 must travel in seats with special restraints.

Traffic on main roads has priority; where 2 roads of equal importance merge, traffic from the right has priority. On 3-lane roads, the central lane is for overtaking.

Minimum driving age: 18.

Tolls (**il pedaggio**) are payable on expressways/motorways (**autostrada**) in Italy. Traffic police can give on-the-spot fines (ask for a receipt).

The use of horns is prohibited in built-up areas except for emergencies.

Alcohol limit in blood: max. 80mg/100ml. Note that any alcohol may impair concentration.

Conversion Chart

km	1	10	20	30	40	50	60	70	80	90	100	110	120	130
miles	0.62	6	12	19	25	31	37	44	50	56	62	68	74	81

Road network

Italy	**autostrada** – toll expressway/motorway; **superstrada** – non-toll expressway/motorway; **strada statale** – main road; **strada provinciale** – secondary road; **stada comunale** – local road
Switzerland	**A** – expressway/motorway toll free; **N** – main road; **E** – secondary

Speed limits *kmph (mph)*	Built-up area	Outside built-up area	(Toll) expressway/highway
Italy	50 (31)	110 (69) main roads 90 (55) sec. roads	130 (81)
car with trailer/caravan	50 (31)	70 (44)	80 (50)
Switzerland	50 (31)	80 (50)	100-120 (62-74)

Car rental L'autonoleggio

Third-party insurance (**R.C.A.**) is included in the basic hire charge, usually with a Collision Damage Waiver.

If you are traveling by air or train, you may want to take advantage of special inclusive arrangements for car rental. Small local firms are generally cheaper than international or major Italian rental companies, but cars can only be booked locally. Some firms require a minimum age of 21; a valid license held for at least one year is a standard requirement.

Where can I rent a car?	**Dove posso noleggiare un'auto(mobile)?** _dovay posso nolaydjaaray oonowto (oonowtomobeelay)_
I'd like to hire a(n) ...	**Vorrei noleggiare ...** _vorrehee nolaydjaaray_
2-/4-door car	**un'auto a due/a quattro porte** _oonowto ah doo-ay/ah kwattro portay_
an automatic	**con cambio automatico** _kon kambeeo owtomaateeko_
with air conditioning	**con aria condizionata** _kon areea kondeetseeonaata_
I'd like it for a day/a week.	**Vorrei noleggiarla per un giorno/una settimana.** _vorrehee nolaydjaaray pehr oon jorno/oona saytteemaana_
How much does it cost per day/week?	**Quanto costa al giorno/alla settimana?** _kwanto kosta al jorno/ alla saytteemaana_
Are mileage and insurance included?	**Il chilometraggio e l'assicurazione sono inclusi?** _eel keelomaytradjo ay lasseekooratseeonay sono eengkloosee_
Can I leave the car at ...?	**Posso lasciare la macchina a ...?** _posso lashaaray la makkeena ah_
What sort of gasoline/fuel does it take?	**Che tipo di benzina prende?** _kay teepo dee bayndzeena praynday_
Where is the high/ low beam?	**Dove sono gli abbaglianti/anabbaglianti?** _dovay sono lyee abbalyeeantee/ anabbalyeeantee_
Could I have full insurance, please?	**Vorrei una polizza di assicurazione completa.** _vorrehee oona poleetsa dee asseekooratseeonay komplayta_

Gas station La stazione di servizio

Where's the next service/filling station, please? | **Dov'è la prossima stazione di servizio?** *doveh la prosseema statseeonay dee sayrveetseeo*

Is it self-service? | **È un distributore automatico?** *eh oon deestreebootoray owtomateeko*

Fill it up, please. | **Il pieno, per favore.** *eel peeayno pehr favoray*

… liters of … gasoline, please. | **… litri di benzina …, per favore.** *leetree dee bayndzeena … pehr favoray*

super/regular | **super/normale** *super/normaalay*

lead-free/diesel | **verde/il diesel** *vayrday/eel diesel*

Where is the air pump/water? | **Dov'è la pompa per l'aria/l'acqua?** *doveh la pompa pehr lareea/lakwa*

◎   **PREZZO AL LITRO**   price per liter/litre   ◎

Parking Parcheggio

Most street parking is limited in town centers. Tokens (**dischi di sosta**) for parking (up to 1 hour) in blue zones are obtained from tourist organizations, automobile clubs and service stations. Set the disc to show when you arrived and when you must leave.

In Rome, central parking (in the **zona tutelata**) on weekdays is prohibited; punishable by a fine and prison sentence.

Is there a parking lot nearby? | **C'è un parcheggio qui vicino?** *cheh oon parkaydjo kwee veecheeno*

What's the charge per hour/per day? | **Quanto costa all'ora/al giorno?** *kwanto kosta allora/ al jorno*

Do you have some change for the parking meter? | **Ha moneta per il parchimetro?** *ah monayta pehr eel parkeemaytro*

My car has been clamped. Who do I call? | **La mia auto è stata bloccata con ceppo bloccaruote. A chi devo rivolgermi?** *la meea owto ay staata blokkaata kon chayppo blokkaroo-otay. a kee dayvo reevoljayrmee*

NUMBERS ➤ 216; DIRECTIONS ➤ 94

Breakdown Guasti

For help in the event of a breakdown:
refer to your breakdown assistance documents; or contact the
ACI (Automobile Club d'Italia) breakdown service:
Italy: ☎ 116.

Where is the nearest garage?	**Dov'è l'autorimessa più vicina?** *do<u>veh</u> lowtoree<u>may</u>ssa pee<u>oo</u> vee<u>chee</u>na*
I've had a breakdown.	**Ho un guasto all'automobile.** *o oon <u>goo</u>sto allowto<u>mo</u>beelay*
Can you send a mechanic/ tow truck?	**Può mandare un meccanico/un carro attrezzi?** *pwo man<u>daa</u>ray oon may<u>kk</u>aneeko/ oon <u>karr</u>o at<u>tray</u>tzee*
I belong to … recovery service.	**Sono socio del servizio soccorso stradale …** *<u>so</u>no <u>so</u>cho dayl sayr<u>vee</u>tseeo so<u>kkor</u>so stra<u>daa</u>lay*
My license plate/registration number is …	**La mia targa è …** *la <u>mee</u>a <u>tar</u>ga eh*
The car is …	**L'auto è …** *<u>low</u>to eh*
on the highway	**sull'autostrada** *soollowtostr<u>aa</u>da*
2 km from …	**a due chilometri da …** *ah <u>doo</u>-ay kee<u>lo</u>maytree da*
How long will you be?	**Fra quanto tempo arriva?** *fra <u>kwan</u>to <u>taym</u>po ar<u>ree</u>va*

What is wrong? Che guasto ha?

My car won't start.	**L'auto non parte.** *<u>low</u>to non <u>par</u>tay*
The battery is dead.	**La batteria è scarica.** *la battay<u>ree</u>a eh <u>ska</u>reeka*
I've run out of gas.	**Ho finito la benzina.** *oh fee<u>nee</u>to la baynd<u>zee</u>na*
I have a flat tire.	**Ho un pneumatico forato.** *oh oon pnayoo<u>ma</u>teeko fo<u>raa</u>to*
There is something wrong with …	**C'è qualcosa che non funziona con …** *cheh kwal<u>ko</u>sa kay non foontsee<u>o</u>na kon*
I've locked the keys in the car.	**Ho chiuso le chiavi dentro la macchina.** *o kee<u>oo</u>zo lay kee<u>aa</u>vee <u>dayn</u>tro la <u>ma</u>kkeena*

Repairs Riparazioni

Do you do repairs?	**Fa riparazioni?** *fa reeparatseeonee*
Can you repair it (temporarily)?	**Può fare una riparazione (provvisoria)?** *pwo faaray oona reeparatseeonay (provveezoreea)*
Please make only essential repairs.	**Faccia solo le riparazioni essenziali, per favore.** *fatcha solo lay reeparatseeonay ayssayntseeaalee pehr favoray*
Can I wait for it?	**Posso aspettare?** *posso aspayttaaray*
Can you repair it today?	**Può ripararla oggi?** *pwo reeparaarla odjee*
When will it be ready?	**Quando sarà pronta?** *kwando sara pronta*
How much will it cost?	**Quanto costerà?** *kwanto kostayra*
That's outrageous!	**Non esageriamo!** *non aysajayreeaamo*
Can I have a receipt for the insurance?	**Mi dia una ricevuta per l'assicurazione, per favore.** *mee deea oona reechayvoota pehr lasseekooratseeonay pehr favoray*

... non funziona.	The ... isn't working.
Non ho i pezzi di ricambio necessari.	I don't have the necessary parts.
Devo ordinare i pezzi di ricambio.	I will have to order the parts.
Posso solo fare una riparazione provvisoria.	I can only repair it temporarily.
La sua macchina è inservibile.	Your car is totaled/a write-off.
Non si può riparare.	It can't be repaired.
Sarà pronta ...	It will be ready ...
oggi più tardi	later today
domani	tomorrow
fra ... giorni.	in ... days

TIME ➤ 220; *NUMBERS* ➤ 216

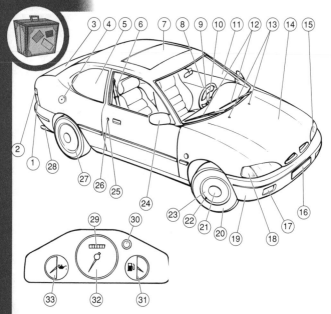

1 tail lights
  i fanali posteriori
2 brakelights le luci dei freni
3 trunk il portabagagli
4 gas cap
  il tappo del serbatoio
5 window il lunotto
6 seat belt la cintura di sicurezza
7 sunroof il tetto apribile
8 steering wheel il volante
9 ignition/starter l'accensione
10 ignition key
   la chiave dell'accensione
11 windshield il parabrezza
12 windshield/windscreen wipers
   il tergicristallo
13 windshield/windscreen washers
   i lavacristalli
14 hood il cofano
15 headlights i fari/gli abbaglianti

16 license/registration plate la targa
17 fog lamp il fanale antinebbia
18 turn signals/indicators
   gli indicatori di posizione
19 bumper il paraurti
20 tires i pneumatici
21 hubcap la coppa
22 valve la valvola
23 wheels le ruote
24 outside mirror
   lo specchietto retrovisore esterno
25 central locking la chiusura centralizzata
26 lock la chiusura
27 wheel rim il cerchione
28 exhaust pipe il tubo di scappamento
29 odometer
   il contachilometri

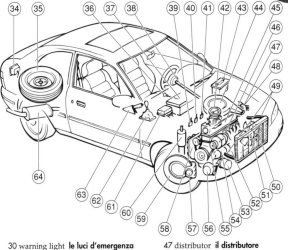

30 warning light **le luci d'emergenza**
31 fuel gauge/pump
   l'indicatore della benzina
32 speedometer **l'indicatore di velocità**
33 oil gauge
   l'indicatore del livello dell'olio
34 backup lights **le luci di
   retromarcia**
35 spare wheel **il pneumatico/
   la gomma di ricambio**
36 choke **la valvola d'aria**
37 heater **l'impianto di riscaldamento**
38 steering column **il piantone**
39 accelerator **l'acceleratore**
40 pedal **il pedale**
41 clutch **la frizione**
42 carburetor **il carburatore**
43 battery **la batteria**
44 alternator **l'alternatore**
45 camshaft **l'albero a camme**
46 air filter **il filtro dell'aria**

47 distributor **il distributore**
48 points **le candele**
49 radiator hose (top/bottom)
   il tubo del radiatore
50 radiator **il radiatore**
51 fan **il ventilatore**
52 engine **il motore**
53 oil filter **il filtro dell'olio**
54 starter motor **il motorino d'avviamento**
55 fan belt **la cinghia del ventilatore**
56 horn **il claxon**
57 brake pads **la ganascia dei freni**
58 transmission/gearbox
   il cambio di velocità
59 brakes **i freni**
60 shock absorbers **gli ammortizzatori**
61 fuses **i fusibili**
62 gear shift **la leva del cambio**
63 handbrake **il freno a mano**
64 muffler **il silenziatore**

Accidents Incidenti

In the event of an accident:

1. put your red warning triangle about 100 meters/metres behind your car;

2. report the accident to the police (compulsory if there is personal injury); don't leave before they arrive;

3. show your driver's licence and green card;

4. give your name, address, insurance company to the other party;

5. report to the appropriate insurance bureaus of the third party and your own company;

6. don't make any written statement without advice of a lawyer or automobile club official;

7. note all relevant details of the other party, any independent witnesses of the accident.

There has been an accident.	**C'è stato un incidente.** *cheh staato oon eencheedayntay*
It's …	**È …** *eh*
on the highway	**sull'autostrada** *soollowtostraada*
near …	**vicino a …** *veecheeno ah*
Where's the nearest telephone?	**Dov'è il telefono più vicino?** *doveh eel taylayfono peeoo veecheeno*
Call …	**Chiami …** *keeaamee*
the police	**la polizia/i carabinieri** *la poleetseea/ee karabeeñehree*
an ambulance	**un'ambulanza** *oon amboolantsa*
a doctor	**un medico** *oon maydeeko*
the fire station	**i pompieri** *ee pompeeehree*
Can you help me please?	**Mi aiuti, per favore!** *mee aeeootee pehr favoray*

Injuries Ferite

There are people injured.	**Ci sono dei feriti.** *chee sono day fayreetee*
No one is hurt.	**Non ci sono feriti.** *non chee sono fayreetee*
He is seriously injured.	**È gravemente ferito.** *eh gravaymayntay fayreeto*
She's unconscious.	**Ha perso conoscenza.** *ah payrso konoshayntsa*

92

INJURIES/DOCTOR ➤ 162; DIRECTIONS ➤ 94

Legal matters Questioni legali

What's your insurance company? **Qual'è la sua compagnia d'assicurazione?** *kwaleh la sooa kompañeea dasseekooratseeonay*

What's your name and address? **Qual'è il suo nome e il suo indirizzo?** *kwaleh eel soo-o nomay ay eel soo-o eendeereetso*

He ran into me. **Mi ha investito.** *mee ah eenvaysteeto*

She was driving too fast/ too close. **Stava guidando troppo veloce/troppo vicino.** *staava gooeedando troppo vaylochay/ troppo veecheeno*

I had right of way. **Avevo la precedenza.** *avayvo la praychaydayntsa*

I was only driving at ... km/h. **Guidavo solo a ... chilometri all'ora.** *gooeedaavo solo ah ... keelomaytree allora*

I'd like an interpreter. **Vorrei un interprete.** *vorrehee oon eentayrpraytay*

I didn't see the sign. **Non ho visto il segnale.** *non oh veesto eel sayñaalay*

The license plate/registration number was ... **Il numero di targa era ...** *eel noomayro dee targa ayra*

Mi faccia vedere ... per favore.	Can I see your ... please?
la patente di guida	driver's license/licence
la polizza d'assicurazione	insurance certificate
i documenti del veicolo.	vehicle registration document
A che ora è successo?	What time did it happen?
Dove è successo?	Where did it happen?
C'erano altre persone coinvolte?	Was anyone else involved?
Ci sono testimoni?	Are there any witnesses?
Lei stava accelerando.	You were speeding.
Le sue luci non funzionano.	Your lights aren't working.
Deve pagare un'ammenda/ una multa ora.	You'll have to pay a fine (on the spot).
Deve fare una dichiarazione in Commissariato.	We need you to make a statement at the station.

POLICE ➤ 152; TIME ➤ 220

Asking directions Chiedere la strada

Excuse me, please.	**Scusi, per favore.** _skoozee pehr favoray_
How do I get to …?	**Come si arriva a …?** _komay see arreeva ah_
Where is …?	**Dov'è … ?** _doveh_
Can you show me on the map where I am?	**Può indicarmi dove sono sulla carta?** _pwo eendeekaarmee dovay sono soolla karta_
I've lost my way.	**Mi sono perso/smarrito.** _mee sono payrso/ smarreeto_
Can you repeat that please?	**Può ripetere, per favore?** _pwo reepaytayray pehr favoray_
More slowly, please.	**Più lentamente, per favore.** _peeoo layntamayntay pehr favoray_
Thanks for your help.	**Grazie (per il suo aiuto).** _graatseeay (pehr eel soo-o aeeooto)_

Traveling by car Viaggiare in automobile

Is this the right road for …?	**È questa la strada per …?** _eh kwaysta la straada pehr_
How far is it to … from here?	**Quant'è lontano/a … da qui?** _kwanteh lontaano/a … da kwee_
Where does this road lead?	**Dove porta questa strada?** _dovay porta kwaysta straada_
How do I get onto the highway?	**Come si entra in autostrada?** _komay see ayntra een owtostraada_
What's the next town called?	**Come si chiama la prossima città?** _komay see keeaama la prosseema cheetta_
How long does it take by car?	**Quanto tempo ci vuole in macchina?** _kwanto taympo chee vwolay een makkeena_

– Scusi, per favore. Come si arriva all'ospedale?
– Prenda la terza svolta a sinistra ed è sempre dritto.
– La terza a sinistra. È lontano?
– È a cinque minuti a piedi.
– Grazie.
– Prego.

È	It's …
(sempre) dritto	straight ahead
a sinistra/a destra	on the left/on the right
dall'altro lato della strada	on the other side of the street
all'angolo	on the corner
dietro l'angolo	round the corner
in direzione di …	in the direction of …
di fronte …/dietro…	opposite …/behind …
vicino a …/dopo …	next to …/after …
Scenda …	Go down the …
la strada laterale/ la strada principale	side street/main street
Attraversi …	Cross the …
la piazza/il ponte	square/bridge
Prenda a terza svolta a destra.	Take the third turn on the right.
Giri a sinistra …	Turn left …
dopo il primo semaforo	after the first traffic lights
al secondo incrocio	at the second intersection/crossroad

È … da qui	It's … of here.
al nord/al sud	north/south
all'est/all'ovest	east/west
Prenda la strada per …	Take the road for …
È sulla strada sbagliata	You're on the wrong road.
Deve ritornare a …	You'll have to go back to …
Segua le indicazioni per …	Follow the signs for …

È …	It's …
vicino/lontano	close/a long way
a cinque minuti a piedi	5 minutes on foot
a dieci minuti in auto	10 minutes by car
a circa dieci chilometri	about 10 km away

TIME ➤ 220; NUMBERS ➤ 216

Road signs La segnaletica

ACCESSO LIMITATO	access only
PERCORSO ALTERNATIVO	alternative route
DEVIAZIONE	detour
METTERSI IN CORSIA	stay in lane (get in lane)
DARE LA PRECEDENZA	yield/give way
PONTE BASSO	low bridge
SENSO UNICO	one-way street
STRADA CHIUSA	road closed
SCUOLA	school
ACCENDERE I FARI	use headlights

Town plans Carte della città

aeroporto (m)	_ayroporto_	airport
attraversamento (m) **pedonale**	_attravayrsamaynto paydonaalay_	pedestrian crossing
campo (m) **sportivo**	_kampo sporteevo_	playing field/ sports ground
chiesa (f)	_kee-ehza_	church
cinema (m)	_cheenayma_	movie theater
città (f) **storica**	_cheetta storeeka_	old town
commissariato (m)	_kommeessareeaato_	police station
edifici (mpl) **pubblici**	_aydeefeechee poobbleechee_	public building
fermata (f) **d'autobus**	_fayrmaata dowtobooss_	bus stop
gabinetti (mpl)	_gabeenayttee_	bathrooms/toilets
lei è qui	_lay eh kwee_	you are here
parcheggio (m)	_paarkaydjo_	parking lot
parco (m)	_parko_	park
percorso (m) **d' autobus**	_pehrkoarsoa dowtoabooss_	bus route
posteggio (m) **tassì**	_postedjo tassee_	taxi stand
sottopassaggio (m)	_sottopassadjo_	underpass
stadio (m)	_stadeeo_	stadium
stazione (f) **(metropolitana)**	_statseeonay (maytropoleetana)_	subway station
ufficio (m) **postale**	_looffeecho_	post office
via (f) **principale**	_veea preencheepaalay_	main street
zona (f) **pedonale**	_dzona paydonaalay_	pedestrian zone

DICTIONARY ➤ 169; SIGHTSEEING ➤ 97–107

Sightseeing

Tourist information office Ufficio turistico

Tourist information offices are often situated in the town center; look for **Ufficio turistico**.

Where's the tourist office?	**Dov'è l'Ufficio turistico?** *doveh looffeecho tooreesteeko*
What are the main points of interest?	**Quali sono i punti principali d'interesse?** *kwalay sono ee poontee preencheepaalay deentayrayssay*
We're here for …	**Siamo qui per …** *seeaamo kwee pehr*
only a few hours	**solo poche ore** *solo pochay oray*
a day	**un giorno** *oon jorno*
a week	**una settimana** *oona saytteemaana*
Can you recommend …?	**Può suggerire …?** *pwo soodjayreeray*
a sightseeing tour	**un giro turistico** *oon jeero tooreesteeko*
an excursion	**una escursione** *oona ayskoorseeonay*
a boat trip	**una gita in barca** *oona jeeta een baarka*
Do you have any information on …?	**Ha informazioni su …?** *a eenformatseeonay soo*
Are there any trips to …?	**Ci sono gite a …?** *chee sono jeetay ah*

Excursions Escursiones

How much does the tour cost?	**Quanto costa il giro?** _kwanto kosta_
Is lunch included?	**Il pranzo è compreso?** _eel prandzo eh komprayzo_
Where do we leave from?	**Da dove si parte?** _da dovay partay_
What time does the tour start?	**A che ora comincia la gita?** _ah kay ora komeencha la jeeta_
What time do we get back?	**A che ora si ritorna?** _ah kay ora see reetorna_
Do we have free time in …?	**C'è del tempo libero a …?** _cheh dayl taympo leebayro ah_
Is there an English-speaking guide?	**C'è una guida di lingua inglese?** _cheh oona gooeeda dee eengglayzay_

On tour Durante la gita turistica

Are we going to see …?	**Andiamo a vedere …?** _andeeaamo ah vaydayray_
We'd like to have a look at the …	**Vorremmo dare un'occhiata a …** _vorrehmmo daaray oonokeeaata ah_
Can we stop here …?	**Possiamo fermarci qui …?** _posseeaamo fayrmaarchee kwee_
to take photographs	**per prendere fotografie** _pehr prayndayray fotografeea_
to buy souvenirs	**per comprare dei souvenirs** _pehr kohmpraaray dayee souvenirs_
for the bathrooms/toilets	**per la toeletta/il gabinetto** _pehr la toaylaytta/eel gabeenaytto_
Would you take a photo of us, please?	**Le dispiace prendere una fotografia di noi?** _lay deespeeachay prayndayray oona fotografeea dee noee_
How long do we have here/in …?	**Quanto tempo abbiamo qui/a …?** _kwanto taympo abbeeaamo kwee/ah_
Wait! … isn't back yet.	**Aspetti! … non è ancora ritornato(-a).** _aspayttee non eh ankora reetornaato(-a)_

Sights Luoghi d'interesse turistico

Town maps are on display in city centers, train, tram and many bus stations, and at tourist information offices.

Where is the …?	**Dov'è …?** *do<u>veh</u>*
abbey	**l'abbazia** *lab<u>bat</u>seea*
art gallery	**la galleria d'arte** la galla<u>ree</u>a <u>dar</u>tay
battle ground	**i luoghi della battaglia** ee <u>loo</u>ogee <u>day</u>lla bat<u>ta</u>lya
botanical garden	**il giardino botanico** eel jar<u>dee</u>no bo<u>ta</u>neeko
castle	**il castello** eel kas<u>tay</u>llo
cathedral	**la cattedrale** la kattay<u>dra</u>alay
cemetery	**il cimitero** eel cheemee<u>tay</u>ro
church	**la chiesa** la kee<u>ay</u>za
downtown area	**il centro città** eel <u>chay</u>ntro <u>chee</u>ta
fountain	**la fontana** la fon<u>taa</u>na
market	**il mercato** eel mayr<u>kaa</u>to
(war) memorial	**il monumento commemorativo** eel monoo<u>mayn</u>to kommaymora<u>tee</u>vo
monastery	**il monastero** eel mona<u>stay</u>ro
museum	**il museo** eel moo<u>za</u>yo
old town	**la città vecchia** la <u>chee</u>tta <u>vay</u>keea
opera house	**il teatro dell'opera** eel tee<u>a</u>tro dayl<u>lo</u>payra
palace	**il palazzo** eel pa<u>laat</u>so
park	**il parco/il giardino** eel <u>par</u>ko/eel jor<u>dee</u>no
parliament building	**il palazzo del Parlamento** eel pa<u>laat</u>so dayl parla<u>mayn</u>to
ruins	**le rovine** lay ro<u>vee</u>nay
shopping area	**la zona dei negozi** la <u>dzo</u>na <u>day</u>ee nay<u>got</u>see
statue	**la statua** la <u>sta</u>too-a
viewpoint	**il punto(m) panoramico** eel <u>poon</u>to panora<u>amee</u>ko
Can you show me on the map?	**Può indicarmi sulla carta?** pwo eendee<u>kahr</u>mee <u>soo</u>llah <u>kahr</u>tah

DIRECTIONS ➤ 94

Admission Ammissione

Check opening times to avoid disappointment: some museums close at 2 p.m. Churches usually close between midday and 4 p.m.

Is the ... open to the public?	**... è aperto(-a) al pubblico?** *eh apayrto(-a) al poobleeko*
Can we look around?	**Possiamo dare un'occhiata in giro?** *posseeaamo daaray oonokeeaata een jeero*
What are the opening hours?	**Qual'è l'orario di apertura?** *kwaleh loraareeo dee apayrtoora*
When does it close?	**A che ora chiude?** *ah kay ora keeooday*
Is ... open on Sundays?	**... è aperto(-a) la domenica?** *eh apayrto(-a) la domayneeka*
When's the next guided tour?	**Quando è la prossima visita guidata?** *kwando eh la prosseema veezeeta gooeedaata*
Do you have a guide book (in English)?	**Ha una guida (in inglese)?** *ah oona gooeeda (een eengglayzay)*
Can I take photos?	**Posso fare fotografie?** *posso faaray fotograafeeay*
Is there access for the handicapped?	**C'è accesso per disabili?** *cheh achaysso pehr deesaabeelee*
Is there an audio guide in English?	**C'è una guida registrata in inglese?** *cheh oona gooeeda rayjeestraata een eengglaysay*

Paying/Tickets Pagare/Biglietti d'ingresso

How much is the entrance/ entry fee?	**Quant'è il biglietto d'ingresso?** *kwanteh eel beelyaytto deenggraysso*
Are there any discounts for ...?	**Ci sono riduzioni/tariffe speciali per ...?** *chee sono reedootseeonee/ tareeffay spaychaalee pehr*
children	**bambini** *bambeenee*
groups	**gruppi** *grooppee*
handicapped	**disabili** *deesaabeelee*
senior citizens	**anziani** *antseeaanee*
1 adult and 2 children, please.	**Un adulto e due bambini, per piacere.** *oon adoolto ay doo-ay bambeenee pehr peeachayray*

TIME ➤ 220

- Cinque biglietti, per favore.
Ci sono tariffe speciali?
– *Sì. Per bambini e anziani
fa ventimila lire.*
- Due adulti e tre bambini, per favore.
– *Fa ottantamila lire, per piacere.*

INGRESSO GRATUITO	free entry
CHIUSO	closed
ARTICOLI PER REGALO/SOUVENIR	gift shop
L'ULTIMO INGRESSO È ALLE ORE DICIASSETTE.	latest entry at 5 p.m.
LA PROSSIMA VISITA ALLE …	next tour at …
INGRESSO VIETATO	no entry
VIETATO USARE IL FLASH.	no flash photography
APERTO	open

Impressions Impressioni

It's …	**È …** *eh*
amazing	**meraviglioso(-a)** *mayraveeleeeoso(-a)*
beautiful	**bello(-a)** *bayllo(-a)*
bizarre	**bizzarro(-a)** *beetsaarro(-a)*
boring	**noioso(-a)** *noeeozo(-a)*
breathtaking	**sensazionale** *saynsatseeonaalay*
brilliant	**splendido(-a)** *splayndeedo(-a)*
great fun	**molto divertente** *molto deevayrtayntay*
interesting	**interessante** *eentayrayssaantay*
magnificent	**magnifico** *mañeefeeko*
romantic	**romantico(-a)** *romanteeko(-a)*
strange	**strano(-a)** *straano(-a)*
stunning	**magnifico(-a)** *mañeefeeko(-a)*
superb	**stupendo(-a)** *stoopayndo(-a)*
terrible	**terribile** *tayrreebeelay*
tremendous	**straordinario(-a)** *straordeenaareeo(-a)*
ugly	**brutto(-a)** *brootto(-a)*
It's good value	**Ne vale la spesa** *nay valay la spayza*
It's a rip-off.	**È una bidonata.** *eh oona beedonaata*
I like it.	**Mi piace.** *mee peeachay*

acquaforte f etching
acquarello m watercolor
affresco m fresco
ala f wing of building
altare m altarpiece
altorilievo m high relief
antichità fpl antiquities
appartamenti mpl **reali** royal apartments
arazzi mpl tapestry
arco m arch
arco m **rampante** buttress
arco m **trionfale** triumphal arch
argenteria f silverware
argento silver
arma f weapon
armeria f armory
artigianato m **d'arte** crafts
atrio m atrium
auriga f charioteer
badia f abbey
basso m **rilievo** bas-relief
biblioteca f library
biga f chariot
campanile m bell tower
camposanto m churchyard
cancello m gate
capolavoro m masterpiece
Cena The Last Supper
ceramica f ceramic
ceramiche fpl pottery
chiesa f church
collezione f collection
completato nel ... completed in
conferenza f lecture
contrafforte f buttress
cornicione m eaves
coro m choirstall

corona f crown
cortile m courtyard
costruito(-a) built in
cupola f dome
d'oro golden
da by person
dagherrotipo m daguerreotype
decorato(-a) da decorated by
decorazione f decoration
dettaglio m detail
dipinto m picture
dipinto(-a) da painted by
disegnato(-a) da designed by
disegno m design, drawing
distrutto(-a) da destroyed by
donato(-a) da donated by
dorato(-a) gilded
duomo m dome
edificio m building
eretto(-a) nel/in erected in
facciata facade
fibula f brooch
finestra f **con vetro colorato** stained-glass window
fondato(-a) nel founded in
fonte f font
foro m forum
fossato m moat
fregio m frieze
frontone m pediment
garguglia f gargoyle
giardino f **formale** formal garden
gioielli mpl jewelry
guglia f spire
imperatore m emperor
imperatrice f empress
in prestito a on loan to
incisione f carving, engraving
ingresso m foyer

iniziò nel started in
liberto m freedman
maestà Madonna and Child
  in majesty
marmo m marble
mattone m brick
mobilia f/mobili mpl furniture
moneta f coin
morto(-a) nel died in
mostra f display, exhibition
muro m wall
nato(-a) nel ... a ...
  born in ... year in ... town
navata f nave
oggetto m esibito/in mostra
  exhibit
orecchini mpl earrings
orologio m clock
padiglione m pavilion
paesaggio m landscape
  painting
palcoscenico m stage
paliotto m altar frontal
Papato m Papacy
pastello m pastel
piano m plan
pietà f Virgin with
  crucified Christ
pietra f stone
pietra f angolare cornerstone
pietra f preziosa gemstone
pietra f tombale headstone
pilastro m pillar
pittore m, pittrice f painter
pittura f murale mural
pitture fpl a olio oils
placca f plaque
ponte m bridge
porta f d'ingresso doorway
ponte m levatoio drawbridge
primo livello m level 1
quadro m painting

rappresenta
  represents
re m king
regina f queen
regno m reign
restaurato nel restored in
ricostruito nel rebuilt in
ritratto m portrait
rocca m fortress/stronghold
rosone m rose window
rovine f ruins
ruderi fpl ruins
sagrestia sacristy
salone m per cerimonie
  stateroom
scala uno:cento scale 1:100
scala f staircase
scavi mpl excavations
scena f drammatica tableau
schiavo m slave
schizzo m sketch
scoperto(-a) nel discovered in
scultore m, scultrice f sculptor
scuola f di school of
secolo m century
sette colli fpl Seven Hills
spalti mpl battlement
a spina f de pesce herringbone
sporgente overhanging
statua f di cera waxwork
tapezzerie fpl tapestry
tela f canvas
terme fpl baths
tetto m roof
tomba f grave, tomb
torre f tower
trittico m triptych
vetro m glass
visse lived
volta f vault
zoccolo m molding

Who/What/When? Chi/Cosa/Quando?

What's that building?	**Cos'è quell'edificio?** *koseh kwayllaydeefeecho*
When was it built/painted?	**Quando fu costruito(-a)/dipinto(-a)?** *kwando foo kostreeto(-a)/ deepeento(-a)*
Who was the ...?	**Chi era ...?** *kee ayra*
architect	**l'architetto** *larkeetaytto*
artist	**l'artista** *larteesta*
What style is that?	**Che stile è?** *kay steelay eh*

Roma repubblicana 500–27 b.c.
After periods of Etruscan (**etrusco**) and Greek (**ellenistico**) influence in Italy, Rome was founded in 753 b.c. The Republic was declared in 509 b.c.; the city expanded its empire across the known world (esp. in Punic Wars against the Carthaginians, ca. 2nd b.c.; and the military successes of Julius Caesar). Caesar's assassination (44 b.c.) brought civil war.

Roma imperiale 27 b.c.–467 a.d.
Caesar's adopted son, Octavius (Augustus), became the first emperor. His descendants (Tiberius, Caligula, Claudius, Nero) were followed by the Flavian, Antonine and Severus dynasties. This period of expansion saw great artistic and architectural achievements. In 382 b.c. Christianity was recognized as the state religion. However, decline set in, the Empire split into two and power was moved to Constantinople. Goths and Vandals plundered Rome, which fell to the Ostrogoths.

Età Mediovale 467–1300
Italy remained fractured, featuring powerful families such as the Medicis, independent city states like Venice, and increasing Papal power (with Rome as the capital of Western Christianity) through the Holy Roman Empire (**Santo impero romano**). Foreign involvement (Norman, German, French, Spanish and Austrian) continued in Italy beyond the Middle Ages into the nineteenth century.

il Risorgimento 1815–1870
The reunification of Italy as one kingdom was achieved by Victor Emmanuel II of Piedmont in 1861, with assistance from his minister Cavour and the exploits of Garibaldi. The final piece came when Rome was captured (1870).

Novocento ca. 20th century
Italy fought with the Allies in World War I, but Benito Mussolini allied with Hitler in World War II with devastating consequences. The Democratic Republic was established in 1946, with numerous fragile governments following. Italy was one of the founding members of the European Economic Community in 1957.

Rulers/Government   Sovrani/Governi

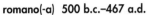

What period is that? **Che periodo è …?**
kay payree_o_do eh

romano(-a) 500 b.c.–467 a.d.
Romans were great builders: ruins remain throughout Italy (esp.
Rome) and Western Europe of their forums, basilicas, arenas, theaters,
amphitheaters, markets, circuses, libraries, triumphal arches, catacombs,
baths, temples, acqueducts, bridges, city walls and mausoleums.

bizantino 400–1100
Byzantine influence from the Eastern Christian Empire emphasized
grandeur and mystery with splendid mosaic-decorated interior (esp.
Ravenna; also later influence in St Mark's in Venice, Sicily and Rome).

Periodo gottico 1300–1400
Gothic style used complex architectural forms, using pointed arches and
rib vaults (esp. cathedrals in Genoa and Siena, ornate window openings of
Venetian houses,artistic work of Giotto in Padua, Assisi and Florence).

il Rinascimento 1400–1650
The Renaissance was a hugely significant cultural and artistic movement,
with a fascination with antiquity and admiration of beauty, colors, light, sta-
bility and poise. It saw stunning artistic creativity in the Quattrocento (ca.
15th cent.) esp. statues of Donatello, paintings of Botticelli; and Cinquecento
(ca. 16th cent.) esp. Michelangelo (statues of David and Moses; Sistine
Chapel ceiling), Leonardo da Vinci, Raphael, and the Venetian School (Tit-
ian, Tintoretto and El Greco).

Mannerismo 1550–1650
Mannerism enjoyed frivolities and exaggerated use of Renaissance features (esp. Tivoli and Bomarzo; artists Caravaggio and Palladio).

Barocco e Rococò 1640–1789
Baroque emphasized movement, using scrolls and ornate embellishments
(e.g. Bernini's facade of St Peter's in Rome; artists Canaletto and Bellotto).

Churches   Chiese
Predominantly Roman Catholic, Italy is rich in cathedrals and churches. Ask
permission before taking photographs; cover bare shoulders before entering.

Catholic/Protestant church	**la chiesa cattolica/protestante** *la kee-eh_za katoleeka/protaystantay*
mosque	**la moschea** *la moskeeah*
synagogue	**la sinagoga** *la seenagoga*
What time is …?	**A che ora è ….?** *ah kay oara eh*
mass/the service	**la messa/il servizio** *la mayssa/eel sayrveetseeo*

In the countryside In campagna

I'd like a map of …	**Vorrei una carta di …**
	vorrehee oona karta dee
this region	**questa regione** *kwaysta rayjonay*
walking routes	**percorsi a piedi** *pehrkorsee ah pee-ehdee*
cycle routes	**percorsi per ciclisti**
	pehrkorsee pehr cheekleestee
How far is it to …?	**Quanto dista …?** *kwanto deesta*
Is there a right of way?	**C'è diritto di passaggio?**
	cheh deereetto dee passadjo
Is there a trail/scenic route to …?	**C'è un sentiero/una strada panoramica per …?** *cheh oon saynteeehro/oona straada panorameeka pehr*
Can you show me on the map?	**Puo indicarmi sulla carta?**
	pwo eendeekaarmee soolla karta
I'm lost.	**Mi sono smarrito(-a).** *mee sono smareeto(-a)*

Organized walks Escursioni organizzate

When does the guided walk/hike start?	**A che ora comincia la passeggiata/ l'escursione?** *ah kay ora komeencha la passaydjaata/layskoorseeonay*
When will we return?	**Quando ritorneremo?**
	kwando reetornayrehmo
What is the walk/hike like?	**Com'è la passeggiata?**
	komeh la passaydjaata
gentle/medium/tough	**facile/di media difficoltà/difficile** *facheelay/dee maydeea deeffeekolta/deeffeecheelay*
I'm exhausted.	**Sono esausto(-a).**
	sono aysaoosto(-a)
What kind of … is that?	**Che tipo di … è quello?**
	kay teepo dee … eh kwayllo
animal/bird	**animale/uccello**
	aneemaalay/oochayllo
flower/plant/tree	**fiore/pianta/albero**
	feeoray/peeanta/albayro

Geographic features Aspetti geografici

bridge	**il ponte**	*eel pontay*
cave	**la caverna/la grotta**	*la kavayrna/la grotta*
cliff	**la scogliera/la rupe**	*la sholee-ehra/ la roopay*
farm	**la fattoria/la cascina**	*la fattoreea/ la kasheena*
field	**il campo**	*eel kampo*
foot path	**il sentiero pedestre**	*eel sayntee-ehro paydaystray*
forest	**la foresta**	*la foraysta*
hill	**la collina**	*la kolleena*
lake	**il lago**	*eel lago*
mountain	**la montagna**	*la montaaña*
mountain pass	**il passo di montagna**	*eel passo dee montaaña*
mountain range	**la catena di montagne**	*la katayna dee montaañay*
nature reserve	**l'oasi naturale**	*loazee natooraale*
panorama	**il panorama/la vista**	*eel panoraama/ la veesta*
park	**il parco**	*eel parko*
peak	**il picco/la cima**	*eel peeko/la cheema*
picnic area	**l'area per pic nic**	*laraya pehr peekneek*
pond	**lo stagno**	*lo staaño*
rapids	**le rapide**	*lay rapeeday*
river	**il fiume**	*eel feeoomay*
sea	**il mare**	*eel maaray*
stream	**il ruscello/il torrente**	*eel rooshayllo/ eel torrayntay*
valley	**la valle**	*la vallay*
viewpoint	**il punto panoramico**	*eel poonto panorameeko*
village	**il paese**	*eel pa-ehsay*
vineyard/winery	**le vigne**	*lay veeñay*

Leisure

What's playing on? Cosa danno?

Local papers and, in large cities, weekly entertainment guides will tell you what's on.

Do you have a program of events?	**Ha un programma delle manifestazioni?** *ah oon progr<u>a</u>ma d<u>ay</u>llay maneef<u>ay</u>statsee<u>o</u>nee*
Can you recommend a good ...?	**Può suggerire un(a) buon(a) ...?** *pwo soodjay<u>ree</u>ray oon(a) bwon(a)*
Is there a ... on somewhere?	**C'è ...?** *cheh*
ballet/concert	**un balletto/un concerto** *oon ball<u>ay</u>tto/oon kon<u>chay</u>rto*
film/movie	**un film** *oon film*
opera	**un'opera** *oon<u>o</u>payra*

Tickets for concerts, theater, and other cultural events are on sale at special ticket agencies (e.g. *Anteprima, Prenoticket, Prontobiglietto*) or major music stores (e.g. *Messaggerie Musicali, Ricordi*).

Availability Disponibilità

When does it start?	**A che ora comincia?** *ah kay <u>o</u>ra ko<u>mee</u>ncha*
When does it end?	**A che ora finisce?** *ah kay <u>o</u>ra fee<u>nee</u>eshay*
Are there any seats for tonight?	**Ci sono posti per questa sera?** *chee <u>so</u>no p<u>o</u>stee pehr k<u>way</u>sta <u>say</u>ra*
Where can I get tickets?	**Dove si comprano i biglietti?** *<u>do</u>vay see <u>ko</u>mpraano ee beel<u>yay</u>ttee*
There are ... of us.	**Siamo in ...** *see-<u>aa</u>mo een*

Tickets Biglietti

How much are the seats?	**Quanto costano i posti?** _kwanto kostano ee postee_
Do you have anything cheaper?	**Ha qualcosa di meno caro?** _ah kwalkosa dee mayno karo_
I'd like to reserve … 3 for Sunday evening	**Vorrei prenotare …** _vorrehee praynotaaray_ **tre posti per domenica sera** _tray postee pehr domayneeka sayra_
1 for Friday matinée	**un posto per lo spettacolo di venerdì pomeriggio** _oon posto pehr lo spayt takolo dee vaynayrdee pomayreedjo_

Mi dica … della sua carta di credito?	What's your credit card …?
il numero	number
il titolare	type
la data di scadenza	expiration date
Ritiri i biglietti … per favore.	Please pick up the tickets …
alle … di sera	by … p.m.
al banco prenotazioni	at the reservations desk

| May I have a program/ programme, please? | **Ha un programma, per piacere?** _ah oon programma pehr peeachayray_ |
| Where's the coat room? | **Dov'è il guardaroba?** _doveh eel goo-ardarob_ |

– Pronto. Teatro Puccini.
– Buongiorno. Vorrei due biglietti per La Bohème di questa sera.
– Sì, certo. Mi dia il numero della sua carta di credito, per favore.
– Sì, è il numero zero cinque zero sei cinque sette otto cinque quattro.
– Bene. E qual'è la data di scadenza?
– Luglio novantasette.
– Grazie. Può ritirare i biglietti al botteghino.

PRENOTAZIONI IN ANTICIPO	Advance bookings
ESAURITO	Sold out
BIGLIETTI PER LO SPETTACOLO DI OGGI	Tickets for today's show

NUMBERS ➤ 216

109

Movies   Al cinema

Foreign films are always dubbed into Italian, but a few movie houses show films in the original version. Italy has a film industry of its own, with famous directors such as Fellini, Antonioni and Visconti, and more recently Bertolucci, the Taviani Brothers, Salvatores and Nanni Moretti. For a view of Italian humor, try a film by Carlo Verdone.

Is there a multiplex cinema near here?	**C'è un cinema multisala qui vicino?** *cheh oon cheenayma moolteesala/ kwee veecheeno*
What's playing at the movies (What's on at the cinema) tonight?	**Cosa danno al cinema questa sera?** *kosa danno al cheenayma*
Is the film dubbed/subtitled?	**Il film è doppiato/ha i sottotitoli?** *eel film eh doppeeaato/af ee sottoteetolee*
Is the film in the original English?	**Il film è in lingua originale inglese?** *eel film eh een leengwa oreejeenaalay eengglayzay*
A ..., please.	**..., per favore.** *pehr favoray*
box of popcorn	**Una scatola del popcorn** *oona skatola dayl popcorn*
chocolate ice cream	**Un pinguino** *oon peengweeno*
hot dog	**Una salciccia calda** *oona salcheecha kalda*
soft drink/soda	**Una bibita frizzante** *oona beebeeta freetsantay*
small/regular/large	**piccolo(-a)/medio(-a)/grande** *peekolo(a)/maydeeo(-a)/graanday*

Theater   A teatro

What's playing at the ... Theater?	**Cosa danno al Teatro ...?** *...kosa danno al teeatro*
Who's the playwright?	**Chi è il commediografo?** *kee eh eel kommaydeeograafo*
Do you think I'd enjoy it?	**Pensa che mi piacerà?** *paynsa kay mee peeachayra*
I don't know much Italian.	**Non conosco l'italiano molto bene.** *non konosko leetaleeaano molto baynay*

110

Opera/Ballet/Dance
All'opera/Balletto/Danza

In addition to the internationally renowned La Scala in Milan, excellent productions are found at the opera houses in Bologna, Florence, Naples, Parma, Rome and Turin. Also look for open-air productions in the summer, often held in Greek and Roman ruins.

Where's the opera house?	**Dov'è il teatro dell'Opera?** *doveh eel teeatro dayllopayra*
Who's the composer/soloist?	**Chi è il compositore/il (la) solista?** *kee eh eel komozeetoray/eel (la) soleesta*
Is formal dress required?	**È necessario indossare abiti da sera?** *eh naychayssaareeo eendossaaray abeetee da sayra*
Who's dancing?	**Chi sono i ballerini?** *kee sono ee ballayreenee*
I'm interested in contemporary dance.	**Mi interessa la danza contemporanea.** *mee eentayraysa la dantsa kontoymporaaneha*

Music/Concerts Musica/Concerti

Where's the concert hall?	**Dov'è la sala concerti?** *doveh la sala konchayrtee*
Which orchestra/band is playing?	**Che orchestra/gruppo sta suonando?** *kay orkaystra/groopo sta soo-onando*
What are they playing?	**Cosa stanno suonando?** *kosa stanno soo-onando*
Who is the conductor/soloist?	**Chi è il direttore d'orchestra/il (la) solista?** *kee eh eel deerayttoray dorkaystra/ eel (la) soleesta*
Who is the support band?	**Chi è il gruppo di supporto?** *kee eh eel grooppo dee soopporto*
I really like …	**Mi piace molto…** *mee peeachay molto*
country music	**la musica country** *la moozeeka country*
folk music	**la musica folcloristica** *la moozeeka folkloreesteeka*
jazz	**il jazz** *eel djaz*
pop	**la musica pop** *la moozeeka pop*
rock music	**il rock** *eel rock*
soul music	**la musica soul** *la moozeeka soul*

Nightlife Vita notturna

What is there to do in the evenings?	**Cosa c'è da fare di sera?** _kosa cheh da faaray dee sayra_
Can you recommend a …?	**Può suggerire …?** _pwo soodjayreeray_
Is there a … in town?	**C'è … in città?** _cheh een cheetta_
bar	**un bar** _oon bar_
casino	**un casinò** _oon kazeeno_
discotheque	**una discoteca** _oona deeskotayka_
gay club	**un locale gay** _oon lokaalay gay_
nightclub	**un nightclub** _oon nightclub_
restaurant	**un ristorante** _oon reestorantay_
What type of music do they play?	**Che tipo di musica suonano?** _kay teepo dee moozeeka soo-onano_
How do I get there?	**Come si arriva?** _komay see arreeva_

Admission Ammissione

What time does the show start?	**A che ora comincia lo spettacolo?** _ah kay ora komeencha lo spayttakolo_
Is evening dress required?	**È necessario l'abito da sera?** _eh naychayssareeo labeeto da sayra_
Is there a cover charge?	**Si deve pagare il coperto?** _see dayvay pagaaray eel kopayrto_
Is a reservation necessary?	**Si deve prenotare?** _see dayvay praynotaaray_
Do we need to be members?	**È necessario essere soci?** _eh naychayssaareeo ayssayray sochee_
How long will we have to wait/stand in line?	**Per quanto tempo si deve aspettare/fare la coda?** _pehr kwanto taympo see dayvay aspayttaaray/faaray la koda_
I'd like a good table.	**Vorrei un buon tavolo.** _vorrehee oon bwon tavolo_

È COMPRESA UNA BIBITA GRATUITA	includes 1 complimentary drink

Children Bambini

Can you recommend something for the children?	**Può suggerire qualcosa per i bambini?** *pwo soodjay<u>ree</u>ray kwal<u>ko</u>sa pehr ee bam<u>bee</u>nee*
Are there changing facilities here for infants?	**Dove si possono cambiare i pannolini?** <u>do</u>vay see <u>po</u>ssono kambee<u>aa</u>ray ee panno<u>lee</u>nee
Where are the bathrooms/ toilets?	**Dove sono le toelette/i gabinetti?** <u>do</u>vay <u>so</u>no lay toay<u>lay</u>ttay/ ee gabeen<u>ay</u>ttee
video arcade	**la sala da giochi** la <u>sa</u>la <u>dah jo</u>kee
fairground	**la fiera** la fee-<u>eh</u>ra
kiddie pool	**la piscina per bambini** la pee<u>shee</u>na pehr bam<u>bee</u>nee
playground	**il parco giochi** eel <u>par</u>ko <u>jo</u>kee
playgroup	**un club per bambini/un miniclub** oon kloob pehr bam<u>bee</u>nee/oon meenee<u>kloob</u>
zoo	**uno zoo** <u>oo</u>no dzoh

Baby-sitting Servizio di babysitter

Can you recommend a reliable baby-sitter?	**Può raccomandare una buona babysitter?** pwo rakoman<u>daa</u>ray <u>oo</u>na <u>bwo</u>na babysitter
Is there constant supervision?	**C'è sorveglianza continua?** cheh sorvayl<u>yaan</u>tsa kon<u>tee</u>noo-a
Are the helpers properly trained?	**Gli assistenti sono tutti addestrati?** lyee asseesta<u>yn</u>tee <u>so</u>no <u>too</u>ttee addays<u>traa</u>tee
When can I drop them off?	**Quando posso lasciarli(-le)?** <u>kwan</u>do <u>po</u>sso lashaa<u>rlee</u>(-lay)
I'll pick them up at …	**Li (Le) passo a prendere alle …** lee (lay) <u>pa</u>sso ah <u>pray</u>ndayray a<u>lla</u>y
We'll be back by …	**Ritorno alle …** ree<u>tor</u>no a<u>lla</u>y
She's 3 and he's 18 months.	**Lei ha tre anni e lui ha diciotto mesi.** <u>la</u>yee ah tray <u>a</u>nnee ay <u>loo</u>ee ah dee<u>chot</u>to <u>ma</u>yzee

Sports Lo sport

Soccer/football, tennis, boxing, wrestling, windsurfing and bicycle, car and horse racing are among popular spectator sports.

If you like sailing, fishing, horseback riding, golf, tennis, hiking, cycling, swimming or golf, you'll find plenty of opportunity to satisfy your recreational bent.

il calcio *eel kalcho*

Soccer is the overriding passion in Italy, which boasts probably the best league in the world (Serie A) with teams of the calibre of Juventus (Turin), Inter Milan, AC Milan, Roma and Sampdoria (Florence). The intensity with which fans support their team creates a thrilling atmosphere during matches. In addition, the stadiums in Rome (Stadio Olimpico), Milan (Stadio San Siro) and Naples (Stadio del Vomero) are particularly striking.

Spectator Sports Assistere

Is there a soccer game/match this Saturday?	**C'è una partita di calcio questa sera** *cheh oona parteeta dee kalcho kwaysta sayra*
Which teams are playing?	**Quali squadre giocano?** *kwalee skwadray jokano*
Can you get me a ticket?	**Può comprarmi un biglietto?** *pwo kompraaray oon beelyaytto*
What's the admission charge?	**Quanto costa l'entrata?** *kwanto kosta layntraata*
Where's the racetrack?	**Dov'è l'ippodromo?** *doveh leeppodromo*
Where can I place a bet?	**Dove si scommette?** *dovay see skommayttay*
What are the odds on ...?	**Qual'è il pronostico su ....?** *kwaleh eel pronosteeko soo*
athletics	**l'atletica** *l'atlayteeka*
basketball	**la pallacanestro** *la pallakanaystro*
cycling	**il ciclismo** *eel cheekleesmo*
golf	**il golf** *eel golf*
horse racing	**l'ippica** *leepeeka*
soccer	**il calcio** *eel kalcho*
swimming	**nuoto** *noo-oto*
tennis	**tennis** *tennis*
volleyball	**pallavolo** *pallavollo*

Playing Giocare

Where's the nearest …?	**Dov'è … più vicino(-a)?** *doveh peeoo veecheeno(-a)*
golf course	**il campo di golf** *eel kampo dee golf*
sports club	**la palestra sportiva** *la palaystra sporteevo*
Where are the tennis courts?	**Dove sono i campi da tennis?** *dovay sono ee kampee da tennis*
What's the charge per …?	**Quanto costa per …?** *kwanto kosta pehr*
day/round/game/hour	**giorno/giro/partita/ora** *jorno/jeero/parteeta/ora*
Do I need to be a member?	**È necessario essere soci?** *eh naychayssaareeo ayssayray sochee*
Where can I rent …?	**Dove posso noleggiare …?** *dovay posso nolaydjaaray*
boots	**gli scarponi** *lyee skaarponee*
clubs	**le mazze** *lay matsay*
equipment	**l'attrezzatura** *lattraytsatooray*
a racket	**la racchetta** *la rakaytta*
Can I get lessons/tuition?	**Vorrei prendere qualche lezione?** *vorrehee prayndayray kwalkay laytseeonay*
Do you have a fitness room?	**C'è una sala di allenamento?** *cheh oona sala dee allaynamaynto*
Can I join in?	**Posso partecipare?** *posso partaycheepaaray*

Mi dispiace, è tutto prenotato.	I'm sorry, we're booked up.
C'è una caparra/un anticipo di …	There is a deposit of …
Che taglia/che misura ha ?	What size are you?
Deve avere una fotografia formato passaporto.	You need a passport size photo.

SPOGLIATOI	Locker rooms
PESCA VIETATA	No fishing
RISERVATO AI DETENTORI DI LICENZA	Permit holders only

At the beach In spiaggia

Italy abounds in beaches and sea resorts, and it is not too difficult to locate near-deserted coves for a quieter time. The most developed resorts offer a full range of facilities for watersports.

Nearly all beaches have private bathing establishments, where you can rent cabins, deck chairs and sunbeds. Often the beach boys (**bagnini**) are also lifeguards, distinguished by their red shorts and vests.

A red flag signifies rough sea, a white flag denotes calm sea with safe bathing.

Is the beach …?	**La spiaggia è …?** *la speeadja eh*
pebbly/sandy	**pietrosa/sabbiosa** *peeehtroso/sabbeeosa*
Is there a … here?	**C'è … qui?** *cheh … kwee*
children's pool	**una piscina per bambini** *oona peesheena pehr bambeenee*
swimming pool	**una piscina** *oona peesheena*
indoor/open-air	**invernale/all'aperto** *eenvayrnaalay/allapayrto*
Is it safe to swim/dive here?	**Si può nuotare tuffare senza pericolo?** *see pwo noootaaray too-fah-ray sayntsa payreekolo*
Is it safe for children?	**È sicuro per i bambini?** *eh seekooro pehr bambeenee*
Is there a lifeguard?	**C'è un bagnino?** *cheh oon bañeeno*
I want to rent some…	**Vorrei noleggiare …** *vorrehee nolaydjaaray*
deck chair	**una sedia a sdraio** *oona saydeea ah sdraeeo*
jet ski	**una moto acquatica** *oona moto akwatika*
motorboat	**una barca a motore** *oona barka ah motoray*
skin-diving equipment	**attrezzature da sub** *attraytsatooray da soob*
umbrella	**un ombrellone** *oon ombrayllonay*
surfboard	**una tavola da surf** *oona tavola da surf*
waterskis	**degli sci d'acqua** *daylyee shee dakwa*
For … hours.	**Per … ore.** *pehr … oray*

116

Skiing Lo sci

There is excellent skiing for enthusiasts, both beginners and experts, in the Dolomites and the Italian Alps (Valle D'Aosta); further south, the Apennines and the slopes of Etna also offer skiing.

Is there much snow?	**C'è molta neve?** *cheh molta nayvay*
What's the snow like?	**Com'è la neve?** *komeh la nayvay*
heavy/icy	**spessa/ghiacciata** *spayssa/geeachaata*
powdery/wet	**farinosa/bagnata** *fareenosa/bañaata*
I'd like to rent …	**Vorrei noleggiare …** *vorrehee nolaydjaaray*
poles	**i bastoncini** *ee bastoncheenee*
skates	**i pattini (da ghiaccio)** *ee patteenee (da geeacho)*
ski boots	**gli scarponi (da sci)** *lyee skarponee (da shee)*
skis	**gli sci** *lyee shee*
These are too …	**Questi(-e) sono troppo …** *kwaystee(-ay) sono troppo*
big/small	**grandi/piccoli(e)** *graandee/peekolee(-ay)*
They're uncomfortable.	**sono scomodi(-e).** *sono skomodee(-ay)*
A lift pass for a day/ 5 days, please.	**Una tessera per la sciovia per un giorno/cinque giorni, per favore.** *oona tayssayra pehr la sheeoveea pehr oon jorno/cheengkway jornee pehr favoray*
I'd like to join the ski school.	**Vorrei iscrivermi alla scuola sci.** *vorrehee eeskreevayrmee alla skooola shee.*
I'm a beginner.	**Sono un principiante.** *sono oon preencheepeeantay*
I'm experienced.	**Ho esperienza.** *oh ayspayree-ehntsah*

LA FUNIVIA	cable car/gondola
LA SEGGIOVIA	chair lift
LA SCIOVIA	tow lift

117

Making Friends

Introductions Presentazioni

Greetings vary according to how well you know someone.
The following is a guide:

It's polite to shake hands, both when you meet and say good-bye.

Begin any formal conversation, whether with a shop assistant or policeman, with a "**Buongiorno**".

Ciao! is an informal, universal expression, meaning both "hello, hi" and "so long, good-bye."

In Italian, there are two forms for "you" (taking different verb forms):

   tu (singular) and **voi** (plural) are used when talking to relatives, close friends and children (and between young people);

   Lei (singular) and **Loro** (plural) are used in all other cases (with the 3rd person singular/plural of the verb).

Hello, we haven't met.	**Buongiorno, non ci conosciamo.** *bwonjorno non chee* *konosheeaamo*
My name is …	**Sono …** *sono*
May I introduce …?	**Posso presentarle …?** *posso praysayntaarlay*
Pleased to meet you.	**Piacere/Molto lieto(-a).** *peeachayray/molto leeehto(-a)*
What's your name?	**Come si chiama?** *komay see keeaama*
How are you?	**Come sta?** *komay sta*
Fine, thanks. And you?	**Bene, grazie, e Lei?** *baynay graatseeay ay layee*

> – Buongiorno, signora. Come sta?
> – *Molto bene, grazie e Lei?*
> – Bene, grazie.

Where are you from? Da dove viene?

Where do you come from?	**Da dove viene?** *da dovay veeaynay*
Where were you born?	**Dove è nato(-a)?** *dovay eh naato(-a)*
I'm from …	**Vengo …** *vaynggo*
Australia	**dall'Australia** *dallowstraaleea*
Britain	**dalla Gran Bretagna** *dalla gran braytaña*
Canada	**dal Canada** *dal kanada*
England	**dall'Inghilterra** *dalleenggeeltayrra*
Ireland	**dall'Irlanda** *dalleerlanda*
Scotland	**dalla Scozia** *dalla skotseea*
U.S.	**dagli Stati Uniti** *dalyee staatee ooneetee*
Wales	**dal Galles** *dal gallayss*
Where do you live?	**Dove vive?** *dovay veevay*
What part of … are you from?	**Da quale parte … viene?** *da kwalay partay … vee-ehnay*
Italy	**dell'Italia** *daylleetaaleea*
Sicily	**della Sicilia** *daylla seecheeleea*
Switzerland	**della Svizzera** *daylla sveetsayra*
We come here every year.	**Veniamo ogni anno.** *vayneeaamo oñee anno*
It's my/our first visit.	**È la mia/nostra prima visita.** *eh la meea/nostra preema veezeeta*
Have you ever been to …?	**È già stato in …?** *eh ja staato een*
Britain/the U.S.	**Gran Bretagna/negli Stati Uniti** *gran braytaña/naylyee staatee ooneeteee*
Do you like it here?	**Le piace questo posto?** *lay peeachay kwaysto posto*
What do you think of the …?	**Cosa pensa di …?** *kosa paynsa dee*
I love the … here.	**Mi piace molto … qui.** *mee peeachay molto … kwee*
I don't really like the … here.	**Non mi piace molto … qui.** *non mee peeachay molto kwee*
food/people	**la cucina/la gente** *la koocheena/la jayntay*

Who are you with?/Family
Con chi è/La famiglia

Who are you with?	**Con chi è?** *kon kee eh*
I'm on my own.	**Sono (da) solo.** *sono (da) solo*
I'm with a friend.	**Sono con un amico/un'amica.** *sono kon oonameeko/oonameeka*
I'm with my …	**Sono con …** *sono kon*
wife	**mia moglie** *meea molyeeay*
husband	**mio marito** *meeo mareeto*
family	**la mia famiglia** *la meea fameelya*
children	**i miei figli** *ee meeayee feelyee*
parents	**i miei genitori** *ee meeayee jayneetoree*
boyfriend/girlfriend	**il mio ragazzo/la mia ragazza** *eel meeo ragatso/la meea ragatsa*
my father/son	**mio padre/figlio** *meeo padray/feelyo*
my mother/daughter	**mia madre/figlia** *meea madray/feelya*
my brother/uncle	**mio fratello/mio zio** *meeo fratayllo/meeo dzeeo*
my sister/aunt	**mia sorella/zia** *meea sorraylla/dzeea*
What's your son's/wife's name?	**Come si chiama suo figlio/sua moglie?** *komay see keeama soo-o feelyo/soo molyeeay*
Are you married?	**È sposato(-a)?** *eh sposaato(-a)*
I'm …	**Sono …** *sono*
married/single	**sposato(-a)/celibe** *sposaato(-a)/chayleebay*
divorced/separated	**divorziato(-a)/separato(-a)** *deevortseeaato(-a)/saypayraato(-a)*
engaged	**fidanzato(-a)** *feedantsaato(-a)*
We live together.	**Viviamo insieme.** *veeveeaamo eensee-ehmay*
Do you have any children?	**Ha bambini/figli?** *ah bambeenee/feelyee*
2 boys and a girl	**Due ragazzi e una ragazza** *doo-ay ragatsee ay oona ragatsa*
How old are they?	**Quanti anni hanno?** *kwantee annee anno*

120

What do you do? Che cosa fa?

What do you do?	**Che cosa fa?**	*kay kosa fa*
What line are you in?	**Che lavoro fa?**	*kay lavooro faa*
What are you studying?	**Che cosa studia?**	*kay kosa stoodeea*
I'm studying …	**Studio …**	*stoodeeo*
I'm in …	**Mi occupo di …**	*mee okoopo dee*
business	**commercio**	*kommayrcho*
engineering	**ingegneria**	*eenjayñayreea*
retail	**commercio al dettaglio**	*kommayrcho al dayttalyo*
sales	**vendite**	*vayndeetay*
Who do you work for?	**Per chi lavora?**	*pehr kee lavora*
I work for …	**Lavoro per …**	*lavoro pehr*
I'm a(n) …	**Sono …**	*sono*
accountant	**ragioniere(-a)**	*rajonee-ehray(-a)*
housewife	**casalinga**	*kazaleengga*
student	**studente(ssa)**	*stoodayntay(ssa)*
retired	**in pensione**	*een paynseeonay*
between jobs	**fra un lavoro e l'altro**	*fra oon lavoro ay laltro*
I'm self-employed.	**Lavoro in proprio.**	*lavoro een propreeo*
What are your interests/hobbies?	**Quali sono i suoi interessi/hobbies?**	*kwalee sono ee sooee eentayrayssee/hobbies*
I like …	**Mi piace/piacciono …**	*mee peeachay/peeachono*
music	**la musica**	*la moozeeka*
reading	**leggere**	*laydjayray*
sport	**lo sport**	*lo sport*
I play …	**Gioco …**	*joko*
Would you like to play …	**Le piacerebbe giocare …**	*lay peeachayraybbay jokaaray*
cards	**a carte**	*ah kartay*
chess	**a scacchi**	*ah skaakee*

What weather! Che tempo!

What a lovely day!	**Che bella giornata!** *kay baylla jornaata*
What awful weather!	**Che tempo orribile!** *kay taympo orreebeelay*
Isn't it cold/hot today!	**Che caldo/freddo oggi!** *kay kaldo/frayddo odjee*
Is it usually as warm as this?	**È così caldo di solito?** *eh kosee kaldo dee soleeto*
Do you think it's going to ... tomorrow?	**Pensa che domani ...?** *paynsa kay domaanee*
be a nice day	**sarà una bella giornata** *sara oona baylla jornaata*
rain	**pioverà** *peeovayra*
snow	**nevicherà** *nayveekayra*
What is the weather forecast?	**Che previsioni ci sono?** *kay prayveeseeonay chee sono*
It's ...	**È ...** *eh*
cloudy	**nuvoloso** *noovoloso*
foggy	**nebbioso** *naybbeeoso*
frosty	**gelato** *jaylaato*
icy	**ghiacciato** *geeachaato*
thundery	**temporalesco** *taymporalaysko*
windy	**ventoso** *vayntoso*
It's raining.	**Piove.** *peeovay*
It's snowing.	**Nevica.** *nayveeka*
It's sunny.	**C'è il sole.** *chay eel solay*
Has the weather been like this for long?	**Il tempo è così da molto tempo?** *eel taympo eh kosee da molto taympo*
What's the pollen count?	**Com'è il conteggio del polline?** *komeh eel kontaydjo dayl polleenay*
high/medium/low	**alto/medio/basso** *alto/maydeeo/basso*
What's the forecast for skiing?	**Che previsioni ci sono per sciare?** *kay prayveeseeonee chee sono pehr sheeaaray*

Enjoying your trip? Si sta divertendo?

È in vacanza?	Are you on vacation?
Come è arrivato qui?	How did you travel here?
Dove alloggia?	Where are you staying?
Da quanto tempo è qui?	How long have you been here?
Quanto tempo si trattiene?	How long are you staying?
Cosa ha fatto finora?	What have you done so far?
Dove andrà dopo?	Where are you going next?
Si sta divertendo?	Are you enjoying your vacation?

I'm here on …	**Sono qui …** _sono kwee_
a business trip	**per affari** _pehr affaaree_
vacation	**in vacanza** _een vakantsa_
We came by …	**Siamo venuti(-e) in …** _seeaamo vaynootee(-ay) een_
train/bus/plane	**treno/pullman/aereo** _trayno/pullman/aayreeo_
car/ferry	**auto/traghetto** _owto/tragaytto_
I have a rental car.	**Ho noleggiato una macchina** _o nolaydjaato oona makeena_
We're staying in …	**Alloggiamo …** _allodjaamo_
an apartment	**in un appartamento** _een oon appartamaynto_
a hotel/campsite	**in un albergo/un campeggio** _een oon albayrgo/oon kampaydjo_
with friends	**con amici** _kon ameechee_
Can you suggest …?	**Può suggerire …?** _pwo soodjayreeray_
things to do	**cose da fare** _kosay da faaray_
places to eat	**posti per mangiare** _postee pehr manjaaray_
places to visit	**luoghi di interesse** _loo-ogee dee eentayrassay_
We're having a great/ boring time.	**Ci stiamo divertendo/annoiando.** _chee steeaamo deevayrtayndo/ annoeeando_

Invitations Inviti

Would you like to have dinner with us on …?	**Vuole venire a cena da noi il …?** _vwo_lay vay_nee_ray a <u>_chay_na</u> da <u>_no_ee eel</u>
May I invite you to lunch?	**Posso invitarLa a pranzo?** _pos_so eenvee_taar_la ah _pran_dzo
Can you come for a coffee this evening?	**Vuole venire a prendere il caffè da noi questa sera?** _vwo_lay vay_nee_ray ah _prayn_dayray eel _kaf_feh da _no_ee _kway_sta _say_ra
We are having a party. Can you come?	**Facciamo una festa. Vuole venire?** fach_aa_mo _oo_na _fay_sta. _vwo_lay vay_nee_ray
May we join you?	**Possiamo venire anche noi?** passee_aa_mo vay_nee_ray _an_kay _no_ee
Would you like to join us?	**Vuole venire anche Lei?** _vwo_lay vay_nee_ray _an_kay _la_yee

Going out Uscire

What are your plans for …?	**Cosa fa …?** _ko_sa fa
today/tonight	**oggi/questa sera** _od_jee/kw_ay_sta _say_ra
tomorrow	**domani** do_maa_nee
Are you free this evening?	**È libero(-a) questa sera?** eh _lee_bayro(-a) kw_ay_sta _say_ra
Would you like to …?	**Le piacerebbe …?** lay pee-achay_rayb_bay
go dancing	**andare a ballare** an_daa_ray ah balla_aa_ray
go for a drink/meal	**andare al bar/al ristorante** an_daa_ray al bar/al reesto_ran_tay
go for a walk	**fare una passeggiata** _faa_ray _oo_na passaydj_aa_ta
go shopping	**fare acquisti** _faa_ray akwee_stee
I'd like to go to …	**Mi piacerebbe andare …** mee pee-achay_rayb_bay an_daa_ray
I'd like to see …	**Mi piacerebbe vedere …** mee pee-achay_rayb_bay vay_day_ray
Do you enjoy …?	**Le piace …?** lay pee-_a_chay

Accepting or declining
Accettare o declinare

Great. I'd love to.	**Sarebbe magnifico.** sa*raybb*ay ma*ñee*feeko
Thank you, but I'm busy.	**Grazie, ma ho un'altro impegno.** *graatsee*ay ma ho oon <u>al</u>tro eem*payño*
May I bring a friend?	**Posso portare un amico(-a).** *po*sso por*taa*ray oon a*mee*ko(-a)
Where shall we meet?	**Dove ci incontriamo?** *do*vay chee eenkontree*aa*mo
I'll meet you …	**La incontro …** la een*kon*tro
in front of your hotel	**di fronte al suo albergo** dee *fron*tay al *soo*-o al*bayr*go
I'll pick you up at 8 p.m.	**La chiamo alle otto/venti.** la kee*aa*mo *al*lay *ot*to/*vayn*tee
Could we make it a bit later/earlier?	**Facciamo un po' più tardi/presto?** fach*aa*mo oon po pee*oo tar*dee/ *pray*sto
How about another day?	**Facciamo un'altro giorno?** fach*aa*mo oon*al*tro *jor*no
That will be fine.	**Va bene.** va *bay*nay

Dining out/in Mangiare al ristorante/a casa

Punctuality varies from region to region in Italy. 15 minutes late may be acceptable in the south, but even 5 minutes would be frowned upon in the north.

Let me buy you a drink.	**Mi permetta di offrirLe una bibita.** mee payr*mee*ta dee of*free*rlay *oo*na bee*bee*ta
Do you like …?	**Le piace …?** lay pee*a*chay
What are you going to have?	**Cosa prende?** *ko*sa *prayn*day
That was a lovely meal.	**Che pasto squisito!** kay *paa*sto skwee*zee*to

Encounters Incontri

Do you mind if I ...?	**Le dispiace se ...?** *lay deespee<u>a</u>chay say*
sit here/smoke	**mi siedo qui/fumo** *mee see-<u>eh</u>do kwee/<u>foo</u>mo*
Can I get you a drink?	**Posso offrirLe una bibita?** <u>pos</u>so offreerlay <u>oo</u>na beeb<u>ee</u>ta
I'd love to have some company.	**Mi piacerebbe avere un po' di compagnia.** *me pee-achayr<u>a</u>ybbay av<u>a</u>yray oon po dee kompa<u>ñee</u>a*
Why are you laughing?	**Perchè ride?** *payr<u>keh</u> <u>ree</u>day*
Is my Italian that bad?	**Parlo tante male l'italiano?** *p<u>a</u>rlo t<u>a</u>nte m<u>aa</u>le leetalee<u>aa</u>no*
Shall we go somewhere quieter?	**Andiamo in un posto più tranquillo?** *andee<u>aa</u>mo een oon p<u>o</u>sto pee<u>oo</u> trankw<u>ee</u>llo*
Leave me alone, please!	**Mi lasci in pace!** *mee <u>la</u>shee een p<u>a</u>chay*
You look great!	**Sei stupendo(-a)!** <u>sa</u>yee stoop<u>a</u>yndo(-a)
May I kiss you?	**Posso baciarti?** <u>pos</u>so ba<u>chaa</u>rtee
Would you like to come back with me?	**Vuoi venire da me?** *voo-<u>oe</u>e vayn<u>ee</u>ray da may*
I'm not ready for that.	**Non sono pronto(-a) per questo.** *non <u>so</u>no pr<u>o</u>nto(-a) pehr kw<u>a</u>ysto*
Thanks for the evening.	**Grazie per la serata.** <u>graa</u>tseeay pehr la sayr<u>aa</u>ta
I'm afraid we've got to leave now.	**Penso che sia ora di partire.** *p<u>e</u>nso che <u>see</u>-a <u>o</u>ra dee part<u>ee</u>ray*
Can I see you again tomorrow?	**Posso rivederLa domani?** <u>pos</u>so reevay<u>day</u>rla dom<u>aa</u>nee
See you soon.	**A presto.** *ah pr<u>ay</u>sto*
Can I have your address?	**Posso avere il suo indirizzo?** <u>pos</u>so av<u>ay</u>ray eel <u>soo</u>-o eendeer<u>ee</u>tso

PARTS OF THE BODY ➤ 166; SAFETY ➤ 65

Telephoning Telefonare

Modern payphones take coins (100, 200 and 500 coins) and phonecards (L.5,000 or 10,000). You can also use your telephone credit card for calling home.

Many public cafés and bars have public phones for local calls. You might have to pay after the call or buy a token (**gettone**) to put in the phone.

To phone home from Italy, dial 00 followed by: Australia 61; Canada 1; Ireland 353; New Zealand 64; South Africa 27; UK 44; US 1. Note that you will usually have to omit the initial 0 of the area code.

Can I have your telephone number?	**Mi da il suo numero di telefono?** mee da eel _soo_-o _noo_mayro dee tay_lay_fono
Here's my number.	**Ecco il mio numero.** _ehko_ eel _meeo noo_mayro
Please call me.	**Mi chiami, La prego.** mee kee_aa_mee la _pray_go
I'll give you a call.	**La chiamerò.** la keeamay_ro_
Where's the nearest telephone booth?	**Dov'è il telefono pubblico più vicino?** do_veh_ eel tay_lay_fono _poob_bleeko pee_oo_ vee_chee_no
May I use your phone?	**Posso usare il suo telefono?** _pos_so oo_zaa_ray eel _soo_-o tay_lay_fono
It's an emergency.	**È un'emergenza.** eh oon aymayr_jaynt_sa
I'd like to call someone in England.	**Vorrei fare una chiamata in Inghilterra.** vor_reh_ee _faa_ray _oo_na kee_amaa_ta een eengeel_tayr_ra
What's the area code for ...?	**Qual'è il prefisso per ...?** kwa_leh_ eel pray_fee_sso pehr
What's the number for Information?	**Qual'è il numero per Informazione Elenco Abbonati?** kwa_leh_ eel _noo_mayro pehr eenformatsee_o_ny ay_layn_ko abbo_naa_tee
I'd like the number for ...	**Vorrei il numero per ...** vor_reh_ee eel _noo_mayro pehr
I'd like to reverse the charges/call collect.	**Vorrei telefonare a carico del destinatario.** vor_reh_ee taylayfo_naa_ray ah _ka_reeko dayl daysteena_ta_reeo

Speaking Telefonare

Hello. This is …	**Pronto. Parla …** *pronto. parla*
I'd like to speak to …	**vorrei parlare a …** *vorrehee parlaaray ah*
Extension …	**Interno …** *eentayrno*
Speak louder/more slowly, please.	**Parli più forte/più lentamente, per piacere.** *parlee peeoo fortay/peeoo laynta maynt ay pehr peeachayray*
Could you repeat that, please.	**Può ripetere, per piacere?** *pwo reepaytayray pehr peeachayray*
I'm afraid he/she's not in.	**Mi dispiace, non è qui.** *mee deespeeaachay non eh kwee*
You have got the wrong number.	**Ha sbagliato numero.** *ah zbalyaato noomayro*
Just a moment.	**Un momento.** *oon momaynto*
Hold on, please.	**Resti in linea, per piacere.** *een leeneea pehr peeachayray*
When will he/she be back?	**Quando rientra?** *kwando reeayntra*
Will you tell him/her that I called?	**Per favore, gli/le dica che ho chiamato.** *pehr favoray lyee/lay deeka kay o keeamaato*
My name is …	**Mi chiamo …** *mee keeamo*
Would you ask him/her to phone me?	**Può dirgli/dirle di richiamarmi?** *pwo deerlyee/deerlay dee reekeeamaarmee*
I must go now.	**Devo andare ora.** *dayvo andaaray ora*
Nice to speak to you.	**È stato un piacere parlare con lei.** *eh staato oon peeachayray parlaaray kon layee*
I'll be in touch.	**La contatterò.** *la kontattayro*
Bye.	**Arrivederci.** *arreevaydayrchee*

128

Stores & Services

ESSENTIAL

I'd like …	**Vorrei …** *vorrehee*
Do you have …?	**Ha …?** *ah*
How much is that?	**Quanto costa?** *kwanto kosta*
Thank you.	**Grazie.** *graatseeay*

For a view of what Italians are buying, take a look in the big chain stores **La Rinascente**, **Upim** and **Standa**, which have branches in most towns.

Check locally for the location and times of open-air markets, generally held at least once a week in most tourist resorts.

APERTO	open
CHIUSO	closed

Stores and services
Negozi e servizi
Where is ...? Dov'è ...?

Where's the nearest ...?	**Dov'è ... più vicino(-a)?** *doveh ... peeoo veecheeno*
Where's there a good ...?	**Dove c'è un(a) buon(a) ...?** *dovay cheh oon (a) bwon(a)*
Where's the main shopping mall/centre?	**Dov'è la zona dei negozi?** *doveh la dzona dayee naygotsee*
Is it far from here?	**È lontano da qui?** *eh lontaano da kwee*
How do I get there?	**Come ci arrivo?** *komay chee arreevo*

Shops Negozi

antique shop	**il negozio di antiquariato** *eel naygotseeo dee anteekwareeaato*
bakery	**la panetteria** *la panayttayreea*
bank	**la banca** *la banka*
bookshop	**la libreria** *la leebrayreea*
butcher shop	**la macelleria** *la machayllayreea*
camera shop	**il negozio di ottica/foto** *eel naygotseeo dee otteeka/foto*
pharmacy	**la farmacia** *la farmacheea*
clothing store	**il negozio di abbigliamento** *eel naygotseeo dee abbeelyamaynto*
delicatessen	**la salumeria** *la saloomayreea*
department store	**il grande magazzino** *eel granday magatseeno*
drugstore	**la farmacia** *la farmacheea*
fish store	**la pescheria** *la payskayreea*
florist's	**il fioraio** *eel feeoraeeo*
gift shop	**il negozio di articoli da regalo** *eel naygotseeo de arteekolee da raygalo*
produce store/greengrocer's	**il fruttivendolo** *eel frooteevayndolo*
grocery store	**la drogheria** *la drogayreea*
health food store/shop	**il negozio di dietetica** *eel naygotseeo dee deeaytayteeka*

jewelry store	**la gioielleria** *la joeeayllay<u>ree</u>a*
liquor store	**la bottiglieria** *la* *botteelyay<u>ree</u>a*
market	**il mercato** *eel mayr<u>kaa</u>to*
newsstand	**l'edicola** *lay<u>dee</u>kola*
pastry shop	**la pasticceria** *la pasteetchay<u>ree</u>a*
record (music) shop	**il negozio di musica** *eel nay<u>got</u>seeo dee <u>moo</u>zeeka*
shoe store	**il negozio di scarpe/la calzoleria** *eel nay<u>got</u>seeo dee <u>skar</u>pay/la kaltsolay<u>ree</u>a*
shopping mall	**il centro commerciale** *eel <u>chayn</u>tro kommayr<u>chaa</u>lay*
souvenir store	**il negozio di ricordi** *eel nay<u>got</u>seeo dee ri<u>kor</u>dee*
sporting goods store	**il negozio di articoli sportivi** *eel* *nay<u>got</u>seeo dee ar<u>tee</u>kolee spor<u>tee</u>vee*
supermarket	**il supermercato** *eel soopayrmayr<u>kaa</u>to*
cigarette stand	**la tabaccheria** *la tabakkay<u>ree</u>a*
toy store	**il negozio di giocattoli** *eel nay<u>got</u>seeo dee jo<u>kat</u>tolee*

Services Servizi

dentist	**il/la dentista** *eel/la daynt<u>ees</u>ta*
doctor	**il medico/il dottore(-ressa)** *eel <u>may</u>deeko/eel dot<u>tor</u>ay(-<u>ray</u>ssa)*
dry cleaner's	**la tintoria/la lavanderia a secco** *la teent<u>or</u>eea/la lavanday<u>ree</u>a ah saykko*
hairdresser's (ladies/men)	**il parrucchiere/la parrucchiera** *eel* *parrookkee<u>ay</u>ray/parrookkee<u>ay</u>ra*
hospital	**l'ospedale** *lospay<u>daa</u>lay*
launderette	**la lavanderia a gettone** *la lavanday<u>ree</u>a ah jay<u>to</u>nay*
library	**la biblioteca** *la beebleeoo<u>tay</u>ka*
optician	**l'ottico/il negozio di ottica** *<u>lot</u>teeko/eel nay<u>got</u>seeo dee <u>ot</u>teeka*
police station	**il commissariato/la questura** *eel kommeessaree<u>ea</u>to/la kways<u>too</u>ra*

Opening hours Orario di apertura

In major cities like Rome, Milan, Bologna and Florence, stores usually close on Saturday afternoon during the Summer; during the August holidays (**Ferragosto**) you may find very few stores open as most locals have fled to the sea or mountains to escape the humidity.

General times for:	Opening	Closing	Lunch break	Closed
stores (winter)	9	7.30	1-3/4	Sun, one half day
(summer)	9	8	1-4/5	during the week
some shopping areas	10	7	none	Sun, Mon a.m
post office (main)	8.30	6	none	Sat p.m., Sun
(smaller)	8.30	6	none	Sat p.m., Sun
banks	8.30	4	1-3	weekend
main offices				

When does the … open/close?	**Quando apre/chiude …?**
	kwando apray/keeooday
Are you open in the evening?	**È aperto la sera?** _eh apayrto la sayra_
Do you close for lunch?	**Chiude per pranzo?**
	keeooday pehr prandzo
Where is the …?	**Dov'è …?** _doveh_
cashier/cash desk	**la cassa** _la kassa_
escalator	**la scala mobile** _la skala mobeelay_
elevator	**l'ascensore** _lashaynsoray_
store guide	**la guida al magazzino**
	la gooeeda al magatseeno
(U.S.) first/ground floor	**pianterreno** _peeano tayrra_
(U.S.) second/first floor	**primo piano** _preemo peeano_

ORARIO DI APERTURA	business hours
CHIUSO PER LA PAUSA DI MEZZOGIORNO	closed for lunch
APERTO TUTTO IL GIORNO	open all day
L'USCITA	exit
L'INGRESSO	entrance
LA SCALA MOBILE	escalator
L'USCITA D'EMERGENZA	emergency/fire exit
L'ASCENSORE	elevator
LE SCALE	stairs

Service Servizi

Can you help me?	**Può aiutarmi?** *pwo aeeootaarmee*
I'm looking for ...	**Cerco ...** *chayrko*
I'm just browsing.	**Sto solo dando un'occhiata.** *sto solo dando oonokkeeaata*
It's my turn.	**È il mio turno.** *eh eel meeo toorno*
Do you have any ...?	**Ha ...?** *ah*
I'd like to buy ...	**Vorrei comprare ...** *vorrehee kompraaray*
Could you show me ...?	**Può farmi vedere ...?** *pwo faarmee vaydayray*
How much is this/that?	**Quant'è questo/quello?** *kwanteh kwaysto/kwayllo*
That's all, thanks.	**È tutto, grazie.** *eh tootto graatseeay*

Buongiorno/buonasera signora/signore.	Good morning/afternoon madam/sir.
Desidera?	Are you being served?
Cosa desidera?	What would you like?
Glielo(-a) controllo subito.	I'll just check that for you.
È tutto?	Is that everything?
Nient'altro?	Anything else?

– *Desidera qualcosa?*
– No grazie. Sto solo dando un'occhiata.
– *Bene.*
– Scusi.
– *Sì, desidera?*
– Quanto costa quello?
– *Um, controllo subito ... Costa trentamila lire.*

IL SERVIZIO (ASSISTENZA) CLIENTI	customer service
SALDI/LIQUIDAZIONI	sale

133

Preference Preferenze

I want some-thing …	**Voglio qualcosa di …** *volyo kwalkosa dee*
It must be …	**Deve essere …** *dayvay ayssayray*
big/small	**grande/piccolo(-a)** *granday/ peekkolo(-a)*
cheap/expensive	**economico(-a)/caro(-a)** *aykonomeeko(-a)/kaaro(-a)*
dark/light	**scuro(-a)/chiaro(-a)** *skooro(-a)/ keearo(-a)*
light/heavy	**leggero(-a)/pesante** *laydjayro(-a) payzantay*
oval/round/square	**ovale/rotondo(-a)/quadrato(-a)** *ovaalay/ rotondo(-a)/kwadraato(-a)*
genuine/imitation	**genuino(-a)/imitazione** *jaynooeeno(-a)/ eemeetatseeonay*
I don't want anything too expensive.	**Non voglio niente di troppo caro.** *non volyo neeayntay dee troppo kaarao*
about … lira.	**Sulle … lire.** *soollay … leeray*
Do you have anything …?	**Ha qualcosa di …?** *ah kwalkosa dee*
larger	**più largo** *peeoo largo*
better quality	**di qualità migliore** *dee kwaleeta meelyoray*

Che … desidera/vuole?	What … would you like?
colore/forma	color/shape
qualità/quantità	quality/quantity
Che tipo preferisce?	What sort would you like?
Su che prezzi vuole rimanere?	What price range are you thinking of?

cheaper	**più economico/meno caro** *peeoo aykonomeeko/mayno karo*
smaller	**più piccolo** *peeoo peekkolo*
Can you show me …?	**Può mostrarmi …?** *pwo mostraarmee*
that/this one	**quello/questo** *kwayllo/kwaysto*
these/those ones	**questi/quelli** *kwaystee/kwayllee*

Conditions of purchase
Condizioni di vendita

Is there a guarantee?

C'è una garanzia?
cheh oona garantseea

Are there any instructions with it?

Ci sono anche delle istruzioni? chee *sono ankay dayllay eestrootseeonee*

Out of stock Esaurito

Mi dispiace, non ne abbiamo.	I'm sorry, we haven't any.
È esaurito(-a)	We're out of stock.
Posso mostrarLe qualcos'altro/ un tipo diverso?	Can I show you something else/ a different sort?
Glielo(-a) ordino?	Shall we order it for you?

Can you order it for me?

Può ordinarmelo(-a)?
pwo ordeenaarmaylo(-la)

How long will it take?

Quanto tempo occorre?
kwanto taympo okkorray

Where else could I get …?

In quale altro negozio posso comprare …?
een kwalay altro naygotseeo posso kompraaray

Decision Decisioni

That's not quite what I want.

Non è esattamente quello che voglio. non *eh ayssattamayntay kwayllo kay volyo*

No, I don't like it.

No, non mi piace. *no non mee peeachay*

That's too expensive.

È troppo caro. *eh troppo karo*

I'd like to think about it.

Vorrei pensarci. *vorrehee paynsaarchee*

I'll take it.

Lo (La) prendo. *lo (la) prayndo*

– Buongiorno, signora. Vorrei una blusa.
  – Certo. Che tipo preferisce?
– Bianca, per piacere. Deve essere larga.
  – Ecco. Sono duecentomila lire.
– Non è esattamente quello che voglio.
  Grazie comunque.

Paying Pagare

Most stores, restaurants and hotels, and some highway service stations accept major credit cards, traveler's checks and Eurocheques–look for the signs on the door.

Tax can be reclaimed on larger purchases when returning home (outside the EU).

Where do I pay?	**Dove si paga?** _dovay see paga_
How much is that?	**Quant'è/Quanto costa?** _kwanteh/kwanto kosta_
Could you write it down, please?	**Può scrivermelo, per favore?** _pwo skreevayrmaylo pehr favoray_
Do you accept traveler's checks?	**Accetta assegni turistici?** _atchaytta assañee tooreesteechee_
I'll pay ...	**Pago ...** _pago_
by cash	**in contanti** _een kontantee_
by credit card	**con carta di credito** _kon karta dee kraydeeto_
I don't have any smaller change.	**Non ho spiccioli.** _non o speecholee_
Sorry, I don't have enough money.	**Mi dispiace, non ho abbastanza soldi.** _mee deespeeachay non o abbastantsa soldee_
Could I have a receipt please?	**Mi dà la ricevuta, per favore?** _mee da la reechayvoota pehr favoray_
I think you've given me the wrong change.	**Credo che si sia sbagliato(-a) nel darmi il resto.** _kraydo kay see see-a zbalyeeaato(-a) nayl daarmee eel raysto_

Come paga?	How are you paying?
Questa operazione non è stata approvata/accettata.	This transaction has not been approved/accepted.
Questa carta non è valida.	This card is not valid.
Può mostrarmi un altro documento d'identità?	May I have further identification?
Ha spiccioli?	Have you got any smaller change?

CASSA	cashier
I TACCHEGGIATORI SARANNO PUNITI A NORMA DI LEGGE	shoplifters will be prosecuted

Complaints Reclami

This doesn't work.	**Questo è difettoso(-a).** *kwaysto eh deefayttoso(-a)*
Can you exchange this, please?	**Può cambiare questo, per favore?** *pwo kambeeaaray kwaysto pehr favoray*
I'd like a refund.	**Vorrei un rimborso.** *vorrehee oon reemborso*
Here's the receipt.	**Ecco la ricevuta.** *eko la reechayvoota*
I don't have the receipt.	**Non ho la ricevuta.** *non o la reechayvoota*
I'd like to see the manager.	**Vorrei parlare con il gestore.** *vorrehee parlaaray kon eel jaystoray*

Repairs/Cleaning Riparazioni/Pulitura

This is broken. Can you repair it?	**Questo è rotto(-a). Può ripararlo(-a)?** *kwaysto eh rotto(-a) pwo reeparaarlo(-la)*
Do you have … for this?	**Ha … per questo?** *ah … pehr kwaysto*
a battery	**una pila** *oona peela*
replacement parts	**dei pezzi di ricambio** *dayee paytsee dee reekambeeo*
There's something wrong with …	**C'è qualcosa che non va con …** *cheh kwalkosa kay non va kon*
Can you … this …?	**Può … questo(-a) …?** *pwo … kwaysto(-a)*
clean	**pulire** *pooleeray*
press	**stirare** *steeraaray*
mend	**riparare** *reeparaaray*
Can you alter this?	**Può aggiustarmi questo(-a)?** *pwo ajeeoostaarmee kwaysto(-a)*
When will it be ready?	**Quando sarà pronto(-a)?** *kwando sara pronto(-a)*
This isn't mine.	**Questo non è mio.** *kwaysto non eh meeo*
There's … missing.	**Manca …** *manka*

Bank/Currency Exhange
Banca/Ufficio Cambio

At some banks, cash can be obtained from ATMs with Visa, Eurocard, American Express and many other international cards. Instructions are often given in English.

You can also change money at most hotels, but the rate will not be as good. Main railway stations and airports also have currency exchange offices.

Remember your passport when you want to change money.

Where's the nearest …?	**Dov'è … più vicino(-a)?** *doveh … peeoo veecheeno(-a)*
bank	**la banca** *la banka*
currency exchange office	**l'ufficio cambio** *looffeecho kambeeo*

TUTTE LE OPERAZIONI	all transactions
SPINGERE/TIRARE/PREMERE	push/pull/press
APERTO/CHIUSO	open/closed
CASSA	cashiers

Changing money Cambiare la valuta

Can I exchange foreign currency here?	**Si può cambiare la valuta straniera qui?** *see pwo kambeeaaray la valoota strañehray kooee*
I'd like to change some dollars/pounds into lira.	**Vorrei cambiare alcuni dollari/sterline in lire.** *vorrehee kambeeaaray alkoonee dollaree/stayrleenay een leeray*
I want to cash some traveler's checks.	**Voglio incassare dei traveller's cheques/ Eurocheques.** *volyo eenkassaaray travellers cheques/eurocheques*
What's the exchange rate?	**Quant'è il cambio?** *kwanteh eel kambeeo*
How much commission do you charge?	**Quanto prende di commissione?** *kwanto praynday dee kommeesseeonay*
Could I have some smaller bills/change, please?	**Posso avere delle banconote di taglio più piccolo/spiccioli?** *posso avayray dayllay bankonotay dee talyo peekkolo/speetcholee*
I've lost my traveler's checks. These are the numbers.	**Ho perso i miei traveller's cheques. Ecco i numeri.** *oa payrso ee meeayee travellers cheques. eko ee noomayree*

Security Misure di sicurezza

Posso vedere …?	Could I see …?
il suo passaporto	your passport
un documento d'identità	some identification
la sua carta bancaria	your bank card
Qual'è il suo indirizzo?	What's your address?
Dove alloggia?	Where are you staying?
Compili/riempia questo modulo, per favore.	Fill in this form, please.
Per favore firmi qui.	Please sign here.

Cash machines/ATMs Bancomat/Cassa automatica

Can I withdraw money on my credit card here?

Posso fare un prelievo con la mia carta di credito qui? _posso faaray oon prayleeayvo kon la meea karta dee kraydeeto kwee_

Where are the cash machines/ATMs?

Dove sono i Bancomat/le casse automatiche? _dovay sono ee bankomat/lay kassay owtomateekay_

Can I use my … card in the cash machine?

Posso usare la mia carta … nel Bancomat? _posso oozaaray la meea karta … nayl bankomat_

The cash machine has eaten my card.

Il Bancomat ha mangiato la mia carta. _eel bankomat ah manjaato la meea karta_

BANCOMAT/ CASSA AUTOMATICA		automated teller/ cash machine

Currency	Lira (plural lire); abbreviation L. or Lit.; Switzerland: 100 centesimi = 1 franco
Italy	_Coins:_ 50, 100, 200, 500 lire _Notes:_ 1,000, 2,000, 5,000, 10,000, 50,000, 100,000 lire
Switzerland	_Coins:_ 5, 10, 20, 50 ct.; 1/2, 1, 2, 5 Fr. _Notes:_ 10, 20, 50, 100, 500, 1000 Fr.

Pharmacy La farmacia

Pharmacies are easily recognized by their sign: a green cross, usually lit up.

If you are looking for a pharmacy at night, on Sundays or holidays, you'll find the address of duty pharmacies (**farmacia di turno**) listed in the newspaper or displayed in all pharmacy windows.

Where's the nearest (all-night) pharmacy?	**Dov'è la farmacia (notturna) più vicina?** doveh la farmacheea (nottoorna) peeoo veecheena
What time does the pharmacy open/close?	**A che ora apre/chiude la farmacia?** ah kay ora apray/keeooday la farmacheea
Can you make up this prescription for me?	**Può farmi questa ricetta?** pwo faarmee kwaysta reechaytta
Shall I wait?	**Devo aspettare?** dayvo aspayttaaray
I'll come back for it.	**Passerò a ritirarla.** passayro ah reeteeraarla

Dosage instructions Dosi e uso

How much should I take?	**Quanto devo prenderne?** kwanto dayvo prayndayrnay
How often should I take it?	**Con quale frequenza devo prenderlo(-la)?** kon kwalay fraykwehntsa dayvo prayndayrlo(-la)
Is it suitable for children?	**È adatto per bambini?** eh adatto pehr bambeenee

Prenda ... pastiglie/cucchiaini ...	Take ... tablets/teaspoons ...
prima/dopo i pasti	before/after meals
con acqua	with water
intero(-a)	whole
la mattina/la sera	in the morning/at night
per ... giorni	for ... days

DOCTOR ➤ 151

Asking advice Chiedere consiglio

What would you recommend for ...?	**Che cosa consiglia per ...?** *kay kosa konseelya pehr*
a cold	**un raffreddore** *oon raffraydoray*
a cough	**la tosse** *la tossay*
diarrhea	**la diarrea** *la deearraya*
a hangover	**i postumi di una sbornia** *ee postoomee dee oona zborneea*
hayfever	**la febbre del fieno** *la faybbray dayl fee-ayno*
insect bites	**le punture d'insetto** *lay poontooray deensaytto*
a sore throat	**il mal di gola** *eel mal dee gola*
sunburn	**una scottatura solare** *oona skottatoora solaaray*
travel sickness	**la cinetosi** *la cheenaytozee*
an upset stomach	**mal di stomaco** *mal dee stomako*
Can I get it without a prescription?	**Si può comprare senza ricetta?** *see pwo kompraaray sayntsa reechaytta*

Over-the-counter treatment Trattamento senza ricetta

Can I have ...?	**Ha ...?** *ah*
antiseptic cream	**della pomata antisettica** *dayllay pomaata anteesaytteeka*
(soluble) aspirin	**dell'aspirina (solubile)** *dayllaspeereena (soloobeelay)*
bandage	**delle bende** *dayllay baynday*
condoms	**dei profilattici** *dayee profeelatteechee*
cotton	**del cotone idrofilo** *dayl kotonay eedrofeelo*
insect repellent/spray	**della pomata contro gli insetti/dello spray insetticida** *daylla pomaata kontro lyee eensayttee/dayllo spray eensaytteecheeda*
pain killers	**dell'antinevralgico** *dayllanteenayvraljeeko*
vitamin tablets	**delle vitamine** *dayllay veetameenay*

Toiletries Articoli da toeletta

I'd like …	**Vorrei …** vor<u>reh</u>ee
after shave	**un dopobarba** oon dopo<u>bar</u>ba
after-sun lotion	**una lozione doposole** <u>oo</u>na lotsee<u>o</u>nay dopo<u>so</u>lay
deodorant	**un deodorante** oon deeodo<u>ran</u>tay
moisturizing cream	**una crema idratante** <u>oo</u>na <u>kray</u>ma eedra<u>tan</u>tay
razor blades	**delle lamette da barba** <u>dayl</u>lay la<u>may</u>ttay da <u>bar</u>ba
sanitary napkins	**degli assorbenti** <u>day</u>lyee assor<u>bayn</u>tee
soap	**del sapone** dayl sa<u>po</u>nay
sun block	**un blocco antisolare** oon block anteeso<u>laa</u>ray
suntan cream/lotion	**una crema/una lozione abbronzante** <u>oo</u>na <u>kray</u>ma/<u>oo</u>na lotsee<u>o</u>nay abbrond<u>zan</u>tay
factor …	**fattore …** fat<u>to</u>ray
tampons	**dei tamponi** <u>day</u>ee tam<u>po</u>nee
tissues	**dei fazzoletti di carta** <u>day</u>ee fatso<u>lay</u>ttee dee <u>kar</u>ta
toilet paper	**della carta igienica** <u>dayl</u>la <u>kar</u>ta eejay<u>nee</u>ka
toothpaste	**un dentifricio** oon dayntee<u>free</u>cho

Haircare Prodotti per i capelli

comb	**un pettine** oon payt<u>tee</u>nay
conditioner	**del balsamo** dayl <u>bal</u>samo
hair mousse	**della schiuma volumizzante** <u>dayl</u>la skee<u>oo</u>ma voloomeedz<u>an</u>tay
hair spray	**della lacca per capelli** <u>dayl</u>la <u>lak</u>ka pehr ka<u>pay</u>llee
shampoo	**dello shampoo** <u>dayl</u>lo shampoo

For the baby Per il neonato

baby food	**degli alimenti per neonati** <u>day</u>lyee alee<u>mayn</u>tee pehr neo<u>naa</u>tee
baby wipes	**dei fazzolettini/delle salviette per neonati** <u>day</u>ee fatzolayt<u>tee</u>nee/<u>dayl</u>lee salvee<u>ay</u>ttee pehr neeo<u>naa</u>tee
diapers	**dei pannolini** <u>day</u>ee panno<u>lee</u>nee

Clothing Abbigliamento

The fashion capital of Italy is Milan, where many of the great designers, such as **Armani**, **Versace**, **Trussardi**, **Ferré**, **Moschino** and **Krizia**, have salons.

You'll find that airport boutiques offering tax-free shopping may have cheaper prices but less selection.

General Generale

I'd like …	**Vorrei …** *vorrehee*
Do you have any …?	**Avete ….?** *avaytay*

ABBIGLIAMENTO PER DONNA	ladies wear
ABBIGLIAMENTO PER UOMO	menswear
ABBIGLIAMENTO PER BAMBINI	children's wear

Color Colore

I'm looking for something in …	**Cerco qualcosa in …** *chayrko kwalkosa een*
beige	**beige** *beige*
black	**nero** *nayro*
blue	**blu** *bloo*
brown	**marrone** *marronay*
green	**verde** *vayrday*
gray	**grigio** *greejo*
orange	**arancione** *aranchonay*
pink	**rosa** *rosa*
purple	**viola** *veeola*
red	**rosso** *rosso*
white	**bianco** *beeanko*
yellow	**giallo** *jallo*
light …	**chiaro** *keeaaro*
dark …	**… scuro** *… skooro*
I want a darker/lighter shade.	**Vorrei una tonalità più scura/chiara.** *vorrehee oona tonaleeta peeoo skoora/keeaara*
Do you have the same in …?	**Ce l'ha anche in …?** *chay la ankay een*

Clothes and accessories
Capi di abbigliamento e accessori

belt	**la cintura** *la cheentoora*
bikini	**il bikini** *eel beekeenee*
blouse	**la camicetta** *la kameechaytta*
bra	**il reggiseno** *eel raydjeesayno*
briefs	**le mutandine** *lay mootandeenay*
cap	**il berretto** *eel bayrraytto*
coat	**il cappotto** *eel kappotto*
dress	**il vestito** *eel vaysteeto*
handbag	**la borsetta** *la borsaytta*
hat	**il cappello** *eel kapayllo*
jacket	**la giacca** *la jakka*
jeans	**i jeans** *ee jeans*
jumper	**la maglia** *la malya*
leggings	**i fuseaux** *ee fooso*
pants	**i pantaloni** *ee pantalonee*
pullover	**il maglione** *eel malyonay*
raincoat	**l'impermeabile** *leempayrmeeabeelay*
scarf	**la sciarpa/il foulard** *la sharpa/eel foolar*
shirt	**la camicia** *la kameecha*
shorts	**gli shorts** *lyee shorts*
skirt	**la gonna** *la gonna*
socks	**i calzini** *ee kaltseenee*
stocking	**le calze** *lay kaltsay*
suit	**il completo** *eel komplayto*
sweatshirt	**la felpa** *la faylpa*
swimming trunks	**i calzoncini da bagno** *ee kaltsoncheenee da baño*
swimsuit	**il costume da bagno** *eel kostoomay da baño*
T-shirt	**la T-shirt/la maglietta** *la tee shirt/la malyaytta*
tie	**la cravatta** *la kravatta*
tights	**il collant** *eel kollant*
tracksuit	**la tuta da ginnastica** *la toota da jeennasteeka*
underpants	**le mutande** *lay mootanday*

Shoes Scarpe

A pair of ...	**un paio di** *oon pa-yo dee*
boots	**gli scarponi** *lyee skarponay*
flip-flops	**le ciabatte** *lay cheeabattay*
sandals	**i sandali** *ee sandalee*
shoes	**le scarpe** *lay skarpay*
slippers	**le pantofole** *lay pantofolay*
running shoes/trainers	**le scarpe da ginnastica** *lay skarpay da jeennasteeka*

Walking/hiking gear Abbigliamento escursionismo

windbreaker	**la giacca a vento** *la jakka ah vaynto*
knapsack	**lo zaino** *lo dza-eeno*
walking boots	**gli scarponi** *lyee skarponee*
waterproof jacket	**la giacca a vento** *la jakka ah vaynto*

Fabric Stoffe

I want something in ...	**Vorrei qualcosa in ...** *vorrehee kwalkosa een*
cotton	**cotone** *kotonay*
denim	**tela jeans** *tayla "jeans"*
lace	**pizzo** *peetso*
leather	**pelle** *payllay*
linen	**lino** *leeno*
wool	**lana** *lana*
Is this ...?	**È ...?** *eh*
pure cotton	**in puro cotone** *een pooro kotonay*
synthetic	**in fibra sintetica** *een feebra seentayteeka*
Is it hand washable/ machine washable?	**Si può lavare a mano/in lavatrice?** *see pwo lavaaray ah maano/ een lavatreechay*

LAVARE A SECCO	dry clean only
LAVARE A MANO	handwash only
NON STIRARE	do not iron
COLORI SOLIDI	colorfast

Does it fit? Come le va?

Can I try this on?	**Me lo/la posso provare?**
	may lo/la posso provaaray
Where's the fitting room?	**Dov'è la cabina di prova?**
	doveh la kabeena dee prova
It fits well. I'll take it.	**Mi va bene. Lo/La prendo.**
	mee va baynay. lo/la prayndo
It doesn't fit.	**Non mi va bene.** *non mee va baynay*
It's too…	**È troppo …** *eh troppo*
short/long	**corto(-a)/lungo(-a)** *korto(-a)/loonggo(-a)*
tight/loose	**stretto(-a)/largo(-a)** *straytto(-a)/largo(-a)*
Do you have this in size …?	**Ha questo nella taglia/misura …?**
	ah kwaysto naylla talya/meesoora
What size is this?	**Che taglia è?** *kay talya eh*
Could you measure me, please?	**Può misurarmi, per piacere?**
	pwo meesooraarmee pehr peeachayray
What size do you take?	**Cha taglia/misura prende?**
	kay talya/meesoora praynday
I don't know Italian sizes.	**Non conosco le misure italiane.**
	non konosko lay meesooray eetaleeaanay

Size Misure

	Dresses/Suits							Women's shoes			
American	8	10	12	14	16	18		6	7	8	9
British	10	12	14	16	18	20		4½	5½	6½	7½
Continental	36	38	40	42	44	46		37	38	40	41

	Shirts				Men's shoes								
American) British)	15	16	17	18	5	6	7	8	8½	9	9½	10	11
Continental	38	41	43	45	38	39	41	42	43	43	44	44	45

EXTRA GRANDE	extra large (XL)
GRANDE	large (L)
MEDIA	medium (M)
PICCOLA	small (S)

1 centimeter (cm.) = 0.39 in.	1 inch = 2.54 cm.
1 meter (m.) = 39.37 in.	1 foot = 30.5 cm.
10 meters = 32.81 ft.	1 yard = 0.91 m.

Health and beauty
Salute e bellezza

I'd like a …	**Vorrei …** *vorrehee*
facial	**un trattamento per il viso** *oon trattamaynto pehr eel veezo*
manicure	**una manicure** *oona maneekooray*
massage	**un massaggio** *oon massadjo*
waxing	**una ceretta** *oona chayraytta*

Hairdresser's/Hairstylist Parrucchiere

Tipping: up to 15% is normal.

I'd like to make an appointment for …	**Vorrei un appuntamento per …** *vorrehee oon appoontamaynto pehr*
Can you make it a bit earlier/later?	**Può un po' più presto/tardi?** *pwo oon po peeoo praysto/tardee*
I'd like a …	**Vorrei …** *vorrehee*
cut and blow-dry	**un taglio e asciugatura con fon** *oon talyo ay ashoogatoora kon fon*
shampoo and set	**uno shampoo e messa in piega** *oono shampoo ay mayssa een peeayga*
trim	**una spuntatina** *oona spoontateena*
I'd like my hair …	**Vorrei …** *vorrehee*
colored/tinted	**fare il colore** *faaray eel koloray*
permed	**una permanente** *oona payrmanayntay*
Don't cut it too short.	**Non li tagli troppo corti.** *non lee talyee troppo kortee*
A little more off the …	**Tagli ancora un po' …** *talyee ankora oon po*
back/front	**dietro/davanti** *deeaytro/davantee*
neck/sides	**al collo/ai lati** *al kollo/lattee*
top	**in cima** *een cheema*
That's fine, thanks.	**Va bene, grazie.** *va baynay graatseeay*

Household articles
Articoli casalinghi

I'd like a(n)/some ... **Vorrei ...** _vorrehee_

adapter	**una presa multipla** _oona praysa moolteepla_
aluminum foil	**della carta stagnola** _daylla karta stañolay_
bottle opener	**un apribottiglie** _oon apreebotteelyay_
candles	**delle candele** _dayllay kandaylay_
clothes pins	**delle mollette da bucato** _dayllay mollayttay da bookaato_
plastic wrap	**della pellicola** _daylla paylleekola_
corkscrew	**un cavatappi** _oon kavatappee_
lightbulb	**una lampadina** _oona lampadeena_
matches	**dei fiammiferi** _dayee feeammeefayree_
paper napkins	**dei tovaglioli di carta** _dayee tovalyolee dee karta_
plug	**una spina elettrica** _oona speena aylayttreeka_
scissors	**un paio di forbici** _oon paeeo dee forbeechee_
screwdriver	**un cacciavite** _oon katchaveetay_
can opener	**un apriscatole** _oon apreeskatolay_

Cleaning items Articoli di pulizia

bleach	**della candeggina** _daylla kandaydjeena_
dish cloth	**uno strofinaccio per i piatti** _oono strofeenatcho pehr ee peeattee_
dishwashing detergent	**un detersivo per lavastoviglie** _oon daytayrseevo pehr lavastoveelyay_
garbage bags	**dei sacchetti per i rifiuti** _dayee sakkayttee pehr ee reeffeeootee_
laundry soap	**un detersivo per lavatrice** _oon daytayrseevo pehr lavatreechay_
dishwashing liquid	**un detersivo per i piatti** _oon daytayrseevo pehr ee peeattee_

Crockery/Cutlery Stoviglie e posate

cups	**delle tazze** _dayllay tatsay_
forks	**delle forchette** _dayllay forkayttay_
glasses	**dei bicchieri** _dayee beekkeeehree_
knives	**dei coltelli** _dayee koltayllee_
mugs	**dei boccali** _dayee bokkaalee_

Jeweler In gioielleria

Even if you can't afford the wares of **Bulgari** and **Buccellati**, Italy's most famous jewelers, you will find the jewelry is generally beautifully crafted and 18-carat gold is a good buy.

Could I see …?	**Vorrei vedere …?** *vorrehee vaydayray*
this/that	**questo/quello** *kwehsto/kwehllo*
It's in the window/ display cabinet.	**È in vetrina/nell'armadietto vetrina.** *eh een vaytreena/nayllarmadeeaytto vaytreena*
I'd like a(n)/some …	**Vorrei …** *vorrehee*
alarm clock	**un orologio sveglia** *oon orolojo zvaylya*
bracelet	**un braccialetto** *oon bratcheealaytto*
brooch	**una spilla** *oona speella*
chain	**una catenina** *oona katayneena*
clock	**un orologio** *oon orolojo*
earrings	**degli orecchini** *daylyee oraykkeenee*
necklace	**una collana** *oona kollana*
ring	**un anello** *oon anayllo*
watch	**un orologio da polso** *oon orolojo da polso*
watch battery	**una pila per orologi** *oona peela pehr orolojee*

Materials Materiali

Is this real silver/gold?	**È argento/oro vero?** *eh arjaynto/oro vayro*
Is there a certificate for it?	**C'è un certificato di garanzia?** *cheh oon chayrteefeekaato dee garantseea*
Do you have anything in …?	**Ha qualcosa …?** *ah kwalkosa*
copper	**in rame** *een ramay*
crystal	**in cristallo** *een kreestallo*
cut glass	**in vetro tagliato** *een vaytro talyaato*
diamond	**con diamante** *kon deeamantay*
enamel	**in smalto** *een smalto*
gold	**in oro** *een oro*
gold plate	**placcato d'oro** *plakaato doro*
pearl	**con perle** *kon payrlay*
pewter	**in peltro** *een payltro*
platinum	**in platino** *een plateeno*
silver	**in argento** *een arjaynto*

Newsstand Il giornalaio

Foreign newspapers can usually be found at rail stations or airports, or on newsstands in major cities.

Tobacco is a state monopoly in Italy. Licensed tobacconists are marked by a large white "T" on a black background. Cigarettes are also sold in some cafés and bars with a tobacco license.

Do you sell English-language books/newspapers?	**Ha libri/giornali inglese?** *ah leebree/jornaalee eengglayzay*
I'd like a(n)/some …	**Vorrei …** *vorraiee*
book	**un libro** *oon leebro*
candy	**delle caramelle** *dayllay karamayllay*
chewing gum	**della gomma da masticare** *daylla gomma da masteekaaray*
chocolate bar	**una tavoletta di cioccolata** *oona tavolaytta dee chokkolaata*
pack of cigarettes	**un pacchetto di sigarette** *oon pakkaytto dee seegaraytlay*
cigars	**dei sigari** *dayee seegaaray*
dictionary	**un dizionario** *oon deetseeonaareeo*
Italian-English	**Italiano-Inglese** *eetaleegno eengglayzay*
envelopes	**delle buste** *dayllay boostay*
guidebook of …	**una guida di …** *oona gooeeda dee*
lighter	**un accendino** *oon atchayndeeno*
magazine	**una rivista** *oona reeveesta*
road map of …	**una carta stradale di …** *oona karta stradaalay*
matches	**dei fiammiferi** *dayee feeaammeefayree*
newspaper	**un giornale** *oon jornaalay*
American/English	**americano/inglese** *amayreekaano/eengglayzay*
paper	**della carta** *daylla karta*
pen	**una penna** *oona paynna*
pencil	**una matita** *oona mateeta*
postcard	**una cartolina** *oona kartoleena*
stamps	**dei francobolli** *dayee frankobollee*
candy	**dei dolci** *dayee dolchee*
tobacco	**del tabacco** *dayl tabako*

Photography La fotografia

I'm looking for a(n) … camera.	**Cerco una macchina fotografica …** *chayrko oona makkeena fotografeeka*
automatic	**automatica** *owtomateeka*
compact	**compact** *kompakt*
disposable	**usa-e-getta** *ooza ay jaytta*
SLR	**SLR** *ayssay ayllay ayrray*
I'd like a (an/) …	**Vorrei …** *vorrehee*
battery	**la pila** *la peela*
camera case	**la custodia per macchina fotografica** *la koostodeea pehr makkeena fotografeeka*
(electronic) flash	**il flash (elettronico)** *eel flash (aylayttroneeko)*
filter	**il filtro** *eel feeltro*
lens	**l'obiettivo** *lobeeaytteevo*
lens cap	**il cappuccio per l'obiettivo** *eel kappootcho pehr lobyaytteevo*

Film/Processing Pellicole/Sviluppo

I'd like a … film for this camera.	**Vorrei una pellicola … per questa macchina (fotografica).** *vorrehee oona paylleekola … pehr kwaysta makkeena (fotografeeka)*
black and white	**in bianco e nero** *een beeanko ay nayro*
color	**a colori** *ah koloree*
24/36 exposures	**da 24/36 pose** *da vaynteekwatro/trayntasay pozay*
I'd like this film developed, please.	**Vorrei fare sviluppare questo film.** *vorrehee faaray zveeloopaaray kwehsto film*
Would you enlarge this, please?	**Può ingrandire questa, per favore?** *pwo eenggrandeeray kwaysta pehr favoreh*
How much do … exposures cost?	**Quanto costa lo sviluppo …?** *kwanto kosta lo zveelooppo*
When will the photos be ready?	**Quando saranno pronte le foto?** *kwando saranno prontay lay foto*
I'd like to pick up my photos. Here's the receipt.	**Vorrei ritirare le mie foto. Ecco la ricevuta.** *vorrehee reeteeraaray lay meeay foto. eko la reechayvoota*

Police Polizia

In Italy, dial ☎ 113 for all emergency services and ☎ 118 for fire. Dial ☎ 7 for the police in Switzerland.

Beware of pickpockets, particularly in crowded places. Report all thefts to the local police within 24 hours for your own insurance purposes.

Where's the nearest …?	**Dov'è … più vicino(-a)?** *do<u>veh</u> … pee<u>oo</u> veech<u>ee</u>no(-a)*
police station	**il Commissariato/la Questura** *eel kommeessaree<u>aa</u>to/la kwehs<u>too</u>ra*
Does anyone here speak English?	**C'è qualcuno che parla inglese?** *cheh kwal<u>koo</u>no kay <u>par</u>la eeng<u>glay</u>zay*
I want to report a(n) …	**Voglio denunciare …** <u>vol</u>yo daynoon<u>chaa</u>ray
accident/attack.	**un incidente/un'aggressione** *oon eenchee<u>day</u>ntay/oonaggraysseeo<u>nay</u>*
mugging/rape	**un'aggressione per rapina/uno stupro.** *oonaggraysseeo<u>nay</u> pehr ra<u>pee</u>na/<u>oo</u>no <u>stoo</u>pro*
My child is missing.	**Il/La mio(-a) bambino(-a) è scomparso(-a).** *eel/la <u>mee</u>o(-a) bam<u>bee</u>no(-a) eh skom<u>paar</u>so(-a)*
Here's a photo of him/her.	**Ecco la sua foto.** <u>eh</u>ko la <u>soo</u>-a <u>fo</u>to
Someone's following me.	**Qualcuno mi sta seguendo.** *kwal<u>koo</u>no mee sta saygoo-<u>ay</u>ndo*
I've seen a suspicious package.	**Ho visto un pacco sospetto.** *o <u>vee</u>sto oon <u>pak</u>ko sos<u>pay</u>tto*
I need an English-speaking lawyer.	**Vorrei un avvocato che parla l'inglese.** *vor<u>reh</u>ee oon avvo<u>kaa</u>to kay <u>par</u>la leeng<u>glay</u>zay*
I need to make a phone call.	**Devo fare una telefonata.** *<u>day</u>vo <u>faa</u>ray <u>oo</u>na taylayfo<u>naa</u>ta*
I need to contact the … Consulate.	**Devo contattare il Consolato …** *<u>day</u>vo konta<u>taa</u>ray eel konso<u>laa</u>to*
American	**americano** *ahmayree<u>kaa</u>noa*

Lo/la può descrivere?	Can you describe him/her?
uomo/donna	male/female
biondo(-a)/bruno(-a)	blonde/brunette
con capelli rossi/grigi	red-headed/gray
con capelli lunghi/corti/stempiato	long/short hair/balding
altezza approssimativa …	approximate height …
di (circa) … anni	aged (approximately) …
indossava …	He/She was wearing …

Lost property/Theft Oggetti smarriti/Furti

I want to report a theft/break-in.	**Voglio denunciare un furto/una rapina.** _volyo daynoonchaaray oon foorto/oona rapeena_
I've been mugged/robbed.	**Sono stato aggredito/derubato.** _sono staato aggraydeto/dayroobaato_
I've lost my …	**Ho perso …** _o payrso_
My … has been stolen.	**Mi hanno rubato …** _mee anno roobaato_
bicycle	**la bicicletta** _la beecheeklaytta_
camera	**la macchina fotografica** _la makeena fotografeeka_
(rental) car	**l'auto (noleggiata)** _lowto (nolaydjaata)_
credit cards	**le carte di credito** _lay kartay dee kraydeeto_
handbag	**la borsetta** _la borsaytta_
money	**i soldi** _ee soldee_
passport	**il passaporto** _eel passaporto_
purse	**il portamonete** _eel poartamonaytay_
ticket	**il biglietto** _eel beelyaytto_
wallet	**il portafoglio** _eel portafolyo_
watch	**l'orologio** _lorolojo_
What shall I do?	**Cosa faccio?** _kosa fatcho_
I need a police report/certificate for my insurance claim.	**Devo avere una copia della mia denuncia per la mia assicurazione.** _dayvo avayray oona kopeea daylla meea daynooncha pehr la meea asseekooratseeonay_

Cosa manca?	What's missing?
Quando è successo?	When did it happen?
Dove alloggia?	Where are you staying?
Da dove è stato(-a) preso(-a)?	Where was it taken from?
Dov'era lei in quel momento?	Where were you at the time?
Le abbiamo chiamato un interprete.	We're getting an interpreter for you.
Ci occuperemo della faccenda.	We'll look into the matter.
Compili questo modulo, per favore.	Please fill in this form.

Post office L'Ufficio Postale

Italian post offices bear the sign PT. Mail boxes are red in Italy, though some post offices have yellow boxes for express mail.

In major towns, the main post offices are normally open from 8.30 a.m. through to 6 p.m., while smaller branches close at 2 p.m. Stamps can be bought from tobacconists **(tabaccaio)**, some hotel desks, as well as from the Post Office.

General queries Informazioni generali

Where is the main post office? **Dov'è l'ufficio postale principale?** *dovai looffeecho postaalay preencheepaalay*

What time does the post office open/close? **A che ora apre/chiude l'ufficio postale?** *ah kay oray apray/keeooday looffeecho postaalay*

Does it close for lunch? **Chiude per pranzo?** *keeooday pehr prandzo*

Where's the mailbox/postbox? **Dov'è la cassetta delle lettere?** *doveh la kassaytta dayllay layttayray*

Where's the general delivery? **Dov'è il Fermo Posta?** *doveh eel fayrmo posta*

Is there any mail for me? My name is … **C'è posta per me? Mi chiamo …** *cheh posta pehr may. mee keeaamo*

Buying stamps Comprare francobolli

A stamp for this postcard, please. **Un francobollo per questa cartolina, per favore.** *oon frankobollo pehr kwaysta kartoleena pehr favoray*

A …-Lira stamp, please. **Un francobollo da … lire, per favore.** *oon frankobollo da … leeray pehr favoray*

What's the postage for a letter to …? **Quanto costa spedire una lettera a …?** *kwanto kosta spaydeeray oona layttayra ah*

Is there a stamp machine here? **C'è un distributore automatico di francobolli qui?** *cheh oon deestreebootoray owtomaateeko dee frankobollee*

> – Buongiorno, vorrei spedire queste cartoline
> negli Stati Uniti, per piacere.
> – *Quante?*
> – Dieci, per favore.
> – *Fa settecentocinquanta lire per dieci.*

Sending parcels Mandare pacchi

I want to send this package by …	**Voglio spedire questo pacco …** _volyo spaydeeray kwaysto pahkko_
airmail	**per via aerea** _pehr veea aayreea_
express/special delivery	**per espresso** _pehr ayspraysso_
It contains …	**Contiene …** _konteeaynay_

Telecommunications Telecomunicazioni

Deve compilare il modulo per la dogana.	Please fill in the customs declaration form.
Che valore ha?	What is the value?
Cosa c'è dentro?/Cosa contiene?	What's inside?

I'd like a phonecard, please.	**Vorrei una carta telefonica, per favore.** _vorraiee oonah kahrtah taylayfoneekah pair fahvoray_
5000/10.000 lira.	**Da cinquemila/diecimila lire.** _da cheenkwaymeela/deeaycheemeela leeray_
Do you have a photocopier?	**Ha un servizio fotocopie?** _ah oon sayrveetseeo fotokopeeay_
I'd like … copies.	**Vorrei … copie.** _vorrehee … kopee-eh_
I'd like to send a message …	**Vorrei trasmettere un messaggio.** _vorrehee trasmayttayray oon mayssajeeo_
by E-mail/fax	**per posta elettronica/fax.** _pehr posta aylaytroneeka/fax_
What's your E-mail address?	**Qual'è il suo indirizzo di e-mail?** _kwalay eel soo-o eendeereetso dee e-mail_
Can I access the Internet here?	**Posso accedere all'internet da qui?** _posso achaydayray aleentaytnet da kwee_
What are your charges per hour?	**Quanto si paga all'ora?** _kwanto see paaga allora_
How do I log on?	**Come ci si collega?** _komay chee see kollayga_

Souvenirs Ricordi

Italy is a shopping wonderland and you'll find no shortage of souvenirs and gifts to take home.

Italian designer clothes for men, women and children are internationally renowned, as well as shoes, accessories and other leather goods (handbags, beauty cases, luggage). You'll also find knitwear, cloth (silk, linen) and lace; or jewelry, including gold and silverware.

Regional crafts include pottery, ceramics, olivewood, glass and crystal work, straw and raffia goods. If you're still stuck for a souvenir, try a bottle of fine Italian wine, liqueur or aperitifs or an art book or reproduction.

antiques	**gli oggetti di antiquariato** *lyee ojayttee dee anteekwareeaato*
ceramics	**la ceramica** *la chayraameeka*
doll	**la bambola** *la bambola*
glassware	**gli articoli di vetro** *lyee arteekolee dee vehtro*
jewelry	**i gioielli** *ee joeeehllee*
knitware	**la maglieria** *la malyayreea*
needlework	**il ricamo** *eel reekaamo*
silk	**la seta** *la sehta*
woodwork	**il lavoro in legno** *eel lavoro een lehño*

Gifts Regali

bottle of wine	**una bottiglia di vino** *oona botteelya dee veeno*
box of chocolates	**una scatola di cioccolatini** *oona skatola dee chokkolaateenee*
calendar	**un calendario** *oon kalayndaareeo*
key ring	**un portachiavi** *oon portakeeavee*
postcard	**una cartolina** *oona kartoleena*
souvenir guide	**una guida-ricordo** *oona gooeeda reekordo*
ceramic plate	**un piatto in ceramica** *oon peeatto*
T-shirt	**una maglietta** *oona malyaytta*

Music Musica

I'd like a ...	**Vorrei ...** *vorrehee*
cassette	**un nastro/una cassetta** *oon nastro/oona kassaytta*
compact disc	**un compact/un CD** *oon compact/oon cheedee*
record	**un disco** *oon deesko*
videocassette	**una videocassetta** *oona veedeeokassaytta*
Who are the popular Italian singers/bands?	**Chi sono i cantanti/gruppi italiani più famosi?** *chee sono ee kantantee/ grooppee eetaleeaanee peeoo famozee*

Toys and games Giocattoli e giochi

I'd like a toy/game ...	**Vorrei un giocattolo/un gioco ...** *vorrehee oon jokattolo/oon joko*
for a boy	**per un bambino** *pehr oon bambeena*
for a 5-year-old girl	**per una bambina di cinque anni** *pehr oona bambeena dee cheenkway annee*
pail and shovel	**un secchiello e una paletta** *oon saykeeayllo ay oona palaytto*
chess set	**un gioco degli scacchi** *oon joko daylyee skakee*
doll	**una bambola** *oona bambola*
electronic game	**un gioco elettronico** *oon joko aylayttroneeko*
teddy bear	**un orsacchiotto** *oon orsakkeeotto*

Antiques Oggetti di antiquariato

How old is this?	**Quanti anni ha questo(-a)?** *kwantee annee a kwehsto(-a)*
Do you have anything of the ... era?	**Ha qualcosa del periodo ...?** *ah kwalkosa dayl payreeodo*
Can you send it to me?	**Può spedirmelo(-la)?** *pwo spaydeermeelo(-la)*
Will I have problems with customs?	**Avrò problemi con la dogana?** *avro proablaymee kon la dogaana*
Is there a certificate of authenticity?	**C'è un certificato di autenticità?** *cheh oon chayrteefeekato dee owtaynteecheeta*

ARTISTIC PERIODS ➤ 104

Supermarket/Convenience store
Il supermercato/Il negozio di alimentari

Supermarkets and convenience stores are found in most tourist resorts and all towns; however, Italy is still rich in markets, smaller stores and delicatessens (**salumeria**), where it can be more fun to shop.

At the supermarket   Al supermercato

Excuse me. Where can I find ...?	**Scusi. Dove posso trovare ...?**
	skoozee. dovay posso trovaaray
Do I pay for this here or at the checkout?	**Pago qui o alla cassa?**
	pago kwee o alla kassa
Where are the baskets/ shopping carts?	**Dove sono i cestelli/carrelli?**
	dovay sono ee karrayllee/chestayllee
Is there a ... here?	**C'è ... qui?**
	cheh ... kwee
delicatessen	**una salumeria** *oona saloomayreea*
pharmacy	**farmacia** *farmacheea*

PANE E DOLCI	bread and cakes
PRODOTTI DI PULIZIA	cleaning products
LATTICINI	dairy products
PESCE FRESCO	fresh fish
CARNI FRESCHE	fresh meat
PRODOTTI FRESCHI	fresh produce
PRODOTTI SURGELATI	frozen foods
ARTICOLI CASALINGHI	household goods
POLLAMI	poultry
FRUTTA E VERDURA	fruit and vegetables
VINI E LIQUORI	wines and spirits

Weights and measures

- **1 kilogram** or **kilo (kg.)** = 1000 grams (g.); **100 g.** = 3.5 oz.; **1 kg.** = 2.2 lb [1 oz. = **28.35 g.**; 1 lb. = **453.60 g.**]
- **1 liter (l.)** = 0.88 imp. quart or 1.06 U.S. quart [1 imp. quart = **1.14 l.** 1 U.S. quart = **0.951 l.** 1 imp. gallon = **4.55 l.** 1 U.S. gallon = **3.8 l.**]

Food hygiene Igiene alimentare

CONSUMARE ENTRO ...	eat within ...
DAL GIORNO DI APERTURA.	days of opening
TENERE IN FRIGORIFERO	keep refrigerated
ADATTO(-A) ALLA COTTURA	microwaveable
NEL FORNO A MICROONDE	
DATA DI SCADENZA ...	sell by ...
PER VEGETARIANI	suitable for vegetarians

At the convenience store Al negozio di alimentazione

I'd like some of that/these.	**Vorrei un pò di quello/questo.**
	vorrehee oon po dee kwayllo/kwaysto
This one/those	**Questo/quelli** *kwaysto/kwayllee*
To the left/right	**A sinistra/destra** *ah seeneestra/daystra*
Over there/Here	**Lì/qui** *lee/kwee*
Which one/ones?	**Quale/quali** *kwalay/kwalee*
That's all, thanks.	**È tutto, grazie.** *eh tootto graatseeay*
I'd like a(n) ...	**Vorrei ...** *vorrehee*
kilo of apples	**un chilo di mele** *oon keelo dee maylay*
half-kilo of tomatoes	**mezzo chilo di pomodori** *maytso keelo dee pomodoree*
100 grams of cheese	**100 grammi di formaggio** *chaynto grammee dee formadjo*
liter of milk	**un litro di latte** *oon leetro dee lattay*
half-dozen eggs	**mezza dozzina di uova** *maytsa dotseena dee ooova*
... slices of ham	**... fette del prosciutto affettato** ... *fehttay dayl proshootto affayttaato*
piece of cake	**un pezzo di torta** *oon paytso de torta*
box of chocolates	**una scatola di cioccolatini** *oona skatola dee chokkolateenee*
bottle of wine	**una bottiglia di vino** *oona botteelya dee veeno*
carton of milk	**una scatola di latte** *oona skatola dee lattay*
jar of jam	**un vasetto di marmellata** *oon vasaytto dee marmayllaata*

– Vorrei un chilo di quel formaggio,
per favore.
– *Questo?*
– Sì, il gorgonzola, per piacere.
– *Certo … E' tutto?*
– E 300 grammi di quel prosciutto a
sinistra, per favore.

Provisions/Picnic   Provviste/Picnic

butter	**burro** *boorro*
cheese	**formaggio** *for<u>ma</u>djo*
cookies	**biscotti** *bees<u>ko</u>ttee*
chips	**patatine** *pata<u>tee</u>nay*
eggs	**uova** *oo-<u>o</u>va*
French fries	**patate fritte** *pa<u>ta</u>tay <u>free</u>ttay*
grapes	**uva** *<u>oo</u>va*
ice cream	**gelato** *jay<u>laa</u>to*
instant coffee	**caffè solubile** *ka<u>ffeh</u> solo<u>o</u>beelee*
loaf of bread	**pagnotta di pane** *pa<u>ño</u>tta dee <u>pa</u>nay*
margarine	**margarina** *marga<u>ree</u>na*
milk	**latte** *<u>la</u>ttay*
rolls	**i panini** *ee pa<u>nee</u>nee*
sausages	**salciccie** *sal<u>chee</u>chay*
six-pack of beer	**una confezione di sei lattine di birra** *<u>oo</u>na konfayt<u>see</u>onay dee <u>sa</u>yee <u>la</u>tteenay dee <u>bee</u>rra*
soft drink/soda	**bibita analcolica** *bee<u>bee</u>ta anal<u>ko</u>leeka*
tea bags	**bustine di tè** *boo<u>stee</u>nay dee teh*
bottle of wine	**bottiglia di vino** *bot<u>tee</u>lyay dee <u>vee</u>no*

del pane   *dayl <u>paa</u>nay*
Bread; look for **pane all'olio** (olive oil white bread), **pane al latte** (milk bread), **panettone** (Christmas bread enriched with butter and candied fruit, sultanas and raisins), **pandoro** (a large sponge cake topped with powdered vanilla), **pangiallo** and **panforte** (firm nut and honey cake), **panpepato** (spicy nut cake) and **veneziana** (sweet holiday bread with whole almonds).

focaccia   *fo<u>ka</u>tcha*
Savory flatbread; which may be flavored ~ **alla salvia** (sage bread), ~ **alla salsiccia** (sausage bread) or ~ **alle noci** (walnut bread).

Health

Insurance and payment (➤ 168 for phrases)

Before you leave, make sure your health insurance policy covers any illness or accident while on vacation/holiday. If not, ask your insurance representative, automobile association or travel agent for details of special health insurance. In Italy, EU citizens with a Form E111 are eligible for free medical treatment from the Italian national health system.

Hospital emergency departments (**Pronto Soccorso**) will treat all emergencies. However, it you are a non-EU citizen or without an E111 form, you will later have to sign a declaration that either you or your consulate will pay.

Doctor/General Dottore/Espressioni generali

Where can I find a doctor/dentist?	**Dove posso trovare un medico/ un dentista?** _dovay posso trovaaray oon maydeeko/oon daynteesta_
Where's there a doctor who speaks English?	**C'è un medico che parla inglese?** _cheh oon maydeeko kay paarla eengglayzay_
What are the office hours?	**Quando apre l'ambulatorio?** _kwando apray lamboolatoreeo_
Could the doctor come to see me here?	**Posso avere una visita domiciliare?** _posso avayray oona veeseeta domeecheelyaaray_
Can I make an appointment for …?	**Vorrei (fissare) un appuntamento per …?** _vorrehee (feessaaray) oon appoontamaynto pehr_
tomorrow	**domani** _domaanee_
as soon as possible	**al più presto** _al peeoo praysto_
It's urgent.	**È urgente.** _eh oorjayntay_
I've got an appointment with Doctor …	**Ho un appuntamento con il dottor/ la dottoressa …** _oh oon apoontamaynto kon eel dottor/dottorayssa_

TIME ➤ 220; DATE ➤ 218

- Vorrei un appuntamento al più presto possibile.
- Oggi è tutto prenotato. E' urgente?
- Sì.
- Beh, possiamo farla passare alle 10.15 domani con il dottor Rossi.
- Dieci e un quarto. Molte grazie.

Accident and injury Incidenti e lesioni

My … is hurt/injured.	**… si è fatto(-a) male/è ferito(-a).** *see eh fatto(-a) malay/eh fayreeto(-a)*
husband/wife	**Mio marito/Mia moglie** *meeo mareeto/meea molyeeay*
son/daughter	**Mio figlio/Mia figlia** *meeo feelyo/meea feelya*
friend (m./f.)	**Il mio amico/La mia amica** *eel meeo ameeko/la meea ameeka*
baby (m./f.)	**Il mio bambino/La mia bambina** *eel meeo bambeeno/la meea bambeena*
He/She is unconscious.	**Ha perso conoscenza.** *ah payrso konoshayntsa*
He/She is bleeding (heavily).	**Perde (molto) sangue.** *payrday (molto) sanggway*
He/She is (seriously) injured.	**È ferito(-a) (gravemente).** *eh fayreeto(-a) gravamayntay*
I've got a/an …	**Ho …** *o*
blister	**una vescica** *oona vaysheeka*
bruise	**una contusione/un livido** *oona kontooseeonay/oon leeveedo*
burn	**una scottatura** *oona skottatoora*
cut	**un taglio** *oon talyo*
graze	**un'escoriazione** *oonayskoreeatseeonay*
insect bite	**una puntura d'insetto** *oona poontoora deensaytto*
lump	**un bernoccolo** *oon bayrnokkolo*
rash	**un'eruzione della pelle** *oonayrootseeonay dayllay payllay*
sting	**una puntura** *oona poontoora*
swelling	**un gonfiore** *oon gonfeeoray*
My … hurts.	**Mi fa male …** *mee fa malay*

PARTS OF THE BODY ➤ 166

Short-term symptoms Sintomi recenti

I've been feeling ill for … days.	**Mi sento male da … giorni.** *mee saynto malay da … jornee*
I feel faint.	**Mi sento svenire.** *mee saynto svayneeray*
I feel feverish.	**Mi sento la febbre.** *mee saynto la faybbray*
I've been vomiting.	**Ho vomitato.** *o vomeetaatao*
I've got diarrhea.	**Ho la diarrea.** *o la deeaarraya*
I've have …	**Ho …** *o*
backache	**male alla schiena** *malay allay sheeayna*
cold	**il raffreddore** *eel raffrayddoray*
cramps	**i crampi** *ee krampee*
earache	**male alle orecchie** *malay allay orraykkeeay*
headache	**mal di testa** *mal dee taysta*
sore throat	**mal di gola** *mal dee gola*
stiff neck	**il collo rigido** *eel kollo reejeedo*
stomachache	**mal di stomaco** *mal dee stomako*
sunstroke	**un colpo di sole** *oon kolpo dee solay*

Health conditions Stato di salute

I have arthritis.	**Ho l'artrite** *o lartreetay*
I have asthma.	**Ho l'asma** *o lasma*
I am …	**Sono …** *sono*
deaf	**sordo(-a)** *sordo(-a)*
diabetic	**diabetico(-a)** *deeabayteeko(-a)*
epileptic	**epilettico(-a)** *aypeelaytteeko(-a)*
handicapped	**disabile** *deesabeelay*
(… months) pregnant	**incinta di … mesi** *eencheenta dee … maysee*
I have a heart condition.	**Ho disturbi cardiaci.** *o deestoorbee kardeeachee*
high blood pressure.	**Ho la pressione alta.** *o la praysseeonay alta*
I had a heart attack … years ago.	**Ho avuto un infarto … anni fa.** *o avooto oon eenfaarto … annee fa*

163

Doctor's inquiries Domande del dottore

Da quanto tempo si sente così?	How long have you been feeling like this?
È la prima volta che ha avuto questo?	Is this the first time you've had this?
Prende altre medicine?	Are you taking any other medicines?
È allergico(-a) a qualcosa?	Are you allergic to anything?
È vaccinato(-a) contro il tetano?	Have you been vaccinated against tetanus?
Ha perso l'appetito?	Have you lost your appetite?

Examination La visita medica

Le prendo la temperatura/ la pressione del sangue.	I'll take your temperature/ blood pressure.
Arrotoli/tiri sù la manica, per favore.	Roll up your sleeve, please.
Si spogli fino alla vita, per favore.	Please undress to the waist.
Si sdrai, per favore.	Please lie down.
Apra la bocca.	Open your mouth.
Respiri profondamente.	Breathe deeply.
Tossisca, per favore.	Cough please.
Dove le fa male?	Where does it hurt?
Fa male qui?	Does it hurt here?

Diagnosis Diagnosi

Deve fare una radiografia.	I want you to have an x-ray.
Voglio un campione di sangue/feci/urina.	I want a specimen of your blood/stools/urine.
Deve farsi visitare da uno specialista.	I want you to see a specialist.
Deve andare in ospedale.	I want you to go to hospital.
È rotto(-a)/slogato(-a).	It's broken/sprained
È dislocato(-a)/strappato(-a).	It's dislocated/torn.

Ha ...	You've got (a/an) ...
l'appendicite	appendicitis
la cistite	cystitis
l'influenza	flu
l'avvelenamento alimentare	food poisoning
una frattura	fracture
la gastrite	gastritis
l'ernia	hernia
un'infiammazione di	inflammation of ...
il morbillo	measles
la polmonite	pneumonia
la sciatica	sciatica
la tonsillite	tonsilitis
un tumore	tumor
una malattia venerea	venereal disease
È infetto(-a).	It's infected.
È contagioso(-a)	It's contagious.

Treatment Cura

Le do ...	I'll give you ...
un antisettico	an antiseptic
un analgesico	a pain killer
Le prescrivo ...	I'm going to prescribe ...
una cura di antibiotici	a course of antibiotics
delle supposte	some suppositories
È allergico(-a) a qualche medicina?	Are you allergic to any medicines?
Prenda una pillola ...	Take one pill ...
ogni ... ore/... volte al giorno	every ... hours/... times a day
prima/dopo dei pasti	before/after meals
in caso di dolore	if there is any pain
per ... giorni	for ... days
Ritorni fra ... giorni.	I'd like you to come back in ... days.
Consulti un medico quando ritorna a casa.	Consult a doctor when you get home.

Parts of the body Parti del corpo

appendix	l'**appendice**	*lappayndeechay*
arm	il **braccio**	*eel bratcho*
back	il **dorso**/la **schiena**	*eel dorso/la skeeehna*
bladder	la **vescica**	*la vaysheeka*
bone	l'**osso**	*losso*
breast	il **petto**/il **seno**	*eel paytto/eel sayno*
chest	il **torace**	*eel toraachay*
ear	l'**orecchio**	*loraykkeeo*
eye	l'**occhio**	*lokkeeo*
face	la **faccia**/il **viso**	*la fatcha/eel veezo*
finger	il **dito**	*eel deeto*
foot	il **piede**	*eel peeehday*
gland	la **ghiandola**	*la geeandola*
hand	la **mano**	*la mano*
head	la **testa**	*la taysta*
heart	il **cuore**	*eel koooray*
jaw	la **mascella**	*la mashehlla*
joint	l'**articolazione**	*larteekolatseeonay*
kidney	il **rene**	*eel raynay*
knee	il **ginocchio**	*eel jeenokkeeo*
leg	la **gamba**	*la gamba*
lip	il **labbro**	*eel labbro*
liver	il **fegato**	*eel faygato*
mouth	la **bocca**	*la bokka*
muscle	il **muscolo**	*eel mooskolo*
neck	il **collo**	*eel kollo*
nose	il **naso**	*eel naaso*
rib	la **costola**	*la kostola*
shoulder	la **spalla**	*la spalla*
skin	la **pelle**	*la payllay*
stomach	lo **stomaco**	*lo stomako*
thigh	la **coscia**	*la kosha*
throat	la **gola**	*la gola*
thumb	il **pollice**	*eel polleechay*
toe	il **dito del piede**	*eel deeto dayl peeehday*
tongue	la **lingua**	*la leenggooy*
tonsils	le **tonsille**	*lay tonseellay*
vein	la **vena**	*la vayna*

Gynecologist Dal ginecologo

I have … **Ho … o**

abdominal pains **dolori addominali**
doloree addomeenaalee

period pains **mestruazioni dolorose**
maystrooatseeonay dolorosay

a vaginal infection **un'infezione vaginale**
ooneenfaytseeonay vajeenaalay

I haven't had my period for … months. **Non ho le mestruazioni da … mesi.** *non o lay maystrootseeonay da … maysee*

I'm on the Pill. **Prendo la pillola (anticoncezionale).**
prayndo la peellola (anteekonchaytseeonaalay)

Hospital Ospedale

Please notify my family. **Per favore informi la mia famiglia.** *pehr favoray eenformee la meea fameelya*

I'm in pain. **Ho dolori.** *o doloree*

I can't eat/sleep. **Non posso mangiare/dormire.**
non posso manjaaray/dormeeray

When will the doctor come? **Quando verrà il dottore?**
kwando vayrra eel dottoray

Which ward is … in? **In che reparto/corsia è …?**
een kay raypaarto/korseea eh

I'm visiting … **Visito …** *veeseeto*

Optician Ottico

I'm nearsighted/farsighted. **Sono miope/presbite.**
sono meeopay/praysbeetay

I've lost … **Ho perso …** *o payrso*

one of my contact lenses **una delle mie lenti a contatto** *oona dayllay meeay layntee ah kontatto*

my glasses **i miei occhiali** *ee meeayee okeeaalee*

a lens **una lente** *oona layntay*

Could you give me a replacement? **Può sostituirmelo(-la)?**
pwo sosteetooeermaylo(-la)

167

Dentist   Dentista

If you need to see a dentist, you'll probably have to pay the bill on the spot; save all receipts for reimbursement.

I have toothache.	**Ho mal di denti.** *o mal dee dayntee*
This tooth hurts.	**Questo dente mi fa male.** *kwaysto dayntay mee fa malay*
I've lost a filling/a tooth.	**Ho perso un'otturazione/un dente.** *o pehrso oonottooratseeonay/oon dayntay*
Can you repair this denture?	**Può riparare questa dentiera?** *pwo reeparaaray kwaysta dayntee-ehra*
I don't want it extracted.	**Non voglio un'estrazione.** *non volyo oon aystratseeonay*

Le faccio un'iniezione/ un'anestesia locale.	I'm going to give you an injection/ a local anesthetic.
Ci vuole un'otturazione/ una capsula/una corona.	You need a filling/cap/crown.
Devo fare un'estrazione.	I'll have to take it out.
Posso fissarlo solo temporaneamente.	I can only fix it temporarily.
Non mangi niente per ... ore.	Don't eat anything for ... hours.

Payment and insurance
Pagamento e assicurazione

How much do I owe you?	**Quanto Le devo?** *kwanto lay dayvo*
I have insurance.	**Sono assicurato.** *sono asseekooraato*
Can I have a receipt for my health insurance?	**Vorrei una ricevuta per la mia assicurazione medica.** *vorrehee oona reechayvoota pehr la meea asseekooratseeonay maydeeka*
Would you fill in this health insurance form, please?	**Compili questo modulo di assicurazione medica, per favore.** *koampeelee kwehsto modoolo dee asseekooratseetseeonay maydeeka pehr favoray*
Do you have... ?	**Ha ...?** *ha*
Form E111/health insurance	**il modulo E111/l'assicurazione medica** *eel modoolo ay-chento-oondeechee/ lasseekooratseeonay*

Dictionary
English - Italian

To enable correct usage, most terms in this dictionary are either followed by an expression or are cross-referenced to pages where the word appears in a full phrase. The notes below provide some basic grammar guidelines.

Nouns

Nouns in Italian are classed as either masculine (m) or feminine (f). Nouns ending in **-o** are generally masculine (to form their plural, change **-o** to **-i**). Nouns ending in **-a** are usually feminine (to form their plural, change **-a** to **-e**). Nouns ending in **-e** can be either gender (to form their plural, change **-e** to **-i**). The articles they take depend on their gender:

	definite article *(the)*		indefinite article *(a)*	partitive *(some, any)*	
	singular	plural		singular	plural
masc. beginning with:					
a vowel	l'amico	gli amici	un amico	dell'amico	degli amici
z or **s**+consonant	lo studio	gli studi	uno studio	dello studio	degli studi
all other consonants	il treno	i treni	un treno	del treno	dei treni
fem. beginning with:					
a vowel	l'ora	le ore	un'ora	dell'ora	delle ore
a consonant	la casa	le case	una casa	della casa	delle case

Adjectives

Adjectives agree in gender and number with the noun they are describing. In this dictionary the feminine form (where it differs from the masculine) is shown in brackets, e.g.

leggero(-a) – light (in weight)   feminine form: **leggera**

If the masculine form ends in **-e** or with a consonant, the feminine keeps in general the same form:

il museo/la casa grande   the large museum/house

Most adjectives form their plurals in the same way as nouns:

il museo italiano – i musei italiani   la cattedrale interessante – le cattedrali interessanti

Verbs

Verbs are generally shown in the infinitive (to say, to eat etc.) Here are three of the main categories of regular verbs in the present tense:

	amare (to love) ends in **-are**	**vendere** (to eat) ends in **-ere**	**partire** (to laugh) ends in **-ire**
io (I)	amo	vendo	parto
tu (you)	ami	vendi	parti
lui, lei (he, she, it)	ama	vende	parte
noi (we)	amiamo	vendiamo	partiamo
voi (you)	amate	vendete	partite
essi/esse (they)	amano	vendono	partono

Note that the subject pronouns are generally omitted, except for emphasis.
Negatives are generally formed by putting non before the verb: **Non vado a Roma.** I am not going to Rome.

A-Z

A

a few pochi(e) 15
a little un poco 15
a lot molto(-a) 15
a.m. di mattina
abbey abbazia f 99
able, to be (also can, could) potere
about (approximately) circa 15
above (place) sopra
abroad all'estero
abscess ascesso
accept, to accettare 136
access accesso m 100
accessories accessori mpl 144
accident incidente 152; (road) incidente stradale m 92
accidentally accidentalmente 28
accommodation sistemazione f
accompaniments condimenti mpl, salse f 38
accompany, to accompagnare 65
accountant ragioniere (a) m/f
ace (cards) asso m
activities le attività fpl
acne acne f
across attraverso
action film film m d'azione
actor/actress attore m/attrice f
adaptor presa f multipla 26, 148
address indirizzo m 32, 84, 93, 94, 126
adhesive bandage bende fpl adesive
adjoining room camera f adiacente 22
admission charge prezzo m d'entrata 114
adult adulti mpl 100
advance, in in anticipo 21
aerial (car/tv) antenna f
aerobics aerobica f
after (time) dopo 13; (place) 95
after shave dopobarba m 142
after-sun lotion lozione f doposole
afternoon, in the nel pomeriggio 218, 221
age: what age? età: quanti anni? 113
aged, to be avere ... anni 152
ago fa 13
agree: I agree sono d'accordo
air conditioning aria f condizionata
air mattress materasso m di gomma 31
air pump pompa f per l'aria 87

air-freshener deodorante m per ambienti
airline linea f aerea
airmail via f aerea 155
airplane aeroplano m
airport aeroporto m 96
air steward/hostess assistente m/f di volo
aisle seat posto m nel corridoio 69
alarm clock orologio m sveglia 149
alcoholic (drink) alcolico(-a)
all tutto(-a)
all-night bar bar m aperto tutta la notte 112
all-night pharmacy farmacia f notturna 140
allergic, to be essere allergico(-a) a 164, 165
allergy allergia f
allowed: is it allowed? è permesso?
almost quasi 19
alone solo(-a) 120
alphabet alfabeto m 9
already già 28
also anche 19
alter, to ritoccare 137
aluminum foil carta f stagnola 148
always sempre 13
am: I am sono
amazing sorprendente 101
ambassador ambasciatore m
amber ambra f
ambulance ambulanza f 92
American (person/adj) americano(-a) m/f 150, 152
American football calcio m americano
amethyst ametista m
amount ammontare m 42
and e 19
anesthetic anestetico m
angling pesca m con lenza
animal animale m 106
announcement: what was that announcement? cos'era quell'annuncio?
another un altro/un'altra 21
another time un'altra volta 125
antacid antiacido m
antibiotics antibiotici mpl 165
antifreeze antigelo m

antique oggetti mpl di antiquariato 157

antique shop negozio m di antiquariato 130

antiseptic antisettico m 165; **~ cream** pomata f antisettica 114

any qualsiasi 15

anyone: does anyone speak English? c'è qualcuno che parla inglese?

anyone else altre persone 93

anything cheaper qualcosa di più economico 21

anything else? nient'altro?

apartment appartamento 28

apologies scuse fpl 10

apologize: I apologize chiedo scusa

appendicitis appendicite f 165

apples mele fpl 160

appointment appuntamento m 161, 168;

approximately circa/approssimativamente 152

architect architetto m

architecture architettura f

area regione f 97

arm braccio m 166

armbands *(swimming)* bracciali mpl salvagente

around *(place)* attorno, intorno 12; *(time)* circa 13

arrange: can you arrange it? può organizzarlo(-a)?

arrest, to be under essere in arresto

arrive, to arrivare 68, 70, 71, 76

art arte f

art gallery galleria d'arte f, pinacoteca f 99

artery arteria f 166

arthritic, to be essere artritico(-a) 163

artificial sweetener zucchero m dietetico 38

artist artista m/f 104

ashtray posacenere m 27, 39

asked for ... ho ordinato ... 41

asking the way chiedere la strada 94

asleep, to be essere addormentato(-a)

aspirin aspirina f 114, 140

asthmatic, to be essere asmatico(-a) 163

astringent astringente m

at *(place)* a 12; *(time)* a/alle 13

at least almeno 23

ATM *(cash dispenser)* Bancomat m 139

attack *(crime)* aggressione f 152; *(medical)* attacco m

attendant guardiano m

attractive attraente m/f

aunt zia f 120

Australian *(n)* australiano(-a) m/f

Austrian *(person)* austriaco(-a) m/f

authentic: is it ? è autentico(-a)?

automatic *(car)* auto f con cambio automatico 86

automatic camera macchina f fotografica automatica 151

autumn autunno m 219

avalanche valanga f

away via 12

awful orribile

A-Z

B **baby** bambino m/bambina f 162; neonato(-a) m/f 113

baby food alimenti per neonati 142

baby seat sedile m per bambini

baby wipes fazzolettini mpl/salviette fpl per neonati 142

baby's bottle biberon f

baby-sitter babysitter f

back dorso m, schiena f 166

backache mal m di schiena 163

backpack zaino m 31

backpacking girare il mondo con lo zaino

bad cattivo(-a) 14

baked al forno

bakery panetteria f 130

ball palla f 157

ballet balletto m 108

ballroom sala f da ballo

bandage bende fpl

bank banca f 130, 138

bank account conto m bancario

bank card carta bancaria f 139

bank loan prestito m bancario

bar *(hotel)* bar m 26

barber barbiere m

barge *(long boat)* lancia f

basic expressions espressioni comuni 10

basin bacino m

basket cestello m 158

basketball pallacanestro f 114

bath towel asciugamano m 27
bath: to take a fare il bagno
bathroom bagno m 26; sala f da bagno 22
battery batteria f 88; pila f 137, 151
be able, to potere 18
be, to essere
beach spiaggia f 107, 116
beard barba f
beautiful bellissimo(-a) 14; bello(-a) 101; stupendo(-a) 126
because perchè 16
because of a causa di 16
bed letto m 21
bed and breakfast pernottamento m e colazione f 24
bed: I'm going to vado a letto
bedding biancheria f da letto 29
bee ape f
beer birra f 49
before (time) prima di 13, 221
begin, to (see also to start) iniziare
beginner principiante m/f 117
beginning inizio m
belong: this belongs to me questo è mio
below 15°C sotto i 15ªC
belt cintura f 144
beneath sotto 12
berth cuccetta f 74, 77
best il migliore 94
better migliore 14
between fra, tra 12
bib bavaglino m
bicycle bicicletta f 75, 83, 153
bicycle parts 82
bicycle rental noleggio (m biciclette) 83
big grande 14, 117, 134
bill conto m 32, 42, 136; **put it on the ~** lo metta sul conto
bin liner sacco m di plastica per bidoni di spazzatura
binoculars binocolo m
bird uccello m 106
birthday compleanno m 219
biscuits biscotti m 160

bite (insect) puntura f
bitten: I've been bitten by a dog sono stato morsicato da un cane
bitter amaro(-a) 41
bizarre bizzarro(-a) 101
black nero(-a) 143
black and white film (camera) in bianco e nero 151
black coffee (weak) caffè m lungo 40
bladder vescica f 166
blanket coperta f 27
bleach candeggina f 148
bleeding, to be perdere sangue 92, 162
blind tapparella f 25
blister vescica f 162
blocked bloccato(-a) 25; **the drain is ~** le fognature sono bloccate; **the road is ~** la strada è bloccata
blood sangue m 164
blood group gruppo m sanguigno
blood pressure pressione f del sangue 163, 164
blouse camicetta f 144
blow-dry asciugatura f a fon 147
blue blu 143
blusher (rouge) rosso m per guance
board, on a bordo
boarding card carta f d'imbarco 69, 70
body: parts of the body parti fpl del corpo 166
boiled bollito
bone osso m 166
book libro m 150
book of tickets blocchetto m di biglietti 79
book, to prenotare 21, 74, 98, 109
booked up, to be essere prenotato(-a) 115, 161
booking prenotazione f 22, 36
booking office ufficio m prenotazioni
bookstore libreria f 130
boots stivali mpl 145; (for sport) scarponi mpl 115
border (country) frontiera f
boring noioso(-a) 101
born: I was born in sono nato a/nel
borrow: may I borrow your ...? posso prendere in prestito il suo...?
bottle bottiglia f 159
bottle-opener apribottiglie m 148

bowel intestino m 166
box of chocolates scatola f di cioccolatini 156
box office biglietteria f
boxing pugilato m
boy bambino m 157; ragazzo m 120
boyfriend ragazzo m 120
bra reggiseno m 144
bracelet braccialetto m 149
brass ottone m
bread pane m 38
break, to rompere 28; ~ **the journey** interrompere il viaggio 75
break-in rapina f 153
breakage rottura f
breakdown guasto m 88
breakfast (prima) colazione f 26, 27
breast petto m, seno m 166
breathe, to respirare 92, 164
breathtaking sensazionale 101
bridge ponte m 107; *(cards)* bridge m
briefcase valigetta f portadocumenti
briefs mutandine fpl 144
brilliant splendido(-a) 101
bring, to portare 37
Britain Gran Bretagna f 119
British *(person/adj)* britannico(-a) m/f
brochure opuscolo m
broken rotto(-a) 25, 137, 164
bronchitis bronchite f
bronze *(adj)* bronzeo(-a)
brooch spilla f 149
broom scopa f
brother fratello m 120
brown marrone 143
browse, to dare un'occhiata 133
bruise contusione f/livido m 162
brush spazzola f
bubble bath schiuma f per bagno
bucket secchiello m 157
buffet car vagone m ristorante
build, to costruire 104
building edificio m
built costruito(-a) 104
buoy boa f
burger hamburger m 40
burger stand chiosco m per hamburger 35
burn scottatura f 162

burn: it's burned è bruciato(-a)
burst tire pneumatico m scoppiato
bus autobus m 70, 78, 79, 98
bus route percorso m d' autobus 96
bus station stazione f autobus 78
bus stop fermata f d'autobus 65, 96
business trip viaggio m d'affari 123
business, on per lavoro 66
businessman uomo m d'affari
businesswoman donna f d'affari
busy, to be *(occupied)* occupato(-a) 125
but ma 19
butane gas campingaz m 30, 31
butcher shop macelleria f 130
butter burro m 38, 160
button bottone m
buy, to comprare 67, 80
bye! arrivederci
bypass circonvallazione f

C **cabaret** cabaret m
cable car funivia f
café bar m 35, 40
cake torta f 40
cake shop pasticceria f
calendar calendario m 156
call, to chiamare 92, 128; *(phone)* telefonare 127; ~ **call the police!** chiami la polizia! 92
camcorder videocamera f
camera macchina f fotografica 151
camera case custodia f per macchina fotografica 151
camera shop/store negozio m di ottica/fotografia 130, 151
campbed lettino m da campo 31
camping campeggio m 30
camping equipment 31
campsite campeggio m 30
can I posso 18
can opener apriscatole m
cancel, to annullare 68
cancer *(disease)* cancro m
candles candele fpl 148
candy caramella f 150

cap berretto m 144
cap *(dental)* capsula f
corona f 168
capital city capitale f
car auto(mobile) f,
macchina f 86-9, 153; **by ~** in
auto/macchina 95
car alarm antifurto m per auto
car hire noleggio auto m,
autonoleggio m 70, 86
car parts 90-1
car pound deposito auto m 87
car repairs 89
car wash lavaggio auto m
cardphone telefono m a scheda
cards carte 121
careful: be careful! faccia attenzione!
carpet *(fitted)* moquette f; *(rug)*
tappeto m
carrier bag sacchetto m 136
carry-cot portabebe m
carton scatola f (di cartone) 159; **~ of**
milk cartone m di latte
cartoon cartoni mpl animati
cash contanti mpl, soldi mpl 136
cash card carta f bancaria 139
cash desk cassa f 132, 136
cash machine Bancomat m 139
cash, to incassare 138
cassette cassetta f, nastro m 157
castle castello m 99
cat gatto m
catch, to *(bus)* prendere (l'autobus)
cathedral cattedrale f 99
cave caverna m, grotta f 107
CD compact m, il CD m
CD-player lettore m per compact
cemetery cimitero m 99
central heating impianto m di
riscaldamento
center of town centro m città 21
ceramics ceramica f
certificate certificato m 157, 168
certification certificato m 149
chain catena f 149
chair sedia f
chair-lift funivia f 117
change *(coins)* moneta f 87; resto m,
spiccioli mpl 136
change lanes, to cambiare corsia 93

change, to cambiare
change, to *(bus, train)* cambiare 78, 79,
84; *(money)* 27, 74, 138; *(reservation)* 68
change: keep the change tenga il resto 84
chapel cappella f
charcoal carbone m 31
charter flight volo m charter
cheap a buon prezzo 14, 134
cheaper più economico(-a) 21, 24, 109
meno caro(-a)
check conto m 32, 42, 136
check in, to registrare 68
check out, to *(hotel)* saldare il conto
checkbook libretto m degli assegni
checkers *(draughts)* gioco m della
dama
checkout cassa f 158
check guarantee card carta f bancaria
cheers! alla salute!
cheese formaggio m 48; 160
chemist farmacia f 130, 140
check book libretto m degli assegni
chess scacchi 121
chess set gioco m degli scacchi 157
chest torace m 166
chewing gum gomma f da masticare 150
chickenpox varicella f
child bambino m/bambina f, figlio
m/figlia f 41, 98, 152
child seat *(in car)* sedile per bambini m 86
children bambini mpl 24, 39, 66, 74,
100, 113; figli mpl 120
children's meals piatti mpl per
bambini 39
Chinese (cuisine) (cucina) Cinese 35
chips patatine fpl 160
choc-ice pinguino m 110
chocolate cioccolata f 40, 160; **box of ~**
scatola f di cioccolatini
chocolate bar tavoletta f di cioccolata 150
chop *(meat)* braciola f 160
Christian *(adj)* cristiano(-a)
Christmas Natale m 219
church chiesa f 96, 99, 105
cigarette machine distributore m
automatico di sigarette
cigarettes, pack of sigarette fpl 150
clamps (car) i ceppi bloccaruote fpl 87
class: first class prima classe f 68
clean *(adj)* pulito(-a) 14, 39, 41

clean, to pulire 137
cleaning person cameriera f 28
cliff scogliera f/rupe f 107
cling film pellicola f trasparente 148
cloakroom guardaroba m 109
clock orologio m 149
close (near) vicino(-a) 95
close, to chiudere 100, 132, 140
clothes abbigliamento m 144
clothes line corda f per il bucato
clothing store (clothing store) negozio
  m di abbigliamento 130
cloudy, to be essere nuvoloso(-a) 122
clown clown, pagliaccio m
clubs (golf) mazze fpl
coach corriera f, pullman 78; (train
  compartment) carrozza f 75, 77
coat cappotto m 144
code (area/dialling) codice m telefonico
coffee caffè m 40
coin moneta f
cold freddo(-a) 14; 41; 122
cold (flu) raffreddore m 141, 163
cold meats affettati mpl 160
collapse: he's collapsed ha avuto un
  collasso
collect, to ritirare 151
color colore m 134, 143; (film) a colori 151
comb pettine m 142
come back , to (return) ritornare 36,
  165; (for collection) passare a ritirare 140
communication difficulties difficoltà di
  comunicazione 11
compact camera macchina f compact 151
company (business) azienda f;
  (companionship) compagnia f 126
compartment (train) scompartimento m
complaints reclami mpl 25, 41; **to make
  a ~** fare un reclamo 137
computer computer m, l'ordinatore m
concert hall sala f concerti 99, 111
concession tariffa f speciale 100
concussion, to have avere la
  commozione cerebrale
condoms profilattici mpl
conductor direttore m d'orchestra
conference conferenza f
confirm, to (reservation) confermare 22, 68
confirmation conferma f 22
congratulations! congratulazioni!

connection (transport)
  coincidenza f
conscious, to be (medical)
  riprendere conoscenza
Consulate consolato m
  152
consult, to consultare 165
consultant (medical) specialista m/f
contact lens lenti fpl a contatto 167
contact, to contattare 28
contact lens fluid fluido m per lenti a
  contatto 167
contagious, to be essere contagioso(-a)
contain, to contenere 39, 69, 155
ccontraceptive contraccettivo m
convenience store nepozio m di
  alimentari 158
convenient conveniente
conversion charts 85, 145, 158
convertible (car) auto f decappottabile
cook cuoco m, cuoca f
cook, to cucinare
cooker cucina f a gas/elettrica 28
cookies biscotti mpl 160
cooking (cuisine) cucina f
copper rame m 149
copy copia f 155
corkscrew cavatappi m 148
corn plaster callifugo m
corner angolo m 95
correct (also right) giusto
cosmetics cosmetici mpl
cottage la villetta f, il rustico m 28
cotton cotone m
cotton wool (absorbent cotton) cotone m
  idrofilo 114, 142
cough tosse f 141
cough syrup sciroppo m per la tosse 114
cough, to tossire 164
counter (shop) banco m (post office,
  bank) sportello m
country (nation) paese m
countryside campagna f 119
couple (pair) paio m
courier (guide) guida m/f,
  l'accompagnatore m
course (meal) portata f
courthouse palazzo m di giustizia 99
cousin cugino m, la cugina f
cover (lid) coperchio m

A-Z

cover charge coperto m 112
craft shop negozio m di artigianato
cramps crampi mpl 163
crash: I've had a crash ho avuto un incidente d'auto
creche asilo-nido m
credit card carta f di credito 42, 136,
credit status posizione f finanziaria
credit, in in credito
crib culla f 22
crisps chips fpl 160 see prev. page.
crockery stoviglie fpl 148
cross, to (road) attraversare 95
cross-country skiing track pista f per sci di fondo
crossroads incrocio m 95
crowded affollato(-a) 30
crown (dental) corona f 168
cruise crociera f
crutches stampelle f
cup tazza f 39, 148
cupboard credenza f, l'armadio m
currency valuta f 67, 138
currency-exchange office ufficio m cambio 70, 73, 138
curtains tende fpl
cushion cuscino m
customs dogana f 67, 157
customs declaration dichiarazione f doganale 155
cut taglio m 162
cut and blow-dry taglio m e asciugatura a fon
cutlery posate fpl 148
cycle helmet casco m per ciclista
cycle path pista f ciclabile
cycling ciclismo m 114
cyclist ciclista m/f
cystitis cistite f 165

D
daily giornalmente 13
damaged, to be essere danneggiato(-a) 28, 71
damp (n) umidità f; (adj) umido(-a)
dance (performance) danza f 111
dancing, to go andare a ballare 124
dangerous pericoloso(-a)
dark scuro(-a) 14, 134, 143; buio(-a) 24

daughter figlia f 120, 162
day giorno m 97; (ticket) giornaliero 79
day trip gita f di un giorno
dead morto(-a); (battery) scarico(-a) 88
deaf, to be essere sordo(-a) 163
dear (greeting) caro(-a)
decide: we haven't decided yet non abbiamo ancora deciso
deck (ship) ponte m
deck chair sedia f a sdraio 116
declare, to dichiarare 67
deduct, to (money) detrarre
deep profondo(-a)
deep frozen surgelato(-a)
defrost, to scongelare
degrees (temperature) gradi mpl
delay ritardo m 70
delicatessen salumeria f 130; reparto m di gastronomia 158
delicious (food) squisito(-a) 125; delizioso(-a) 14
deliver, to consegnare
dental floss filo m per denti
dentist dentista m/f 131, 168
dentures dentiera fsing 168
deodorant deodorante m 142
depart, to (train, bus) partire
department store grande magazzino m 130
departure (train) partenza f 76
departure lounge sala f partenze
depend: it depends on dipende da
deposit caparra f, anticipo m 24, 83, 115
describe, to descrivere 152
design (dress) disegno m
designer stilista m/f
destination destinazione f
details dettagli mpl
detergent detersivo m
develop, to (photos) sviluppare 151
diabetes diabete m
diabetic diabetico(-a)
dialing (area) **code** codice m, prefisso m
diamond diamante m 149; (cards) quadri mpl
diapers pannolini mpl 142
diarrhea diarrea f 141; **to have ~** avere la diarrea
dice dadi mpl
dictionary dizionario m 150
diesel diesel m 87

diet: I'm on a diet sono a dieta
difficult difficile 14
digital digitale 149
dine, to mangiare 112
dining car carrozza ristorante f 75, 77
dining room sala f da pranzo 26
dinner jacket smoking m
dinner, to have cenare 124
direct diretto 75
direct, to indicare la via 18
direct-dial telephone telefono m a linea diretta
direction direzione f 80, 94; **in the ~ of** in direzione 95;
director *(of company)* direttore m; *(film)* regista m/f
directory *(telephone)* elenco m abbonati
Directory Inquiries Informazioni Elenco Abbonati 127
dirty sporco(-a) 14, 28
disabled disabili m/fpl 22, 100
discount sconto m; **can you offer me a ~** può farmi uno sconto?
disgusting disgustoso(-a)
dish *(meal)* piatto m 37
dish cloth strofinaccio m per i piatti 148
dishwashing detergent detersivo m per lavastoviglie 148
dislocated, to be essere dislocato(-a) 164
display cabinet armadietto m vetrina 149
display case astuccio m 134
disposable camera macchina f usa-e-getta 151
distilled water acqua f distillata
district zona f
disturb: don't non disturbare
dive, to tuffarsi 116
diversion deviazione f
divorced, to be essere divorziato(-a) 120
DIY store negozio m del fai-da-te 130
dizzy, to feel avere il capogiro 163
do: things to do cose fpl da fare 123
doctor dottore(ssa) m/f, medico m 131, 161, 167
dog cane m
doll bambola f
door porta f 25, 29
dosage dose f 140
double bed letto m matrimoniale 21
double room camera f doppia 21

down giù 12
downstairs al piano inferiore 12
downtown area centro m città 99
dozen dozzina f 159, 217
drain fognatura f
draught *(wind)* corrente f d'aria
dress vestito m 144
drink bibita f 70, 124, 125, 126
drinking water acqua f potabile 30
drinks bevande f 40
drip: the tap (faucet) drips il rubinetto perde
drive, to guidare 86, 93
driver conducente m 79; *(bus, etc)* autista m/f
driver's/driving licence patente di guida f 86
drop someone off, to fare scendere 83
drowning: someone is drowning qualcuno sta annegando
drugstore farmacia f 130
drunk ubriaco(-a)
dry-clean, to lavare a secco
dry cleaner's lavanderia f a secco 131
dry clothes, to asciugare i vestiti
dubbed, to be essere doppiato 110
during durante 13
dusty polveroso(-a)
duty: to pay duty pagare il dazio 67
duvet piumone m

 E **each: how much each?** quant'è ciascuno?
ear orecchio m 166; **~ache** mal d'orecchia m 163; **~drops** le gocce fpl per orecchie; **~rings** orecchini mpl
earlier più presto 125, 147
early di buon'ora 13;
east est m 12, 95, 106
Easter Pasqua f 219
easy facile 14
eat, to mangiare 21, 41, 167; **places ~** posti mpl per mangiare 123
eaten: have you ~? ha già mangiato?;
we've already ~ abbiamo già mangiato
economical economico(-a)
economy class in classe turistica 68
eggs uova fpl

A-Z

either ... or o...o
elastic (adj) elastico(-a)
electric shaver rasoio m
  elettrico
electrical items articoli
  mpl elettrici
electrician elettricista m 131
electricity elettricità f 28
~meter contatore m dell'elettricità 28
electronic flash flash m elettronico 151
~game gioco m elettronico 157
elevator ascensore m 26, 132
else, something qualcos'altro
embark, to (boat) imbarcarsi
embassy ambasciata f
emerald smeraldo m
emergency emergenza f 127, 152; **it's
  an ~** è un'emergenza; **~ room** pronto
  soccorso m
emergency exit uscita f d'emergenza
empty vuoto(-a) 14
enamel smalto m 149
end, to finire
end: at the end in fondo 95
engaged, to be essere fidanzato(-a) 120
engine motore m 88
engineer ingegnere m/f
England Inghilterra f 119
English (language) inglese m 11, 67,
  110, 150, 152, 161
enjoy, to piacere 124, 125
enlarge, to (photos) ingrandire 151
enough abbastanza 15, 136; sufficiente 42
entertainment: what ~ is there? cosa c'è
  come divertimenti/spettacoli?
entertainment guide guida f spettacoli
entirely completamente 17
entrance fee tariffa f d'ingresso 100
entry visa visto m d'entrata
envelope busta f 150
epileptic epilettico(-a) 140; **to be ~**
  essere epilettico(-a) 163
equally equamente 17
equipment (sports) attrezzatura f
error errore m
escalator scala mobile f 132
essential essenziali 89
estate agent agente m/f immobiliare
EU Unione f Europea

evening dress abito m da sera 112
events manifestazioni fpl 108
every day tutti i giorni 97
every week ogni settimana 13
examination (medical) visita f medica
example, for per esempio
excellent (adj) eccellente 42
except eccetto
excess baggage eccedenza bagaglio f 69
exchange rate tasso m di cambio 138
exchange, to cambiare 138
excluding meals pasti m esclusi 24
excursion escursione f 97
excuse me (apology. attention) scusi 10;
exhausted, to be essere esausto(-a) 106
exhibition mostra f
exit uscita f 70; **at the ~** all'uscita
expensive caro(-a) 14
expiration date data f di scadenza 109
expire, to: when does it expire?
  quando scade?
exposure (photos) posa f 151
expressway autostrada f 94
extension interno 128
extension lead prolunga f
extra (additional) supplementare 23, 27
extracted, to be (tooth) avere
  un'estrazione 168
extremely estremamente 17
eye occhio m 166

F
fabric (material) stoffa f 146
face faccia f, viso m 166
facial trattamento per il viso m
facilities servizi mpl 22, 30;
  attrezzature f
factor (sun protection) fattore 142
factory outlet vendita diretta in
  fabbrica
faint, to feel sentirsi svenire 163
fall (season) autunno m 219
fall: he's had a fall è caduto
family famiglia f 66, 74, 120, 167
famous famoso(-a)
fan (air) ventaglio m 25
far lontano(-a) 12, 95; **how ~ is it?**
  quanto dista? 73; **is it ~?** è lontano?84
farsighted presbite 167
fare tariffa f 79

fashionable, to be essere alla moda
fast-food restaurant tavola calda f, self-service m
fast, to be *(clock)* anticipare 221
fat grasso m
father padre m 120
fault: it's my/your fault è colpa mia/sua
faulty difettoso(-a) 137
faulty, to be essere difettoso(-a)
favorite favorito(-a)
fax facilities servizio m fax
fax, to spedire un fax 155
feeding bottle biberon m
feel ill, to sentirsi male 163
feel sick, to sentirsi male/vomitare
female donna f; femmina f 152
festival festival m
fetch help! chiami aiuto! 92
feverish, to feel sentirsi la febbre 163
few pochi (e) 15
fiancé(e) fidanzato(-a) m/f
field campo m 107
fight *(brawl)* rissa f
fill in , to compilare/riempire 155
filling *(dental)* otturazione f 168; *(in sandwich)* ripieno m
filling station stazione f di servizio 87
film *(camera)* pellicola f 151; film m 108
film speed velocità f della pellicola 151
filter filtro m 151; ~ **paper** *(for coffee)* filtro m per il caffè
find out: could you find that out? può informarsi?
fine *(penalty)* multa f 93; *(well)* bene 118
finger dito m 166
fire alarm allarme m antincendio
fire brigade pompieri (pl) 92
fire escape uscita f di sicurezza
fire extinguisher estintore m
fire: there's a fire! c'è un incendio!
fireplace caminetto m
first primo(-a) 68, 75, 78
first class in prima classe 68; di prima classe 74
first course primo (piatto) m 37
first floor primo piano m
first floor *(US)* pianterreno
first name nome m

first-aid kit astuccio m pronto soccorso
fish store pescheria f
fishing rod canna f da pesca
fishing, to go andare a pesca
fit, to *(clothes)* andare bene 146
fitting room cabina di prova f 146
fix, to: can you fix it? può ripararlo(-a)?
flag bandiera f
flash *(photography)* flash m elettronico 151
flashlight *(torch)* pila 31
flavor: what flavors do you have? che gusti ha?
flea pulce f
flea market mercato m delle pulci
flight volo m 70
flight number numero m del volo 68
flip-flops ciabatte fpl 145
flood inondazione f
floor *(level)* piano m 26, 132
floor mop Vileda (trademark)
floor show spettacolo m di varietà
florist's fiorista m 130
flour farina f 39
flower fiore m 106
flu influenza f 165
fluent: to speak fluent Italian parlare italiano correntemente
fly *(insect)* mosca f
fly, to volare 69
foggy, to be essere nebbioso(-a) 122
folding chair/table sedia/tavola f pieghevole
folk art arte f popolare
folk music musica f folcloristica
follow, to seguire 95, 152
food poisoning avvelenamento m alimentare 165
foot piede m 166
football *(soccer)* calcio m 114
footpath sentiero m pedestre 107
for a week per una settimana 86
forecast previsioni f 122
foreign straniero(-a)
foreign currency valuta f straniera 138
forest foresta f 107
forget, to dimenticare 42

A-Z

fork forchetta f 39, 41, 148; *(in the road)* incrocio m

form modulo m 153, 155, 168

formal dress tenuta f da sera 111

forms moduli mpl 23

fortunately fortunatamente 19

forward: please forward my mail per favore faccia proseguire la mia posta

foundation *(make-up)* crema f base

fountain fontana f 99

four-door car auto f a quattro porte

four-wheel drive auto fuoristrada f

foyer *(hotel/theater)* atrio m

frame *(glasses)* cornice f per occhiali

France Francia f

free *(available, not busy)* libero(-a) 36, 77, 124; *(of charge)* gratuito(-a) 69

French *(cuisine)* (cucina) Francese

French *(language)* francese m

frequent: how frequent? che frequenza? 76

frequently frequentemente

fresh fresco(-a) 14, 41, 134

freshly squeezed fruit juice spremuta f di frutta 40

fridge frigorifero m

fried fritto(-a)

friend amico m/amica f 162

friendly amichevole, simpatico(-a)

fries patate f fritte 38, 40

frightened, to be essere spaventato(-a)

fringe frangia f

from da 12; ~ ... **to** *(time)* da ... a 13

front door porta f d'ingresso 26; ~ **key** chiave f della porta d' ingresso 28

frosty, to be *(weather)* essere gelato(-a)

frozen congelato(-a) 134

fruit juice succo m di frutta 40

fuel *(gasoline/petrol)* carburante (benzina) m 86

full pieno(-a) 14

full board *(A.P.)* pensione f completa 24

full insurance una polizza f di assicurazione completa 86

fun, to have divertirsi

funny *(amusing/odd)* buffo/divertente

furniture i mobili mpl

fuse fusibile m 28

fuse box fusibili mpl 28

fuse wire filo m a piombo

G gallon gallone m

gambling giocare d'azzardo

game *(toy)* gioco m 157

garage garage m, autorimessa f 26, 88

garden giardino m

gardener giardiniere m

gardening giardinaggio m

gas bottle bombola f del gas 28

gas: I smell gas! c'è odore di gas!

gasoline benzina f 87, 88

gastritis gastrite f 165

gate *(airport)* uscita f 70

gay club locale m gay 112

generous: that's very ... è molto generoso

genuine autentico(-a) 134, 157

get, to *(find)* cercare 84

get by: may I get by? permesso? 77

get off, to *(transport)* scendere 79, 80

get out, to *(of vehicle)* scendere 83

get to, to arrivare a 77; **how do I get to ...?** come si arriva a ...? 73, 94

gift regalo m 67, 156

gift shop negozio m di articoli da regalo 130

girl ragazza f 120; bambina f 157

girlfriend ragazza f 120

give way, to *(on the road)* dare la precedenza 93

give, to dare

glacier ghiacciaio m 107

gland ghiandola f 166

glass bicchiere m 37, 39, 41, 148

glasses *(optical)* occhiali mpl 167

gliding volare con il deltaplano

gloomy tetro(-a)

glossy finish *(photos)* smaltato(-a)

glove guanto m

go, to andare; **let's go!** andiamo!; **where does this bus go?** dove va questo autobus?

go away! vada via!

go back, to *(turn around)* ritornare

go for a walk, to fare una passeggiata 124

go out, to *(in evening)* uscire

go shopping, to fare acquisti 124
goggles occhialini per nuoto
gold oro m 149
gold plate placcato d'oro
good buono(-a) 14, 35
good afternoon buonasera *(from 1pm)* 10
good evening buonasera 10
good morning buongiorno 10
good night buonanotte 10
good-bye arrivederci 10
gorge gola f 107
got: have you got any ...? ha del....?
grade *(fuel)* grado del carburante m
gramme *(gram)* grammo m 159
grandparents nonni mpl
grapes uva f 160
grass erba f
gratuity mancia f
gray grigio 143
graze escoriazione f 162
greasy *(hair)* grasso(-a)
great fun molto divertente 101
Greek (cuisine) (cucina) Greca
green verde 143
greengrocer fruttivendolo m 130
greetings saluti 10
greyhound racing corsa f di levrieri
grilled alla griglia
grocer's *(grocery)* drogheria f 130
ground *(camping)* terreno m del campeggio 30
ground floor pianterreno
groundsheet telo m per il terreno 31
group gruppo m 66, 100
guarantee garanzia f 135
guarantee: is it guaranteed? è garantito(-a)?
guide *(tour)* guida m/f 98
guidebook guida f/m turistica 100, 150
guided tour visita f guidata 100
guitar chitarra f
gum *(mouth)* gengiva f 168
gynecologist ginecologo m 167

H hair capelli mpl 147
hair brush spazzola f per capelli
hair dryer asciugacapelli m, il fon m
hair gel gel m per i capelli
hair spray lacca f per capelli 142

haircare prodotti per i capelli 142
haircut taglio di capelli m
hairdresser's parrucchiera f, parrucchiere m 131, 147
half, a mezzo 217
half board *(M.A.P.)* mezza pensione f 24
half fare metà prezzo
half past e mezza/... e trenta 220
hammer martello m 31
hand mano f 166
hand cream crema f per mani
hand luggage bagaglioa mano m 69
hand towel asciugamano m
hand washable lavaggio a mano 146
handbag borsetta f 144, 153
handicapped, to be essere disabile 163
handicrafts artigianato m
handkerchief fazzoletto m
handle maniglia f
hang-gliding fare il deltapiano
hanger gruccia f portabiti 27
hangover postumi mpl della sbornia 141
happen: what happened? che cosa è successo? 93
happy: I'm not happy with the service non sono soddisfatto(-a) del servizio
harbor/harbour porto m
hard shoulder *(road)* corsia f d'emergenza
hardware store negozio m di ferramenta 130
hat cappello m 144
hatchback auto f a cinque porte
have, to avere 18; *(hold stock of)* 133
have to, to *(must)* dovere 79
hayfever febbre f del fieno 141
head testa f 166
head waiter capocameriere m 41
headache mal di testa m 163
heading, to be *(in a direction)* andare verso/in direzione di 83
health food shop/store negozio *m* di dietetica
health insurance assicurazione *f* medica 168
hear, to sentire 11

hearing aid protesi *f* per udito
heart cuore *m* 166
heart attack infarto *m* 163
heart condition condizione *f* del cuore 163
hearts *(cards)* cuori *mpl*
heating riscaldamento *m* 25
heavy pesante 14, 134
height altezza *f* 152
helicopter elicottero *m*
hello buongiorno 118; salve 10
help aiuto *m* 94
help, to aiutare 18; **can you help me?** mi aiuti! 92, può aiutarmi? 71
helper assistente *m/f*
hemorrhoids emorroidi *fpl*
her lei 16; suo(-a) 16
here qui 12, 17
hernia ernia *f* 165
hers suo(-a) 16
hi! ciao! 10
high alto(-a) 106
high/main street via principale *f* 96
high tide alta marea *f*
hike *(walk)* escursione *f* a piedi 106
hiking fare escursioni a piedi
hill collina *f* 107
him lui 16
hire out, to *(rent out, to)* noleggiare 29
hire, for libero 84
hire, to noleggiare 83, 86, 115, 116, 117
his suo(-a) 16
history storia *f*
hitchhike, to fare l'autostop
HIV-positive sieropositivo(-a)
hobby *(pastime)* hobby 121
hockey field campo *m* di hockey
hold, to *(contain)* contenere
hold on, to restare in linea 128
hole *(in clothes)* buco *m*
holiday resort posto *m* di villeggiatura
holiday, on per/in vacanza 66, 123
home casa *f*; **to go ~** rientrare 123
homeopathic remedy rimedio *m* omeopatico
homosexual *(adj)* omosessuale
honeymoon, to be on essere in luna di miele

hopefully con (la) speranza di 19
horse cavallo *m*
horse racing ippica 114
horseback trip escursione *f* a cavallo
hospital ospedale *m*, policlinico *m* 131, 164, 167
hot caldo(-a) 14, 24; *(weather)* caldissimo(-a)
hot chocolate cioccolata *f* calda 40
hot dog salsiccia *f* calda 110
hot spring sorgente *f* calda
hot water acqua *f* calda 25; **~ bottle** bottiglia *f* dell'acqua calda
hotel albergo *m* 21
hour ora *f* 97; **in an ~** fra un'ora 84
hours *(opening)* orario *m* di apertura 161
house casa *f* 104
household articles articoli casalinghi 148
housewife casalinga *f* 121
how? come? 17
how are you? come sta? 118
how far? quanto dista? 106
how long? quanto (tempo)? 23, 75, 76, 78, 84, 100, 135
how many? quanti? 15, 80
how much? quanto? 15, 21, 69, 84; quanto costa? 109
how often? con che frequenza? 140, 165; ogni quanto?
how old? quanti anni? 120
however comunque 19
hungry, to be avere fame
hurry, to be in a avere fretta 84
hurt, to be essere ferito(-a) 92; farsi male 162; **it hurts** fa male 162
husband marito *m* 120, 162

I

I'd like vorrei 18, 36, 40, 74
I'll have prendo 37
I've lost ho perso 153
ice ghiaccio *m* 38
ice cream gelato *m* 40
ice cream parlour gelateria *f* 35
ice dispenser distributore *m* di ghiaccio
ice lolly ghiacciolo *m*
ice pack borsa *f* da ghiaccio 31
ice rink pista *f* di pattinaggio su ghiaccio, il palazzo *m* del ghiaccio

ice-hockey hockey m su ghiaccio
icy, to be essere ghiacciato(-a) 122
identification documento m d'identità 136, 155
ill, to be stare male 152
illegal, to be essere illegale
illness malattia f
imitation imitazione 134
immediately immediatamente 13
impressive di grande effetto 101
in (place) in 12; (time) fra 13
in-law: father/mother-in-law suocero(-a)
included: is it included? è incluso/compreso? 86, 98
inconvenient scomodo(-a)
Indian (cuisine) (cucina) indiana
indicate, to indicare 93
indigestion indigestione f 163
indoor all'interno
indoor pool piscina f invernale 116
inexpensive economico(-a) 35
infection infezione f 167
inflammation infiammazione f 165
informal (dress) abbigliamento m casuale
information informazione f 97
information desk banco m informazioni 73
information office ufficio m informazioni 96
injection iniezione f 168
injured, to be essere ferito(-a) 92, 162
innocent innocente
inquiry desk banco m informazioni
insect insetto m 25
insect bite puntura f d'insetto 141, 162
insect repellent/spray pomata f contro gli insetti/ dello spray insetticida 114
inside dentro 12
inside lane corsia f interna
insist: I insist insisto
insomnia insonnia f
instant coffee caffè m solubile 160
instead of invece di
instructions istruzioni fpl 135
instructor istruttore m
insulin insulina f
insurance assicurazione f 86, 89, 93,

insurance certificate polizza f d'assicurazione 93
insurance claim richiesta f di rimborso assicurazione 153
insurance company compagnia f d'assicurazione 93
interest (hobby) gli interessi 121
interest rate tasso m d'interesse
interesting interessante 101
international internazionale
International Student Card Carta f Internazionale Studenti 29, 100
interpreter interprete m/f 93
intersection intersezione f 95
interval intervallo m
into dentro, in 12
introduce oneself, to presentarsi 118
introductions presentazioni 118
invitation invito m 124
invite, to invitare 124
involved, to be essere coinvolto(-a) 93
iodine iodio m
Ireland Irlanda f 119
Irish (n) irlandese m/f
iron (for clothing) ferro m da stiro
iron, to stirare
is there ...? c'è...? 17
island isola f
it is è 17, 101
Italian (language) italiano m 11, 126; (person) italiano(-a) m/f
itch: it itches prude
itemized bill conto m dettagliato 32

J **jack** (cards) fante m
jacket giacca f 144
jam marmellata f/conserva f di frutta 160
jammed: it's jammed è bloccato(-a) 25
jar vasetto m
jaw mascella f 166
jellyfish medusa f
jet lag: I have soffro il cambiamento di fuso orario
jewelry store/jeweler's gioielleria f 149
Jewish (adj) ebreo(-a)
job: what's your job? che lavoro fa?

A-Z

A-Z

join: may we join you possiamo venire anche noi 124

joint *(body)* articolazione f 166; *(meat)* pezzo m (di carne) 160

joke scherzo m la barzelletta f

joker *(cards)* matta f, il jolly m

journalist giornalista m/f

journey viaggio m 75, 76, 78, 123

jug *(of water)* brocca f

jumper maglia f 144

junction *(exit)* uscita f autostrada

junction *(intersection)* intersezione f autostrada

K **kerosene** cherosene m

ketchup ketchup m

kettle bollitore m

key chiave f 26, 27, 28, 71, 88

key ring portachiavi m 156

kidney rene m 166

kilo(gramme) chilo(grammo) m 69, 159

kilometer chilometro m 86

kind *(pleasant)* gentile 125

kind: what kind of …? che tipo di …?

king *(cards, chess)* re m

kiosk chiosco m

kiss, to baciare 126

kitchen paper carta f assorbente uso cucina

kitchenette zona cottura f

knee ginocchio m 166

knife coltello m 39, 41, 148

knight *(chess)* cavallo m

knocked down, to be essere buttato a terra

know: I don't know non so 23

kosher puro(-a)

L **label** etichetta f

lace pizzo m

ladder scala f

ladies *(toilet)* toeletta f signore

lake lago m 107

lamp lampada f 25, 31

land, to atterrare 70

landing *(house)* pianerottolo m

landlord/landlady locatore m, la locatrice f

lane corsia f 93

language course corso m di lingua

large grande 40, 110

last ultimo(-a) 14, 68, 75, 78, 80

last, to *(time)* durare 108

late *(delayed)* in ritardo 14, 70, 76, 221; tardi 221

later più tardi 125, 147

laugh, to ridere 126

launderette lavanderia f a gettone 131

lavatory gabinetto m

lawn prato m coltivato

lawyer avvocato m

laxative lassativo m

lead, to *(road)* portare 94

lead-free *(gas/petrol)* benzina verde f 87

leader *(of group)* capogruppo m/f

leaflet opuscolo m

leak, to *(roof/pipe)* perdere; *(car)* 88

learn, to *(language/sport)* imparare

learner studente m, la studentessa f

least expensive il meno caro m, la meno cara f

leather pelle f

leave, to *(exit)* partire 32, 70, 73, 76, 78, 86, 98, 126; *(abandon)* lasciare 71, 73, 86; **leave me alone!** mi lasci in pace!

lecturer docente, insegnante m/f

left-hand side dal lato sinistro 95

left, on the a sinistra 76, 95

left-handed mancino(-a)

left-luggage office *(baggage check)* deposito m bagagli 71, 73

leg gamba f 166

legal matters *(car accident)* 93

legal, to be essere legale

lemon limone m 38

lemonade limonata f

lend: could you lend me …? può imprestarmi …?

length lunghezza f

lens obiettivo m 151; lenti fpl 167

lens cap cappuccio m per obiettivo 151

lesbian club club m per lesbiche

less (di) meno 15

lesson lezione f 117

letter lettera f 154; **by ~** per lettera 22

letterbox cassetta f per lettere

level *(ground)* livellato

library biblioteca f

lie down, to sdraiarsi

lifebelt cintura f di salvataggio

lifeboat scialuppa f di salvataggio

lifeguard bagnino m 116

lifejacket giubba f di salvataggio

lift pass tessera f per la sciovia 117

light *(color)* chiaro(-a) 14; *(weight)* leggero(-a) 14, 134

light bulb lampadina f 148

lighter accendino m 150

lighthouse faro m

lightning fulmine m

like, to piacere; **I'd like ...** vorrei ... 133; **I don't like it** non mi piace

like this *(similar)* simile a questo(-a)

limousine berlina f

line *(metro)* linea f 80; *(profession)* professione f, lavoro m 121

line: an outside line, please una linea esterna, per favore

linen lino m

lip(s) labbro m, labbra fpl 166

lipsalve balsamo m per le labbra

lipstick rossetto m

liqueur liquore m

liter/litre litro m 87, 159

little piccolo(-a)

live, to vivere 104; **~ together** abitare insieme 120

liver fegato m 166

loaf of bread pagnotta f di pane 160

lobby *(theater/hotel)* atrio m

local della regione, regionale 37

local anesthetic anestesia f locale 168

local road strada f comunale

lock *(key)* serratura f 25; *(canal)* chiusa f

lock oneself out, to chiudersi fuori 27

locked, to be essere chiuso(-a) 26; **it's locked** è chiuso a chiave

locker armadietto m

locker rooms spogliatoi mpl

lollipop leccalecca m

long *(clothing)* lungo(-a) 117, 146

long *(time)* molto 36; **how long?** quanto tempo? 164; **how much longer?** per quanto tempo? 41

long-distance call telefonata f interurbana

look: I'm just looking sto solo guardando

look for, to cercare 18

loose *(clothing)* largo(-a) 117, 146

lose, to perdere 28, 153; **I've lost ...** ho smarrito ...; **ho perdito**

lost, to be essere smarrito 152

lost-and-found/lost property office ufficio m oggetti smarriti 73

lotion lozione f

lots molti (e)

loud, it's too è troppo rumoroso(-a)

louder più forte 128

love: I love Italian food amo la cucina italiana; **I love you** ti amo

low-fat con grasso minimo

lower berth cuccetta f inferiore f 74

lubricant lubrificante m

luck: good luck buona fortuna 219

luggage *(baggage)* bagaglio m 32, 67

luggage allowance peso m consentito

luggage locker deposito m bagagli automatico 73

luggage tag etichetta f per bagaglio

luggage ticket biglietto m per i bagagli 71

luggage carts *(trolleys)* carrelli mpl portabagagli

lumpy *(mattress)* pieno di protuberanze

lunch pranzo m 42, 98

lung polmone m 166

M **machine washable** lavaggio a macchina 146

madam *(dear)* signora

made: what is it made of? di che cosa è fatto(-a)?

magazine rivista f 150

magician mago m

magnetic north nord m magnetico

magnificent magnifico 101

maid cameriera f 27, 32

maiden name nome m da nubile

mail *(post)* posta f 27, 155

mailbox cassetta f postale

main principale 130

main course secondo (piatto) m 37

main train station stazione f ferroviaria principale 73

main street strada f principale 95

mains conduttura f principale
make *(brand)* marca f
makeup cosmetici mpl trucco m
male uomo, maschio m 152
mallet maglio m 31
man uomo m
manager direttore m, direttrice f 25; gestore m/f 41, 137
manicure manicure f
manual *(car)* manuale m
many molti (e) 15
map carta f 94, 97, 106, 150
margarine margarina f
market mercato m 99; ~ **day** giorno m di mercato
married, to be essere sposato(-a) 120
mascara mascara m
mask *(diving)* maschera f subacquea
mass messa f 105
massage massaggio m 147
match *(game)* partita f 114
matches fiammiferi mpl 148
material *(fabric)* stoffa f
matinée spettacolo m del pomeriggio 109
matter: what's the matter? cosa succede?; **it doesn't matter** non importa
mattress materasso m 31
may I ...? posso ... ? 18, 37
maybe forse
me me 16
meal pasto m 38; 125
mean, to significare 11
measles morbillo m 165
measure, to misurare 146
measurement le misure fpl
meat carne f 41
medical certificate certificato m medico 168
medicine medicina f 141, 164, 165
medium *(regular)* regolare 40; *(steak)* cottura media
meet, to incontrare 106, 125; **pleased to meet you** piacere/molto lieto(-a) 118
meeting place luogo m d'incontro
member *(of club)* socio m 115
memorial monumento m commemorativo
men *(toilets)* gabinetti mpl, signori

mend, to riparare 137
mention: don't mention it prego 10
menu menu m
message messaggio m 27, 128
metal metallo m
meter *(taxi)* tassametro m 84
methylated spirits alcol denaturato 31
microwave *(oven)* forno m a microonde
midday mezzogiorno 220
midnight mezzanotte 220
migraine emicrania f
mileage chilometraggio m
milk latte m 160; **with ~** con latte
milk of magnesia latte m di magnesia
million un milione 216
mince carne f tritata 160
mine mio(-a) 16
mineral water acqua f minerale
minibar minibar m
minibus minibus m
minimum *(n)* minimo m
minister ministro m
minor road strada f secondaria
minute minuto m 221
mirror specchio m
miss, to passare, mancare; **have I missed the bus to ...?** ho perso l'autobus per ...?
missing, to be mancare 137; scomparire 152
mistake errore m 32, 41, 42, 136
misunderstanding: there's been a ~ c'è stato un malinteso
mittens guantoni mpl
mobile home camper m
modern art arte f moderna
moisturizing cream crema f idratante
monastery monastero m 99
money soldi mpl 139, 153
money order vaglia m postale
money-belt cintura f portasoldi
month mese m 218
monthly *(ticket)* mensile 79
monument monumento m 99
moped motorino m
more (di) più 15; **I'd like some more ...** vorrei ancora un po' di ... 39
morning, in the al mattino 218; di mattina 221

moslem (adj) mussulmano(-a)
mosquito zanzara f
mosquito bite puntura f di zanzara
mother madre f 120
motorbike motocicletta f 83
motorboat barca f a motore
motorcycle motocicletta f 83
motorcycle parts 82
motorway autostrada f 94
mountain montagna f 107
mountain pass passo m di montagna 107
mountaineering alpinismo m
mousetrap trappola f per topi
moustache baffi mpl
mouth bocca f 166
move, to cambiare 25; (car) spostare la
macchina; (house) traslocare; **don't
move him!** non lo muova! 92
Mr. signor m
Mrs. signora f
much molto 15
mugged, to be essere aggredito(-a) 153
mugging aggressione per rapina f 152
mugs boccali mpl 148
multiple journey (ticket) biglietto m
multiplo 79
mumps gli orecchioni mpl
muscle muscolo m 166
museum museo m 99
music musica f
music box carillon m
musician musicista m/f
must: I must devo
mustard senape f 38
my mio 16
myself: I'll do it myself lo farò io

N nail polish lo smalto m per
unghie
nail scissors le forbicine f da unghie
name cognome m
name (first name) nome m 22, 36, 93,
118; **what's your name?** come si
chiama? 118, 120
napkin tovagliolo m 39
narrow stretto(-a) 14
national health servizio m sanitario
nationality nazionalità f
natural history storia f naturale

nature reserve oasi f
naturalistica 107
nature trail percorso m
naturalistico 107
nausea nausea f
navy blue blu m marino
near vicino 12, 84
nearsighted miope 167
nearest più vicino(-a) 80, 88, 92, 130
neck collo m 166; (clothes) 144
necklace collana f 149
need: I need to ... ho bisogno di ... 18
needle ago m 27
negative (photo) negativa f
neighbor vicino(-a) m/f
nephew nipote m
nerve nervo m 166
nervous system sistema m nervoso 166
never mai 13
never mind non importa 10
new nuovo(-a) 14
New Year Anno m Nuovo 219
New Zealand Nuova Zelanda f 119
newsagent's giornalaio m 150
newsdealer giornalaio m 150
newspaper giornale m 150
newsstand edicola f 73
next prossimo(-a) 14, 68, 75, 80, 87;
next stop! la prossima fermata! 79
next to accanto(-a) a 12; vicino(-a) a 95
niece nipote f
night, at di notte 218, 221; **per night**
per notte
night porter portiere m di notte
nightdress camicia f da notte
nobody else nessun altro
noisy rumoroso(-a) 14, 24
non-alcoholic non-alcolico(-a) 125
non-smoking area zona non fumatori f 36
none nessuno(-a) 16
noon mezzogiorno 220
no one nessuno(-a) 16, 92
normal normale 67
north nord m 12, 95, 106
Northern Ireland Irlanda f del nord 119
nose naso m 166
nosebleed emoraggia nasale f 163
not yet non ancora 13
note banconota f 139
notebook taccuino m 150

A-Z

nothing else nient'altro 15
nothing to declare nulla da dichiarare
notice board bacheca f 26
notify, to informare 167
now subito 84; ora, adesso 13
nudist beach spiaggia f per nudisti
number numero m 109; *(telephone)* numero (di telefono) m 84
number plate *(registration plate)* numero di targa m 93
nurse infermiere m
nut *(for bolt)* dado m per bullone
nylon nylon m

O **o'clock, it's ...** è ...sono le ... 220
observatory osservatorio m 99
occasionally occasionalmente 13
occupations 121
occupied occupato(-a) 14
of di, da
of course naturalmente, certamente 19
off-peak bassa stagione f
office ufficio m
often sovente/spesso 13
oil olio m 88
oil lamp lampada f a olio
okay d'accordo./va bene 10
old vecchio(-a) 14
old town città f vecchia 99; città f storica 96
old-fashioned antiquato(-a) 14
olive oil olio m d'oliva
omelet frittata f 40
on *(day, date)* il 13
on *(place)* in 12
on the left a sinistra 12
on the other side all'altro lato 12, 95
on the right a destra 12
on/off switch interruttore m
once una volta 217; **~ a week** una volta alla settimana 13
open aperto(-a) 14; **~ to the public** aperto(-a) al pubblico **~ to traffic** aperto(-a) al traffico
open, to aprire 71, 132, 140
open-air pool piscina f all'aperto 116
opening hours orario m d'apertura 100
opera house teatro m dell'opera 99, 111

operation operazione f
operator operatore m
opposite di fronte 12
optician ottico m 131, 167; negozio m di ottica
or o/oppure 19
orange arancione
oranges arance fpl
orchestra orchestra f
order, to ordinare 37, 41, 89, 135; *(taxi)* chiamare 32
our nostro 16
out: he's out è fuori
outdoor all'esterno
outside fuori 12, 36
outside lane corsia f di sorpasso
oval ovale 134
oven forno m
over sopra 12
over there laggiù 76
overcharged: I've been il prezzo è eccesivo
overdone *(adj)* troppo cotto(-a) 41
overdraft scoperto m
overdrawn, to be avere uno scoperto bancario
overheat, to surriscaldare 88
overnight una notte f 23
overnight service servizio m ventiquattro ore 151
owe: how much do I owe you? quanto le devo?
own: on my own da solo(-a) 65
owner proprietario

P **p.m.** di pomeriggio, di sera 220
pacifier tettarella f
pack, to fare i bagagli 69
pack of cards mazzo m di carte
pack of cigarettes pacchetto m di sigarette
package pacco m 152
packed lunch pranzo m al sacco
packet pacco m, pacchetto m 159
padlock lucchetto m
pail secchiello m 157
pain, to be in avere male 167
painkillers antinevralgico m; analgesico m, antidolorifico m 165
paint, to dipingere 104

painted dipinto(-a) 104
painter pittore m, pittrice f 104
painting quadro m
pair of, a un paio di 217
pajamas pigiama m
palace palazzo m 99
palpitations palpitazioni fpl 163
panorama panorama m/vista f 107
pantomime pantomima f
pants pantaloni mpl 144
panty hose collant m 144
paper carta f 150
paper napkins tovaglioli mpl di carta 148
paraffin paraffina f 31
paralysis paralisi f
parcel *(package)* pacco m 155
pardon? prego? 11
parents genitori mpl 120
park parco m, giardini mpl 96, 99, 107
park ranger guardia f forestale
park, to parcheggiare 30
parking parcheggio m 87
parking disk disco m orario 87
parking lot parcheggio m 26, 87, 96
parking meter parchimetro m 87
parliament building palazzo m del
  Parlamento 99
partner *(boyfriend/girlfriend)* compagno
  m, compagna f
parts *(components)* pezzi mpl di
  ricambio 89
party *(social)* festa f 124
pass passo m 107
pass, to passare 77
passenger passeggero m, passeggera f
passport passaporto m 32, 66, 69, 153
passport control controllo m
  passaporti 66
patch, to rattoppare
path sentiero m 107
patient paziente m/f
pavement, on the sul marciapiede m
pay, to pagare 32, 42, 87, 79, 136; **~ a
  fine** pagare un'ammenda/una multa
  93; **~ by credit card** pagare con carta di
  credito 32
pay phone telefono m a gettone/a
  scheda
payment pagamento m
peak picco m/cima f 107

pebbly *(beach)*
  pietroso(-a) 116
pedalo pedalo m
pedestrian crossing
  attraversamento m
  pedonale 96
pedestrian zone/precinct isola
  f/zona f pedonale 96
pedicure pedicure f
pen penna f 150
pencil matita f 150
penicillin penicillina f 165
penknife coltellino m 31
penpal il, corrispondente m/f
people gente f 119
people carrier *(minivan)* furgoncino m
pepper *(condiment)* pepe m 38, 160;
  (vegetable) peperone m 160
per day al giorno 83, 86, 87; per
  giorno 30, 115
per hour all'ora 87; per ora 115
per night per notte 21
per week alla settimana 83, 86
performance spettacolo m 109
perhaps forse 19
period periodo m 104; *(menstrual)*
  mestruazioni fpl 167
period pains dolori mpl mestruali 167
perm permanente f
perm, to fare la permanente 147
permit permesso m, licenza f
personal stereo stereo m personale
pet *(animal)* animale m domestico
pharmacy reparto m di farmacia 158
phone telefono m 88
phone call telefonata f 152
phonecard carta f telefonica 127, 155
photo, to take a fare una fotografia
photo: passport-size photo fotografia f
  formato passaporto 115
photocopy fotocopia f
photographer fotografo m/negozio m
  di ottica 131
photography fotografia f 151
phrase frase f 11
phrase book frasario m 11
piano pianoforte m
pick up, to passare a prendere 28, 113;
  (ticket) ritirare 109

A-Z

pick-up truck autocarro m

picnic picnic m, scampagnata f; **~ area** area f per pic nic 107

piece articolo di bagaglio m 69; pezzo m 159; **a ~ of ...** un pezzo di ... 40

Pill *(contraceptive)*, **to take the** prendere la pillola (contraccettiva) 167

pillow cuscino m 27

pillowcase federa f per cuscino

pilot light luce f-spia

pink rosa 143

pint pinta f

pipe *(smoking)* pipa f

pipe cleaners puliscipipa m

pipe tobacco tabacco m da pipa

piste map carta f delle piste

pitch *(for camping)* posto m tenda

pity: it's a pity è un peccato

place *(space)* posto m 29, 94

place a bet, to scommettere

plain pianura f; *(not patterned)* in tinta unita

plane volo m 68

plans, to have fare 124

plant pianta f 106

plastic bags sacchetti mpl di plastica

plate piatto m 39, 41, 148

platform binario m 73, 76, 77

platinum platino m

play, to *(drama)* rappresentare *(music)* suonare

playground parco m giochi 113

playgroup club m per bambini 113

playing cards carte fpl da gioco

playing field campo m da gioco 115

pleasant gradevole 14

please per piacere./per favore 10

pliers le pinze fpl

plug *(bath)* presa f 25; *(electric)* spina f elettrica 148

plumber idraulico m

pneumonia polmonite f 165

point of interest luoghi mpl d'interesse 97

point to, to indicare 11

poison veleno m 141

poisonous velenoso(-a)

police polizia f, carabinieri (pl) 92, 93, 152

police certificate denuncia f 153

police station commissariato m, questura f 96, 131, 152

pollen count conteggio m del polline 122

polyclinic policlinico m

pond stagno m 107

pony ride passeggiata f in pony

pop music musica f pop

popcorn popcorn m

port *(harbor)* porto m

porter portiere m 27; facchino m 71

portion porzione f 39, 41

possible: as soon as possible appena possibile

possibly possibilmente 19

post, to *(mail, to)* imbucare

post *(mail)* posta f

post office ufficio m postale 96, 131, 154

postbox *(mailbox)* cassetta f delle lettere

postcard cartolina f 100, 150, 154, 156

poster manifesto m

postman postino m

potato patate f 38

pottery ceramica f

pound *(sterling)* lira f sterlina 136, 138

power cut interruzione f della corrente

power point presa f di corrente

practice: to practice speaking Italian praticare l'italiano parlato

pregnant, to be esser incinta 163, 167

prescribe, to prescrivere 165

prescription ricetta f 140, 141

present *(gift)* regalo m

press, to stirare 137

pretty carino(-a) 101

priest prete m

primus stove fornello m da campeggio 31

prison carcere m

private bathroom bagno f privato

probably probabilmente 19

program programma m 109; **~ of events** programma m delle manifestazioni 108

prohibited: is it prohibited? è proibito?

promenade deck ponte m di coperta

pronounce, to pronunciare 11

propelling pencil matita f portamina

properly correttamente

Protestant protestante

pub osteria f 106
public building edifici pubblici mpl 96
public holidays giorni mpl festivi 219
pullover maglione m 144
pump (gas/petrol) pompa f 31, 83
puncture (flat) foratura f 88
pure (material) puro(-a) 146
purple viola 143
purpose motivo m 66
purse portamonete m 153
push-chair passeggino m
put: where can I put ...? dove posso mettere ..?
put by, to (in shop) mettere da parte
put up: can you put me up for the night? può ospitarmi per una notte?
putting course terreno m da golf

Q

quality qualità f 134
quantity quantità f 134
quarantine quarantina f
quarter, a un quarto 217
quarter past (after) e un quarto 220
quarter to (before) meno un quarto 220
quay molo m
queen (cards, chess) regina f
question domanda f
quick veloce 14
quickest: what's the quickest way to ... qual'è la via più breve per ...?
quickly presto 17, 92
quiet silenzioso(-a) 14
quieter più tranquillo(-a) 24, 126

R

rabbi rabbino m
race (cars) gara f automobilistica; (horses) corsa f di cavalli
race course (track) ippodromo m
racing bike bicicletta f da corsa
racket (tennis, squash) racchetta f 115
rail station stazione f ferroviaria 73
railroad/railway ferrovia f
rain, to piovere 122
raincoat impermeabile m 144
rape stupro m 152
rapids rapide fpl 107

rare (unusual) raro(-a); (steak) poco cotta
rarely raramente 13
rash eruzione f della pelle 162
rather piuttosto 17; ~ noisy piuttosto rumoroso(-a) 14
ravine burrone m
razor rasoio m
razor blades lamette fpl da barba 142
re-enter, to rientrare 100
reading (interest) lettura f
reading glasses gli occhiali mpl per lettura
ready, to be essere pronto(-a) 89, 137, 151; **are you ready?** è pronto(-a)?
real (genuine) vero/autentico 149
receipt ricevuta f 32, 86, 89, 136, 137, 151
reception (desk) ricezione f
receptionist ricezionista m/f 27
reclaim tag talloncino m 71
reclaim, to ottenere il rimborso m 136
recommend, to consigliare 35, 141; raccomandare 21; **can you recommend** può suggerire 97
record (lp) (disco) microsolco m
red rosso(-a) 143
red wine vino m rosso 40
reduction sconto m, riduzione f 24, 68, 74, 100
refreshments rinfreschi (pl) 78
refund rimborso m
regards to ... saluti a ... 219
region regione f 106
registered mail posta f raccomandata
registration form modulo m di registrazione 23
registration number numero di targa m 88, 93
regular (gas/petrol) normale 87; (size of drink) medio(-a) 110
regulations: I didn't know the regulations non conoscevo il regolamento
religion religione f
remember: I don't remember non ricordo
removed, to be essere rimossa

A-Z

rent, to noleggiare 86
rent: for rent affittasi
rental car auto f noleggiata 153
repair, to riparare 89, 137, 168
repairs riparazioni fpl 89, 137
repeat, to ripetere 94, 128; **please repeat that** per piacere può ripetere? 11
replacement *(n)* sostituzione f 167
replacement part pezzo di ricambio m
report, to denunciare
representative rappresentante m/f 27
required necessario(-a) 111, 112
reservation prenotazione f 22, 68, 74
reservations desk botteghino m 109
reserve, to prenotare 36, 109
rest, to riposare 106
retired, to be essere in pensione 121
return *(roundtrip)* **ticket** biglietto di andata e ritorno m 68, 74; biglietto circolare m 79
return, to *(travel)* ritornare 74, 75; *(surrender)* restituire 86
reverse the charges, to *(call collect, to)* telefonare a carico del destinatario 127
revolting disgustoso(-a) 14
rheumatism reumatismo m
rib costola f 166
right *(correct)* giusto(-a) 14, 77, 94, 106
right, on the a destra 76, 95
right of way diritto m di passaggio; precedenza f 93
right-handed che usa la mano destra
ring anello m
rip-off bidonata f 101
river fiume m 107, 116
road strada f 94, 95
road accident incidente m stradale
road assistance soccorso m stradale 88
road map carta f stradale 150
road signs segnaletica f, lindicazioni fpl stradali
roasted arrosto(-a)
robbed, to be essere derubato(-a) 153
robbery rapina f
rock climbing alpinismo m di roccia
rock concert concerto m rock
rocks rocce fpl
roller blades roller blades mpl

rolls panini mpl 160
romance *(film/play)* romanzo m
romantic romantico(-a) 101
roof *(house/car)* tetto m
roof-rack portabagagli m esterno
rook *(chess)* torre f
room camera f 21
room service servizio m camera 26
rope corda f
round *(shape)* rotondo(-a) 134; *(of golf)* giro m; **it's my ~** è il mio turno
roundabout rotatoria f
route strada f, percorso m 94, 106
row, to remare
rowing boat barca f a remi
rude, to be essere maleducato(-a)
rugby rugby m
ruins rovine fpl 99
run into, to *(crash)* venire addosso 93
run out, to *(fuel)* finire 88
run over, to *(people)* investire
rush hour ora f di punta

S safe *(lock-up)* cassaforte f 27
   safe *(not dangerous)* sicuro(-a) 116; **to feel ~** sentirsi sicuro(-a)
safety sicurezza f 65
safety pins spille fpl di sicurezza
sailing boat barca f a vela
salad insalata f
sales rep agente m/f di vendita
salt sale m 38, 39, 160
same day lo stesso giorno 75
same: the same again please stesso, per favore
sand sabbia f
sandals sandali mpl
sandwich panino m 40
sandwich bar paninoteca f 35
sandy sabbioso(-a) 116
sanitary napkins assorbenti mpl 142
satellite TV televisione f via satellite
satisfied: I'm not satisfied with this non sono soddisfatto(-a) di
sauce salsa f 38
saucepan pentola f
sausages salcicce fpl 160
saw *(tool)* sega f

say: how do you say ...? come si dice ..?; **what did he say?** cosa ha detto?

scarf sciarpa f 144

scenic route strada f panoramica

scheduled flight volo m di linea

school scuola f 120

sciatica sciatica f 165

scientist scienziato m, scienziata f

scissors un paio di forbici fpl 148

scooter motoretta f

Scotland Scozia f

Scottish *(person/adj.)* scozzese m/f

screw vite f

screwdriver cacciavite m 148

scrubbing brush spazzola f dura

sculptor scultore m, scultrice f

sea mare m 107

seafront passeggiata f a mare

seasick, I feel ho il mal di mare

season ticket tessera f

seasoning condimenti mpl 38

seat posto m 68, 74, 77, 109

second secondo(-a) 217

second class di seconda classe 74

second floor *(US)* primo piano m

secondhand di seconda mano

secretary segretaria f

security guard guardia f di sicurezza

sedative sedativo m

see, to *(inspect, witness)* vedere 24, 93; **~ someone again** rivedere 126

self-catering in affitto 28

sell, to vendere 133

send, to mandare 88, 155; spedire

senior citizens anziani (pl) 74

separated, to be essere separato(-a)

separately *(adv)* separatamente

septic tank fognatura f

serious serio 89

served, to be *(meal)* essere servito 26; sevire 68

service servizio m 105, 131; **~ charge** servizio m; **is service included?** è compreso il servizio? 42

service station stazione f di servizio

serviette tovagliolo m 39

set menu menù m fisso 37

sex *(act)* sesso m

shade sfumatura f

shady ombreggiato

shallow basso(-a)

shampoo shampoo m

shampoo and set shampoo e messa in piega

shampoo for dry/oily hair shampoo m per capelli secchi/grassi

shape forma f 134

sharp tagliente

shatter, to *(glass)* rompere 88

shaver rasoio m elettrico 142

shaver socket presa f per rasoio 26

shaving brush spazzola f per barba

shaving cream crema f per barba

she lei

sheet *(bedding)* le lenzuola fpl 28

shelf scaffale m

ship nave f

shirt camicia f 144

shivery, to feel sentirsi i brividi 163

shock *(electric)* scossa f elettrica

shoe laces lacci mpl delle scarpe

shoe polish lucido m per scarpe

shoe repair riparatura f delle scarpe

shoe-cleaning service servizio m pulizia scarpe

shoe mender's calzolaio m, calzoleria f

shoes scarpe fpl 145

shop *(store)* grande magazzino m 130

shop assistant commesso(-a) m/f

shop/storekeeper negoziante m/f

shopping area zona f dei negozi, centro m commerciale

shopping basket *(bag)* cesto f della spesa; cestello m

shopping centre *(mall)* centro m commerciale 130

shopping list lista f della spesa

shopping trolley carrello m

shopping, to go *(food)* andare a fare la spesa; *(other items)* andare a fare acquisti

shore *(sea/lake)* riva f del mare/lago

short corto(-a) 117, 146

shorts shorts mpl 144

shoulder spalla f 166

show spettacolo m 97

show, to indicare, mostrare 18, 133; **can you show me?** può indicarmi? 94, 106

shower gel gel m per doccia
shower room sala f docce (pl) 26
showers docce f 30
shutter persiana f 25
shy timido(-a)
sick, to feel sentirsi male 163; **I'm going to be** sto per vomitare
side (of road) lato m 95
side order contorno m 37, 38
side street strada f laterale 95
sidewalk sul marciapiede m
sights luoghi mpl d'interesse
sightseeing tour giro m turistico 97
sightseeing, to go visitare luoghi d'interesse
sign (road) segnali (pl), indicazioni stradali fpl 93, 95
signpost indicatore m stradale
silk seta f
silver argento m 149
silver plate placcato d'argento
similar, to be essere simile a 11
since (time) da 13
singer cantante m/f
single, to be essere celibe 120
single (one-way) **ticket** biglietto di andata m 68, 74; biglietto di corsa semplice m 79
single room camera f singola 21
sink lavandino m
sister sorella f 120
sit, to sedersi 36, 77; sedere 125, 126
sit down, please si accomodi, prego
six-pack of beer confezione f di sei lattine di birra
size misura f, taglia f 115; 146
skates pattini mpl da ghiaccio
skating rink palazzo m del ghiaccio
ski bindings gli attacchi mpl per sci
ski boots scarponi mpl da sci 117
ski instructor istruttore m di sci
ski lift sciovia f 117
ski poles bastoncini mpl da sci 117
ski school scuola f di sci 117
ski suit tuta f per sci
ski trousers pantaloni mpl da sci
ski wax cera f per sci
skid: we skidded abbiamo slittato

skiing sci m 117
skin pelle f, epidermide f 166
skin-diving equipment attrezzatura f per l'immersione subacquea
skirt gonna f 144
skis sci mpl 117
sledge slitta f
sledge run pista f per slitte
sleep, to dormire 167
sleeping bag sacco m a pelo
sleeping car vagone m letto 77
sleeping pill sonnifero m in pillola
sleeve manica f
slice fetta f 40, 159
slide film le diapositive fpl
slip (undergarment) sottoveste f
slippers pantofole fpl 145
slope (ski) discesa f
slow lento(-a) 14
slow down! rallenti!
slow, to be (clock) ritardare 221
slowly lentamente 11, 17, 94, 128
small piccolo(-a) 14, 24, 40, 41, 110, 117; basso(-a)
small change moneta f; spiccioli mpl 139
small spoon cucchiaino m
smell: there's a bad smell c'è un cattivo odore
smoke, to fumare 126
smoke: I don't smoke non fumo
smoking area zona fumatori f 69
snacks spuntini mpl 40
sneakers scarpe fpl da tennis
snorkel maschera f da subacqueo
snow neve f 117
snow, to nevicare 122
snowed in, to be essere bloccato dalla neve
snowplow spazzaneve m
soaking solution (contact lenses) soluzione f per pulire lenti a contatto
soap sapone m 142
soap powder detersivo m in polvere
socket presa f
socks calzini mpl 144
sofa divano m
sofa-bed divano-letto m
soft drink (soda) bibita f frizzante 110; bibita f analcolica 160
sold out esaurito(-a) 108

sole *(shoes)* suola f
soluble aspirin aspirina f solubile 114
some alcuni,
  del/dei/dell'/della/delle 15
someone qualcuno 16
sometimes qualche volta 13
son figlio m 120, 162
soon presto 13; **as ~ as possible** al più
  presto 161
sore throat mal m di gola 141, 163
sore: it's sore fa male
sorry! sono spiacente 10
sort tipo m 134
sound-and-light show spettacolo m
  suoni e luci
sour acido(-a) 41
south sud m 12, 95, 106
souvenir regalo m ricordo, souvenir m
  98, 156; **~ guide** guida f ricordo 156
spa stazione f termale
space spazio m 30
spade *(shovel)* paletta f *(cards)* carta f
  di picche
speak, to parlare 11, 41, 67; **~ to**
  someone parlare con qualcuno 128; **do**
  you speak English? parla inglese? 11
special rate condizioni fpl speciali 24;
  tariffa speciale f 86
special requirements le richieste f
  particolari 39
specialist specialista m/f
specimen campione m 164
spectacles occhiali mpl
speed limit limite di velocità m 93
spell, to sillabare 11
spend, to spendere
spicy speziato(-a)
spin-dryer asciugatore m elettrico
spine spina f dorsale 166
sponge spugna f
spoon cucchiaio m 39, 41
sports club palestra f/associazione f
  sportiva
sports ground campo m sportivo
sprained, to be essere slogato(-a)
spring *(season)* primavera f 219; *(water)*
  fonte f
square *(shape)* quadrato(-a) 134; *(street)*
  piazza f
stain macchia f

stainless steel acciaio
  m inossidabile
stairs scale f
stale non fresco(-a) 14
stall: the engine stalls il
  motore s'inceppa
stalls *(orchestra)* platea f
stamp francobollo m 150, 154; **~**
  machine distributore m automatico di
  francobolli 154
stand in line, to aspettare, fare la coda
  112
standby ticket biglietto m non
  prenotato
start inizio m 109
start, to cominciare 109, 112 **starter**
  antipasto m 37
stately home palazzina f 99
statement *(legal)* dichiarazione f,
  denuncia f 93
station stazione f 96
stay, to fermarsi, rimanere 23, 32, 65, 123
sterilizing solution soluzione f
  sterilizzante
stiff neck collo m rigido 163
still: I'm still waiting sto ancora
  aspettando
sting puntura f 162
stocking calze fpl 144
stolen, to be essere rubato(-a) 71
stomach stomaco m 166; **~ ache** dolore
  m allo stomco 163; **~ cramps** crampi
  mpl allo stomaco
stools *(feces)* feci fpl 164
stop *(bus, tram, metro)* fermata f 79, 80
stop, to femarsi 76, 77, 78, 84, 98;
  please stop here si fermi qui, per
  favore 84
stopover sosta f
store detective personale m di
  sicurezza
store guide guida f al magazzino 132
stove stufa 28
straight ahead *(sempre)* dritto 95
strained muscle strappo m al muscolo
strange strano(-a) 101
straw *(drinking)* cannuccia f
strawberry *(flavor)* fragola f 40
stream ruscello m, torrente m 107
string cordino m

strong *(potent)* forte 165
stuck: the key's stuck chiave è bloccata
students studenti pl 74, 100
  study, to studiare 120, 121
stunning magnifico(-a) 101
stupid: how stupid! che stupidaggine!
style stile m
styling mousse schiuma f per messa in piega
subtitled, to be avere i sottotitoli 110
subway metropolitana 80
subway station stazione f (della) metropolitana 80, 96
suede pelle f scamosciata
sugar zucchero m 38, 39, 160
suggest, to suggerire 123
suit completo m 144
suitable for adatto(-a) per 117, 140
summer estate f 219
sun block blocco m antisolare 142
sun lounger sedia f a sdraio
sunbathe, to prendere il sole
sunburn scottatura f solare 141
suncare prodotti solari
Sunday domenica 218
sundeck *(ship)* ponte m superiore
sunglasses occhiali mpl da sole
sunshade *(umbrella)* ombrellone m 116
suntan cream/lotion crema f/lozione f abbronzante 142
sunstroke colpo di sole m 163
super *(gas/petrol)* super 87
superb stupendo(-a) 101
supermarket supermercato m 158
supervision sorveglianza f
supplement supplemento m 68, 69, 74
suppositories supposte fpl 165
sure: are you sure? è sicuro(-a)?
surfboard tavola f da surf 116
surname cognome m
suspicious sospettoso(-a) 152
swallow, to inghiottire 165
sweatshirt felpa f 144
sweet *(taste)* dolce
sweets *(dessert)* dolci mpl 150; *(candy)* caramelle f 160
swelling gonfiore m 162
swim, to nuotare 116

swimming *(activity)* nuoto
swimming pool piscina f 22, 26, 116
swimming trunks calzoncini mpl da bagno 144
swimsuit costume m da bagno 144
Swiss *(person)* svizzero(-a) m/f
switch interruttore m 25
switch on/off, to accendere/spegnere
Switzerland Svizzera f
swollen, to be essere gonfio
symptoms sintomi 163
synagogue sinagoga f
synthetic in fibra sintetica

T

T-shirt maglietta f 144, 156
  table tavolo m 36, 112
table cloth tovaglia f da tavola
table tennis tennis m da tavolo
tablet pastiglia f 140
take away, to da asporto
take photographs/pictures, to prendere fotografie 98; fare fotografie 100
take someone home, to riaccompagnare 126
take, to *(room, bus, medicine)* prendere 24; 78; 140 *(carry)* portare 71, 165;
taken *(occupied)* occupato(-a) 77
talcum powder borotalco m
talk, to parlare
tall alto(-a) 14
tampons tamponi mpl 142
tan abbronzatura f
tap *(faucet)* rubinetto m 25
tape measure metro m a nastro
tarpaulin telo m per il terreno
taste gusto m
taxi tassì m 70, 71, 84
taxi driver autista m/f di tassì
taxi rank posteggio m tassì 84, 96
tea tè m 40
tea bags bustine fpl di tè
teacher insegnante m/f
team squadra f
teaspoon cucchiaino m 140
teat *(for baby)* tettarella f
teddy bear orsacchiotto m
teenager adolescente m/f
telephone telefono m 22, 70, 87, 92, 127

telephone bill *(in hotel)* conto m del telefono 32
telephone booth cabina f telefonica, 32, telefono m pubblico 127
telephone directory elenco m telefonico 127
telephone kiosk cabina f telefonica
telephone number numero m di telefono 127
telephone token gettone m telefonico
telephone, to telefonare 128
television televisione f
telex telex m
tell, to dire 18, 79; **tell me** dirmi 79
temperature temperatura f 116, 164
temporary provvisorio(-a) 89
tendon tendine m 166
tennis ball palla f da tennis
tennis court campo m da tennis
tent tenda f 30, 31
tent pegs picchetti mpl 31
tent pole palo m della tenda 31
terrible terribile 101
tetanus tetano m
thank you grazie 10, 94
that quello(-a)
that one quello(-a) 16, 134
that's all è tutto 133
thawing snow neve f fondente
theater/theatre teatro m 96, 99, 110
theft furto m 71, 153
their loro 16
theirs loro m/f 16
them loro 16
theme park parco m a tema
then *(time)* poi 13
there là 12, 17
there is ... c'è 17
thermometer termometro m
thermos flask termos m
these questi 134
they loro
thick spesso(-a) 14
thief ladro m
thigh coscia f 166
thin sottile 14
think, to credere 77; **I think** penso 42
think about it, to pensarci 135
third terzo(-a) 217; **a ~** un terzo 217
thirsty assetato(-a)

this one questo(-a) 16, 134
those quelli 134
thread filo m 27
throat gola f 166
throat lozenges pastiglie fpl per la gola
thrombosis trombosi f
through per, attraverso 12
thumb pollice m 166
ticket biglietto m 68, 69, 74, 75, 77, 79, 80, 100, 114, 153
ticket agency/office biglietteria f 73
tie cravatta f 144
tie pin spillo m per cravatta
tight *(clothing)* stretto(-a) 117, 146
tights collant m 144
till receipt ricevuta f di cassa
time *(of day)* ora f 76, 220; **on ~** in orario 76; **free time ~** tempo m libero 98; **at what ~?** a che ora? 78
timetable orario m 70, 75
tin *(can)* lattina f; **~ opener** apriscatole m 148
tin foil carta f stagnola
tint, to fare il colore 147
tinted *(glass/lens)* colorati (e)
tip mancia f 32
tipping dare la mancia 42
tire pneumatico m 83, 88
tired, to be essere stanco(-a)
tissues fazzoletti mpl di carta 142
to *(place)* a 12
toaster tostapane m
tobogganing andare in toboga
today oggi 68, 124, 218
toe dito m del piede 166
toilet gabinetto m 26, 87
toilet paper carta f igienica 25, 142
toilets toelette fpl/gabinetti mpl 30, 70, 73, 78, 96, 98, 132
tomorrow domani 68, 84, 124, 166, 218
tongue lingua f
tonic water acqua f brillante
tonight questa sera 110, 124; **for ~** per questa sera 108
tonsillitis tonsillite f
tonsils tonsille fpl 166
too *(also)* anche 19; *(extreme)* troppo 17, 93

A-Z

A-Z

too much troppo 15
tooth dente m 168
toothache mal m di denti
toothbrush spazzolino m
toothpaste dentifricio m 142
top cima f
top floor ultimo piano m
torch pila 31
totally totalmente 17
tough (food) duro(-a) 41
tour giro m, gita f 97
tour guide guida m/f turistica
tour operator agente m di viaggio 26
tour representative rappresentante
  m/f dell'agenzia viaggi 27
tourist turista m/f
tourist office Ufficio Turismo m/Ente
  Turismo m 97
tow, to trainare
tow rope fune f da traino
towards verso 12
towel asciugamano m 142
towelling tela f per asciugamani
tower torre f 99
town città f 70, 94
town hall Municipio m 99
town plans
toy giocattolo m 157
track sentiero m 107
tracksuit tuta f da ginnastica
traditional tradizionale 35
traffic traffico m
traffic jam ingorgo stradale m
traffic light semaforo m 12
traffic offense/violation infrazione f
  stradale
tragedy tragedia f
trail sentiero m 106
trailer roulotte f 30
trailer park parco m roulotte
train treno m 75, 77, 80
train times orario m ferroviario 75
training shoes scarpe fpl da ginnastica
tram tram m 78, 79
transfer (transport) trasferta f
transfer, to trasferire
transit, in durante il viaggio 71
translate, to tradurre 11
translation traduzione f
translator traduttore m, la traduttrice f

trash rifiuti mpl 28
trash bags sacchetti mpl per i rifiuti
  148
trash cans cassetoni m per i rifiuti 30
travel agency agenzia f di viaggio 131
travel sickness (car/air/sea) mal
  d'auto/d'aria/di mare 141
travel, to viaggiare, partire 74
traveler's checks assegni turistici mpl
  27, 42, 136, 138
tray vassoio m
tree albero m 106
tremendous straordinario(-a) 101
trim (hair) spuntatina f 147
trip gita f 97
trolley carrello m 158
trouble: I'm having trouble with ... ho
  difficoltà con ...
trouser press stirapantaloni m
trousers pantaloni mpl 144
truck camion m
true: that's not true non è vero
try on, to provare 146
tube tubo m
tumor tumore m 165
tunnel sotterraneo m
turn, to girare 95
turn down (volume, heat), to abbassare
  (il volume, il riscaldamento)
turn off, to spegnere 25
turn on, to accendere 25
turn up, to (volume, heat) alzare
turning svolta f 95
TV room sala f televisione
tweezers le pinzette fpl
twice due volte 217
twin bed due letti mpl 21
two-door car auto a due porte f 86
type: what type? che tipo? 112
typical tipico(-a) 37
tyre pneumatico m 83, 88

U ugly brutto(-a) 14, 101
UK Regno m Unito
ulcer ulcera f
umbrella ombrello m 144
uncle zio m 120
unconscious, to be perdere conoscenza
  92, 162
under (place) sotto 12

underdone *(adj)* non abbastanza cotto(-a) 41

underpants mutande fpl 144

underpass sottopassaggio m 76

understand, to capire 11; **do you understand?** capisce? 11; **I don't understand** non capisco 11, 67

undress, to spogliarsi 164

uneven *(ground)* in dislivello 30

unfortunately sfortunatamente 19

uniform uniforme m/f

United States gli Stati Uniti mpl

university università f

unleaded gasoline benzina f senza piombo

unlimited mileage chilometraggio m illimitato

unlock, to aprire a chiave, sbloccare

unpleasant sgradevole 14, 101

unscrew, to svitare

until fino a 13, 221

up to fino a 12

upmarket elegante m/f

upper *(berth)* cuccetta superiore f 74

upset stomach mal m di stomaco 141

upstairs al piano superiore 12

urgent urgente 161

us: for/with us per/con noi

U.S. Stati Uniti USA 119

use, to usare 88, 139

use: for my personal use per mio uso personale 67

useful utile m/f

V **vacancy** camere libere 21
vacant libero(-a) 14

vacate, to lasciare lbero(-a) 32

vacation vacanza f

vaccinated against, to be essere vaccinato(-a) contro 164

vaccination vaccinazione f

vaginal infection infezione f vaginale 167

valet service servizio m di pulizia

valid valido 75, 77, 100

validate, to *(ticket)* convalidare 79

valley valle f 107

valuable prezioso(-a)

value valore m 155

vanilla *(flavor)* vaniglia f

VAT IVA f 24

VAT *(sales tax)* I.V.A. (Imposta Valore Aggiunto) f 136

VAT receipt Ricevuta f Fiscale 42

vegan, to be seguire una dieta macrobiotica

vegan: suitable for vegans adatto(-a) per chi non consuma prodotti derivati da animali

vegetables i legumi m/le verdure f 38

vegetarian vegetariano(-a) 35

vegetarian *(n)* vegetariano m la vegetariana f

vehicle veicolo m

vehicle registration document documenti del veicolo (pl) 93

vein vena f 166

velvet velluto m

vending machine distributore m automatico

venereal disease malattia f venerea 165

ventilator ventilatore m

very molto 17

vet veterinario m

video arcade sala f giochi 113

video game videogioco m

video recorder videoregistratore m

view: with a view of the sea con vista sul mare

viewing point punto m panoramico 107

village paese m 107

vineyard/winery vigne fpl 107

visa visto m

visit visita f 66, 119

visit, to visitare 123, 167

visiting hours ore fpl di visita 167

vitamin tablets vitamine fpl

voice voce f

volleyball pallavolo 114

voltage voltaggio m

vomit, to vomitare 163

W **wading pool** piscina perbambini 113

waist vita f ~ **pouch** borsello m a cintura

wait attesa f 36

wait for, to aspettare 41, 76, 84, 89, 126, 140; **wait!** aspetti! 98

waiter/waitress cameriere(-a) m/f 37
waiting room sala f d'aspetto 73
wake, to (self) svegliarsi
wake someone, to svegliare qualcuno 27
wake-up call chiamata f sveglia
Wales Galles m
walk: to go for a walk andare a fare una passeggiata
walk home, to rientrare a piedi 65
walking passeggiare, camminare
walking boots scarponi mpl 145
walking distance, within raggiungibile a piedi
walking route percorso m a piedi
walking gear abbigliamento m escursionismo 145
wall muro m
wallet portafoglio m 42, 153
want, to volere 18
ward (hospital) reparto m, corsia f 167
warm (weather) caldo(-a) 122
warm, to riscaldare 39
warmer più caldo(-a) 24
wash basin lavello m 25
wash, to lavare 137
washbasin lavabo m
washing, to do fare il bucato
washing instructions istruzioni di lavaggio 146
wasp vespa f
watch orologio m da polso 149, 153
watch battery pila f per orologi 149
watch mender's orologeria f
watch strap cinturino m dell'orologio
watch TV, to guardare la televisione
water acqua f 87, 88, 106, 116
water carrier bidone m dell'acqua
water heater boiler m 28
waterskis sci mpl d'acqua 116
waterfall cascata f 107
waterproof impermeabile m/f
waterskiing sci m d'acqua
wave onda f
way (direction) strada f 94; **I've lost my ~** mi sono smarrito 94; **it's in the ~** blocca il passaggio; **on the ~ to** sulla strada di 83
we noi
weak coffee caffè m lungo

weak: I feel weak mi sento debole
wear, to indossare 152
weather tempo m 122
weather forecast previsioni fpl del tempo 122
wedding matrimonio m
wedding ring fede f nuziale
week settimana f 23, 97, 218
weekend fine f settimana 24; **at the ~** al fine settimana 218
weekend rate tariffa f per fine settimana
weekly (ticket) settimanale 79
weight: my weight is … peso …
welcome to … benvenuto(-a) a
well-done (steak) ben cotta
Welsh (person/adj) gallese m/f
west ovest m 12, 95, 106
wetsuit tuta f per immersione
what? cosa? 18
what kind of …? che tipo di … ? 37, 106
what time …? a che ora …? 68, 76
what's the time? che ora è? 220
wheelchair carrozzella f 100
when? quando? 13
where? dove? 12; **~ is …?** dov'è …? 99
where are you from? da dove viene?
where else? in quale altro negozio 135
which? quale? 16; **~ stop?** quale fermata? 80
while mentre 13
whist (cards) gioco m del whist
white bianco 143
who? chi? 16
whole: the whole day tutto il giorno
whose di chi 16
why? perchè? 16
wide largo(-a) 14
wife moglie f 120, 162
wildlife fauna f
windbreaker giacc a f a vento 144
window finestra f 25; finestrino m 77; (shop) vetrina f
window seat posto m accanto al finestrino 69, 74
windscreen parabrezza m 88
windshield parabrezza m 88
windy, to be essere ventoso(-a) 122
wine vino m 40; **~ bottle** bottiglia f di vino
wine list lista f dei vini 37
winter inverno m 219

wishes: **best wishes to ...** migliori auguri mpl a ... 219
with con 17
withdraw, to fare un prelievo 139
without senza 17
witness testimone m/f 93
wood *(forest)* bosco m 107; *(material)* legno m
wool lana f 146
work, to lavorare 121; *(operate)* funzionare 28, 83, 88, 89; **it doesn't work** non funziona 25
worry: I'm worried sono preoccupato(-a)
worse peggiore 14;
  it's got/gotten ~ è peggiorato(-a)
worst *(adv./adj.)* peggio, peggiore m/f
worth: is it worth seeing? vale la pena vederlo?
wound ferita f 162
wrap up, to impacchettare
write-off *(car)* inservibile 89
write: write soon! scriva presto!
writing pad carta f da lettere
wrong sbagliato(-a) 14, 136; *(not right)* non funziona 88; **~ number** numero m sbagliato 128;
  there's something ~ with ... c'è qualcosa che non va con ...; **what's ~?** che guasto ha? 89

x-ray radiografia f 164
yacht yacht m
year anno m 218
yellow giallo 143
yes sì 10
yesterday ieri 218
yield *(give way)* dare la precedenza
yogurt yogurt m
you *(sing/plur/formal)* tu/voi/Lei 16
young giovane 14
your(s) *(formal)* Suo(-a), *(familiar)* tuo(-a) 16
youth hostel ostello m della gioventù 29
zero zero 216
zip(per) cerniera f
zone zona f
zoo zoo m 113
zoology zoologia f

This Italian-English Dictionary covers all the areas where you may need to decode written Italian: hotels, public buildings, restaurants, shops, ticket offices and on transport. It will also help with understanding forms, maps, product labels, road signs and operating instructions (for telephones, parking meters etc.). If you can't locate the exact sign, you may find key words or terms listed separately.

A a passo d'uomo dead slow
a proprio rischio at the owner's risk
a scelta at your choice …
a stomaco vuoto on an empty stomach
abbazia abbey
abbigliamento per bambini children's wear
abbigliamento per signora ladies wear
abbigliamento per uomo menswear
abbigliamento sportivo sportswear
abiti per uomo menswear
accendere i fari/luci switch on headlights
accettazione admissions
acciaio steel
accostarsi a sinistra/destra keep to the left/right
aceto vinegar
acqua non potabile do not drink water
acqua potabile drinking water
aereo plane
affitasi camere rooms to let
affitasi appartamento apartment to let
agenzia di assicurazioni insurance agent's
agenzia di viaggi travel agent's
agenzia immobiliare estate agent's
aggiornato updated
agitare prima dell'uso shake well before use
ai binari to the platforms
al coperto indoor
albergo hotel
alianti gliding
alimentari grocer's

alimenti surgelati frozen foods
aliscafo hydrofoil
all'aperto outdoor/open-air
allacciare le cinture fasten your seatbelt
alle cabine cabin decks
alotto lounge
alpinismo mountaineering, abseiling
alpinismo da roccia free climing
alt stop
alta tensione high voltage
altezza height
altezza massima … metri headroom
altitudine altitude
alzare il ricevitore lift receiver
ambasciata embassy
ambulatorio oculistico eye infirmary
ancora meglio improved
andata one-way/single
andata e ritorno round trip
andata semplice one-way
anti-urto shock-proof
antiquario antique store/shop
aperto open
aperto tutti i giorni anche la domenica open every day including Sundays
aprire qui open here
area di ristoro rest area
area di servizio service area
argenteria silver shop
argento silver
aria condizionata air conditioning
aromi (naturali) (natural) flavoring
arredi per arredamento soft furnishings
arrivi arrivals
articoli di bellezza e profumeria makeup and perfume

articoli per cucina kitchen equipment

articoli per il bagno bathroom accessories

articoli per la camera di letto bedroom accessories

ascensore elevator

aspettare il proprio turno please wait your turn

aspettare il tono wait for tone

attendere prego please wait

attenti ai ladri beware of pickpockets

attenti al cane beware of the dog

attenzione ghiaia loose gravel

attenzione non scendere il gradino prima dell'apertura della porta do not descend steps before doors open *(on buses)*

attenzione, prego please be careful

attenzione, questa macchina non da resto this machine does not give change

attenzione, … avviso/avvertimento warning

attesa di … minuti circa wait: approx … mins.

attrezzatura per pesca subacquea underwater fishing equipment

attrezzatura per scuba scuba diving equipment

autonoleggio car rental

autostrada expressway

autunno fall/autumn

avanti cross now

B **bagno** restroom/toilets
bagno schiuma foambath

baia bay

balconata balcony, dress circle

balcone balcony

ballo dance

bambini children

bambini solo se accompagnati no unaccompanied children

banca bank

banco di pesce fishstall *(at market)*

bancomat cash dispenser

barca a remi rowing boat

barca a vela sailing-boat, yacht

batelli di salvataggio lifeboats

batello a vapore steamer

belvedere view point

benvenuti! welcome

benzina gas

bevande analocoliche soft drinks

bevande extra drinks not included

bevande incluse drinks included

bibite fresche e snacks refreshments available

biblioteca library

biglietteria ticket office

biglietti tickets

biglietti per oggi tickets for today

biglietto di andata e ritorno return ticket

biglietto ordinario day ticket

biglietto settimanale weekly ticket

binario platform

biodegradabile disposable

birra beer

borse handbags

bracciole waterwings

bretella expressway junction

burrone profondo canyon

C **cabina** bathing cabana/hut
cabina di ponte deck cabin

caduta massi falling rocks

caduta slavine avalanche danger

calcio soccer

calle street *(in Venice)*

calzolaio shoe repairs/cobbler's

cambiare a change at

cambiare per change *(to other metro lines)*

cambio exchange rate

cambio valute bureau de change

Camera dei Deputati parliament building

camere libere vacancies/ accommodation available

camerini fitting rooms

camion truck

campeggio campsite

campi di tennis tennis courts

campo field

A-Z

campo di battaglia battle site
campo giochi/sportivo sports ground
cancellato cancelled
cancello gate
canna da pesca fishing rod
canoa canoe
canottaggio canoeing, rowing
cantante singer
cantante lirica opera singer
canto Gregoriano Gregorian chant
capella chapel
Capodanno New Year's Day
capolinea terminal
capsule capsules
carne meat
carozza coach
carozza non fumatori (non)smokers compartment
carozza/vagone ristorante dining-car
carrelli carts/trolleys
carta d'imbarco embarkation card
carta riciclata recycled paper
cartelle cliniche medical records
cartoleria stationer's
casa house
casa di cura privata health clinic
casa patrizia stately home
cascata waterfall
casco crash helmet
cassa cashier, checkout
cassa di risparmio savings bank
cassa rapida express checkout
cassette luggage lockers; cassettes
cassieri cashiers
castello castle
catena di montagne mountain range
cavalcavia road bridge
centralino/centralinista operator
centrifuga dry spin
centro città downtown area
centro commerciale shopping area
centro congressi convention hall
centro direzionale business district
centro sportivo sports center
ceriali cereals
check-in check-in counter
chiamare ... per il ricevimento dial ... for reception

chiamare ... per una linea esterna dial ... for an outside line
chiesa church
chilometro kilometer
chirurgia surgery
chiudere il cancello keep gate shut
chiudere la porta please shut the door
chiuso (per restauro) closed (for restoration)
chiuso al traffico closed to traffic
chiuso fino a ... closed until ...
chiuso per ferie closed for holiday
chiuso per pranzo closed for lunch
chiuso per rinnovo locali closed for repairs
chiusura festiva closed for holidays
chiusura settimanale closed/day off
ciambella rubber ring
ciclismo cycling
ciniglia chenille
cinte belts
cintura di salvataggio lifebelt
cioccolateria confectioner's
circo circus
circonvallazione ring road
città city
città universitaria university
città vecchia old town
cittadini extracommunitari non-EU citizens
cognome surname
collina/colle hill
colonna sonora soundtrack
colori resistenti colorfast
comando polizia/comando Carabinieri police station
comincia alle ore ... begins at ...
commissioni bank charges
completo full up
compreso inclusive
compreso nel prezzo included in the price
compresse tablets
compri due paghi uno buy 2 get 1 free
compriamo a ... currency bought at ...
compro e vendo ... we buy and sell ...

comunicazioni interurbane/internazionali/intercontine ntali (con operatore) long distance calls (with operator): intercity/international/intercontinental

con bagno with in-suite bathroom

con sottotitoli subtitled

con vista sul mare with sea view

concerto concert

conservanti preservatives

consiglio per la consumazione serving suggestion

consultare il proprio medico prima dell'uso consult your doctor before use

consumare entro il ... best before ...

contatore della luce electricity meter

contenitore per batterie vetro/aluminio/latta/plastica battery/bottle/aluminum/tin/plastic/ paper bank *(recycling)*

conto account

conto corrente current account

contorni vari choice of vegetables

contro la forfora against dandruff

controcoperta upper deck

controllo please show your bags before leaving *(in shop)*; check/control

controllo valuta currency control

convalidare il biglietto (prima della prossima fermata/prima di salire sul treno) validate your ticket (before next bus stop/before getting on train)

coperto cloudy

corsia d'emergenza emergency lane

corsa di levrieri greyhound racing

corsi di cavallo horse racing

corsia lane

corsia ciclabile cycle track

corsia di sorpasso passing bay

corsia preferenziale do not walk

corso semplice one-way

costa coast

costiera cliff

costo per chilo (Kg)/etto/litro/metro price per kilo/330 grams/liter/ meter

cotone cotton

crema per le mani hand cream

crociere cruises

cucina cookery

cuffie obbligatorie bathing caps must be worn

cuoio leather

cura intensiva intensive care

curva pericolosa dangerous bend

curve per ... Km bends for ... kilometers

D **da consumarsi entro il ...** best before ...

da non prendere per via orale not to be taken orally

da ... a .../dalle ore... alle ore ... from ... to ...

danza dance

danza classica ballet

danza folcloristica folk dancing

dare la precedenza yield/give way

darsena docks

data di nascita date of birth

degustazione vini winetasting

della casa homemade

della stagione in season

deltaplano hang gliding

depositi deposits

deposito ambulanze ambulance station

deposito bagagli left-luggage office

deviazione alternative route, detour/diversion

deviazione per camions/TIR truck route/alternative lorry

di giornata fresh daily

diagnosi e cura treatment room

diapositive slides

diga dam

diocesi diocese

diretto direct

direttore manager

disco orario parking disk

dissolvere in acqua dissolve in water

divieto d'attracco no anchorage

divieto di balneazione no swimming/bathing

divieto di campeggio no camping

divieto di ingresso esclusi i mezzi degli handicappati access for disabled persons vehicles only

A-Z

divieto di ingresso escluso veicoli autorizzati authorized vehicles only
divieto di scarico no dumping
divieto di sorpasso no passing
divieto di sosta no stopping
docce showers
dogana customs control
domani tomorrow
domenica Sunday
Domenica delle Palme Palm Sunday
domicilio home address
donne women only, women (toilets)
dopo i pasti after meals
dopobarba aftershave
doposole aftersun
doppiato dubbed
doppio senso two-way traffic
durante i pasti with meals

E edicola newsagent's
edificio pubblico public building
elenco telefonico telephone directory
elicottero helicopter
emergenza emergency
emergenza sanitaria medical (health) emergency
entrata entrance
Epifania Epiphany (January 6)
equitazione horse riding
esaurito sold out
esibire documenti/carta d'identità/passaporto proof of identity required
esibire la ricevuta sul paravento place ticket on windshield
espresso made to order
estate summer
estero foreign
estintore fire extinguisher
estuario estuary
etto 330 grams
extra extra charge/supplement

F fabbrica factory
fantascienza science fiction

farina wheat flour
farina integrale fermenti lattici vivi whole wheat flour
farmacia drugstore
faro marina lighthouse
fatto su misura made to measure
fattore 8 factor 8 (sunlotion)
fattoria farm
febbraio February
fermata bus stop
fermata a richiesta request stop
fermata del tram tram stop
fermata service stopping
Ferragosto Assumption Day (August 15)
ferro iron
ferrovia railroad
Festa del Lavoro Labor Day (May 1)
Festa dell'Assunzione Assumption Day (15 August)
Festa dell'Immacolata Concezione (8 dicembre) Immaculate Conception (December 8)
Festa della liberazione (25 aprile) Liberation Day (April 25)
festa nazionale national holiday
fibre alimentari fibres
fiera fair
fila row
film d'orrore horror film
film per famiglia universal (film classification)
filobus trolleybus
filosofia philosophy
fine autostrada/superstrada end of expressway/motorway
fine deviazione end of detour/diversion
fine lavori stradali end of roadworks
finestrino window seat
finire la cura/il trattamento finish the course
fino a … until …
fioraio florist's
Firenze Florence
firma signature
fiume river
fon hairdryer
Fondamenta canal-side (Venice)
fontana fountain

formaggio cheese
fortezza fortress
fotottico photographic store
fragile – vetro fragile – glass
frana landslide
francobolli stamps
franchigia bagagli luggage allowance
freno d'emergenza emergency brake
fresco fresh
frontiera border crossing
frutta fruit
fruttivendolo greengrocer's
fumetti comics
funivia cable car/gondola
funzione religiosa church service
fuochi d'artificio fireworks
fuori servizio out of order

G **gabinetti** toilets
gabinetti pubblici public toilets
galleria shopping mall (dress)
circle; gallery
galleria chiusa (mountain) tunnel closed
galleria d'arte art gallery
gara contest
gas per campeggio camping gas
gennaio January
Genova Genoa
genuino genuine
ghiaccio icy snow
ghiaccio nero black ice
giardini pubblici park
giardino garden
giardino botanico botanical garden
gift omaggio free gift
ginocologo gynecologist
gioccatoli toystore
giornalaio newsagent's
giorni feriali weekdays
giovedì Thursday
giugno June
gocce drops
goielleria jeweler's
gola gorge
gomma rubber
grassi fat content
grassi vegetali vegetable fats
grotta cave

gruppi groups welcome
guanti, cinte e sciarpe
gloves, belts and scarves
guardaroba cloakroom
guida ai piani store guide

H **hockey su ghiaccio** ice hockey

I **il cuoco suggerisce ...** the chef
suggests ...
il migliore del mondo world's best
imbarco ad uscita n° ... boarding at
gate no. ...
imbarco immediato boarding now
immigrazione immigration control
in casi di guasti telefonare al numero ...
in case of breakdown, phone/contact
...
in funzione sistema di vigilanza/allarme
surveillance/alarm system in operation
incrocio crossing
indirizzo address
indirizzo di casa home address
industria cinematografica
movies/cinema
informazioni information desk,
reception
informazioni elenco abbonati enquiries
informazioni nutrizionali nutritional
information
ingoiare intere swallow whole
ingrandimento enlargement service
ingresso access only, entrance
ingresso libero admission free
ingresso per gli handicappati entrance
for disabled persons
ingresso per soli residenti access to
residents only
inizia alle ore ... commencing ...
inizio autostrada freeway entrance
inizio spettacolo curtain up
**innestare la prima marcia prima di
lasciare la macchina** leave your car in
first gear
inserire monete insert coin
inserire carta di credito insert credit
card

A-Z

inserire il denaro nella macchina e ritirare il biglietto insert money in machine and remove ticket
inverno winter
inversione di marcia change direction
irritante per gli occhi e la pelle harmful for eyes and skin
isola pedonale pedestrians only/pedestrian zone
istituto di credito bank
istruzioni per l'uso instructions for use
itinerario naturale nature trail
itinerario panoramico scenic route
itinerario turistico tourist route
IVA VAT/sales tax
IVA compreso/incluso VAT included

L l'originale the original
La Befana (6 gennaio) Epiphany (January 6)
la merce non può essere cambiata goods cannot be exchanged
lago (artificiale) (artificial) lake
lana wool
lastri x-ray
latte e latticini dairy products
latteria dairy
lavaggio macchine car wash
lavanderia laundry, washing facilities
lavare a mano hand wash only
lavare in acqua fredda/tiepida wash in cold/warm water
lavori in corso (a ... metri) roadworks (... m) ahead
leggere attentamente le istruzioni prima dell'uso read instructions carefully before use
legno wood
lettino sunbed
lettura di poesie poetry reading
levate alle ore ... times of collection
libero vacant, for rent
libreria bookstore
libretto di circolazione/documenti registration papers
lino linen
liquidazione clearance sale

liquori liqueurs
lista menu
Livorno Leghorn
lo chef suggerisce ... the chef suggests ...
locanda guest house
luna park amusement park
lunedì Monday
Lunedì dell'Angelo Easter Monday
luogo di nascita place of birth

M macchina car
macelleria butcher's
magazzino department store grande
maggio May
mare sea
mare mosso rough sea
marionette puppets
marmellate e conserve preserves
martedì Tuesday
marzo March
maternità maternity
mattina a.m.
medico doctor
meglio se servito fresco best served chilled
meno di 8 articoli 8 items or less
menù fisso set menu
menù turistico tourist menu
mercato market
mercato coperto covered market
merce da dichiarare goods to declare
mercoledì Wednesday
messa mass
messa vespertina Evensong
metallo metal
metropolitana/metro subway
mezza pensione half board
mimo mime
miniera mine
misura unica one size fits all
mittente sender
mobili ed arredamenti furniture
mobilificio furniture warehouse
molo dock (boarding)
molta neve heavy (snow)
monastero monastery
monsignore monseignor

montagna mountain
monumenti antichi ruins
monumento (ai caduti) (war) memorial
monumento di interesse turistico tourist feature
monumento storico ancient monument
mulino mill
mulino a vento windmill
multicine multiplex cinema
municipio town hall
muro wall
museo museum
musica music
musica da camera chamber music
musica dal vivo live music
musica lirica opera

N **Napoli** Naples
Natale Christmas

nave ship
nazionalità nationality
nebbia fog
negozio di musica music store/shop
neve snow
neve artificiale artificial snow
neve bagnata wet snow
neve fresca fresh snow
neve ghiacciato icy snow
neve leggera powdery snow
niente flash no flash
niente resto exact change/no change given
niente rimborsi no refunds
nocivo harmful
noleggio for hire
noleggio abiti/vestiti dress hire
nome name
nome dei figli name of children
nome del coniuge name of spouse
nome di famiglia surname
nome di ragazza maiden name
non allacciato disconnected
non appoggiarsi alla porta do not lean against door
non asciugare al sole do not dry in direct sunlight
non avvicinarsi keep clear
non bruciare do not burn

non calpestare il prato/l'erba keep off the grass
non compreso exclusive
non danneggia le pellicole film safe
non esporre a fonti di calore do not expose to heat
non gettare rifiuti do not litter
non incluso not included
non lasciare bagagli incustoditi do not leave baggage unattended
non lasciare oggetti di valore nell'automobile do not leave valuables in your car
non parlare al conducente do not talk to the driver
non più di 4 persone no more than 4 persons
non scongelare prima di cucinare cook from frozen
non si accetta nessuna responsabilità per danni o furto the owners can accept no responsibility for any damage or theft
non si accettano assegni no checks
non si accettano carte di credito no credit cards
non stirare do not iron
non superare 375 kg do not exceed 375 kilos (in elevators)
non toccare do not touch
non usare candeggia do not bleach
nulla da dichiarare nothing to declare
numero di targa car registration
numero verde toll free number
numeri di emergenza emergency telephone numbers
numeri utili useful numbers
numero del passaporto passport number
numero della carta di credito credit card number
numero di soccorso pubblico di emergenza general emergency number
numero di volo flight number
nuoto swimming

A-Z

O occupato occupied/engaged

offerta speciale special offer

officina meccanica car repairs

oggetti elettrici electrical shop/store/appliances

oggetti smarriti lost property

oggi today

ogni ... ore every ... hours

Ognissanti All Saints' Day (November 1)

olio oil; sauces

ombrellone sunshade

omeopatico homeopath

operatore operator

orari timetables

orario opening/business/visiting hours

orario continuato open all day

orario di visite visiting hours

orchestra sinfonica symphony orchestra

24 ore su 24 24-hour service

oreficeria jeweler's

oro gold

ospedale hospital

ospizio hospice

osservatoria observatory

ostello della gioventù youth hostel

ottico optician

ottobre October

ottone brass

P pacchi parcels

padiglione pavilion

padre Father

pagare alla cassa please pay at cash desk

pagare qui please pay here

pagato (grazie) paid (with thanks)

pagine gialle yellow pages

palco (pl. palchi) box

palude marsh, swamp

pane bread

panificio bakery/baker's

paracadutismo parachuting

parcheggio parking (permitted); parking lot

parcheggio libero free parking

parcheggio per biciclette parking for bicycles

parcheggio per soli residenti parking for residents only

parcheggio riservato ai clienti customer parking lot

parcheggio sotterraneo underground garage

parcheggio vietato/divieto di sosta no parking

parrucchiere hairdresser's/hairstylist's

partenze departures

partita match

Pasqua Easter Sunday

passaggio a livello railroad/level crossing

passaggio sotteraneo underground passage

passo carrabile do not block entrance

pasticceria pastry shop

pattini skates

pedaggio toll

pedoni pedestrians

pelle leather

pellicola film

pendenza gradient

penisola peninsula

pensione completa full board

pensione guest house

per vegetariani suitable for vegetarians

per ... giorni for ... days

percorso del traghetto ferry route

percorso per autobus/pullmans bus route

pericolo danger

pericolo di bufere storm warning

pericolo di burrasche gale warning

pericolo di ghiaccio icy road

pericolo di slavine danger of avalanches

pericoloso dangerous

personale staff only

pesce fish; angling

pesce fresco fresh fish

pesce surgelato frozen fish

pescheria fish store

pesistica weight-lifting
piatti pronti oven to table
piatto del giorno dish of the day
piazza square
picco peak
piccola colazione breakfast
piccoli prezzi grande qualità low prices, top quality
pillole pills
pinacoteca art gallery
pioggia rain
piscina swimming pool
piscina per tuffi diving pool
pista bianca for beginners (piste)
pista blu e pista rossa for intermediates (piste)
pista chiusa closed
pista ciclabile cycle lane/track
pista nera for advanced skiers
pista per principianti for beginners (piste)
pista pericolosa dangerous slope
platea stalls
polizia police
polizia stradale highway/traffic police
pollame poultry
poltrona n° seat no.
pomata ointment
pomeriggio p.m.
pompa pump
ponte bridge
ponte bassa (altezza ... m.) low bridge (height ... m.)
ponte di coperta upper deck
ponte di passeggiate promenade deck
ponte levatoio drawbridge
porta gate (to town/city); door
porta antincendio fire door
porta automatica automatic door
portiere notturno night porter
porto harbor
posta post office
posto corridoio aisle seat
posto fumatore smoking
posto non fumatore no smoking
posto n° seat no.
posto riservato agli invalidi please give up this seat to the infirm
pozzo well
PP.TT. post office

prato (campeggio) grass (camping site)
prefisso area code
preghiera prayers
prelievi withdrawals
prelievi di sangue blood tests
prendere il biglietto take ticket
prendere la ricevuta dalla cassa automatica pay at the meter
prenotazione biglietti ticket reservation
prenotazioni reservations, advance bookings
prezzi fissi no discounts
prezzi speciali per gruppi special price for groups
prezzo rate
prezzo al litro price per liter/litre
prezzo per chilo (Kg)/etto price per kilo/330 grams
prima classe first class
prima dei pasti before meals
prima di coricarsi before going to bed (medicine dose)
primavera spring
primo piano first floor
prodotti antiallergici antiallergic products
prodotti di bellezza beauty products
proibito circolare nella chiesa durante le funzioni liturgiche/durante la santa messa no entry during services
pronto intervento emergency services
pronto soccorso accident and emergency; medicine box
proprietà privato private property
prossima levata alle ore ... next collection at ...
prossima visita guidata alle ore ... next tour at ...
punto d'imbarco embarkation point
punto d'incontro meeting point
punto di raduno muster station

Q questa macchina non da resto this machine does not give change
questa sera/stasera this evening
qui si vendono carte telefoniche phone cards on sale here

A-Z

R **racchetta** racket/raquet; ski poles/sticks

raccordo anulare ring-road

rallentare slow down

rallentare, scuola/bambini caution, school/children

reclamo bagagli baggage reclaim

referti test results

regali gifts

reggersi ai corrimano hold on to the side (escalator)

resto massimo (L.2000) maximum change given (L.2000)

ricambi per auto car accessory/spares shop/store

ricevimento reception

riduzioni reductions

rifugio ski shelter

rilasciato il ... da ... issued on ...by ...

rimozione forzata unauthorized vehicles will be towed away

rio stream

riparazioni repairs

riserva d'acqua reservoir

riserva naturale nature reserve

riservato reserved

ritardo delayed

rocca castle, fortress

roccia (campeggio) stone (camping site)

romanzi novels

rompere il vetro in caso di pericolo break glass in case of emergency

rotatoria (a ... metri) roundabout/circle (... m. ahead)

roulotte trailer/caravan

rubinetto water tap

rupe cliff

S **sabato** Saturday

sabbia mobile quick sand

sala banchetti reception facilities

sala congressi/conferenze conference room

sala d'attesa waiting room

sala da pranzo dining room

sala giochi games room

sala operatoria operating theater

sala passaggeri passenger lounge

sala TV television room

saldi clearance sale

sale salt

salita entrance (get on)

salotto lounge

salvagenti lifejackets

San Gennaro St. Januarius (19 September, Naples)

San Giovanni Battista St. John The Baptist (24 June, Florence)

San Marco Saint Mark's Day (25 April, Venice)

San Pietro e Paolo Saint Paul's and Peter's Day (29 June, Rome)

San Silvestro New Year's Eve

Sant'Ambrogio Saint Ambrose's Day (December 7, Milan)

Santo Stefano Boxing Day (December 26)

sanzioni per i trasgressori trespassers will be prosecuted

sanzioni per i viaggiatori senza biglietto penalty for traveling without a ticket

sanzioni se viaggiate senza biglietto penalty for traveling without ticket

saporito tasty

scadenza della carta di credito credit card expiration date

scala d'emergenza emergency stairs

scala mobile escalator

scarico merci deliveries only

scarpata escarpment

scarponi da sci ski boots

schiuma per la barba shaving cream

sci skis, skiing

sci di fondo cross-country skiing

sci nautico waterskiing

sciovia tow (ski) lift

sconto di ...% se spendi più di ... % discount if you spend more than ...

scuola school

scuola rallentare slow, school

sdraia deck-chair

se i sintomi persistono consultare il proprio medico if symptoms persist, consult your doctor

seconda scelta sale

secondo piano second floor

segale rye

seggiovia chairlift
selezionare destinazione/zona select destination/zone
semaforo provvisorio temporary traffic lights
senso unico one-way street
sentiero footpath, track
senza grassi fat-free
senza intervallo no intervals
senza piombo unleaded
senza zucchero sugar-free
sereno sunny weather
servizio service charge
servizio compreso/incluso service included
servizio di camera room service
servizio diretto direct service
servizio immediato while you wait
servizio non incluso no service charge included
servizio notturno night service
seta silk
si accettano gruppi parties welcome
si accettano carte di credito we accept credit cards
si prega consegnare le borse please leave your bags here
si prega controllare il resto please check your change
si prega di aspettare dietro la linea please wait behind barrier
si prega di non consumare cibo nella camera no food in the room please
si prega fare un contributo please make a contribution
si prega mantere il silenzio durante le funzioni religiose quiet, service in progress
si prega pulire la camera this room needs making up
si prega rispettare questo luogo sacro please respect this place of worship
si prega tenere il biglietto please retain your ticket
sicurezza security
signore women only; ladies (toilets)
signori gentlemen (toilets)
slittino sledge
soccorso stradale breakdown services
solista soloist

solo ciclisti cyclists only
solo contanti cash only
solo giorni feriali weekdays only
solo giorni festivi Sundays only
solo per gli abbonati season ticket holders only
solo per uso esterno not for internal consumption
solo rasoi shavers only
solo residenti residents only
solo stasera/una serata for 1 night only
solo uso esterno for external use only
sono previste sanzioni per chi non può esibire lo scontrino fiscale/il biglietto You are liable to be fined if you don't keep your receipt/ticket
sopra il livello del mare above sea level
sopraelevata flyover
sorgente spring
spegnere il motore turn off engine
spettacolo spectacular
spettacolo serale evening performance
spettatori spectators
spiaggia beach
spiaggia per nudisti nudist beach
spingere push
spogliatoi changing rooms
SQ subject to availability
squisito delicious
staccare la corrente prima di (togliere) disconnect from electric mains before (removing)
stampa e sviluppo photographic store
stampe prints
stazione degli autobus bus station/terminal
stazione di pedaggio toll booth
stazione di servizio service/filling station
stazione ferroviario train station
stirare a temperatura bassa cool iron
storia history
storia dell'arte art history
strada road
strada a doppia corsia dual carriageway

A-Z

strada a doppio senso traffic from the opposite direction
strada a senso unico one-way street
strada bianca gravel/unpaved road
strada chiusa road closed
strada dissestata uneven road surface
strada in costruzione road under construction
strada nazionale main road/highway
strada principale main street
strada senza uscita cul-de-sac; no throughway
strada stretta narrow road
straniero(-a) foreign
strappare qui tear here
strisce pedonali pedestrian crossing
studio medico doctor's surgery
succhi di frutta fruit juices
suonare la campanella ring the bell
super four-star (gas)
superstrada expressway
supplemento (notturno, aeroporto, bagagli, festivo) supplement (night-time, airport, baggage, Sunday, holiday)
surgelato frozen
sviluppo developing
svincolo junction/interchange

T
tagliare qui cut here
tangenziale bypass
tavola da sci snowboard
tavola da surf surfboard
tavoli al piano superiore seats upstairs
tassì taxi
teatro per ragazzi children's theater
telefono per solo carte card phone
telefono SOS/di emergenza emergency telephone
teleselezione direct dialing
tenere in frigo keep refrigerated
tenere in un ambiente fresco keep in a cool place
tenere lontano dagli occhi keep away from eyes

tenere lontano dai bambini keep out of reach of children
tenere lontano dal sole do not expose to sunlight
tennis da tavola table tennis
terme baths
tessera season ticket
tessera mensile monthly ticket
tessuti per arredamento soft furnishings
tier tribuna stand/grandstand
tintoria dry cleaner's
tintura per capelli hair dye
tipografia printing & copying
tirare pull
tiro all'arco archery
tomba grave, tomb
Torino Turin
torre tower
tossico poisonous, toxic
traffico intenso delays likely
traffico lento slow traffic
traghetto passenger ferry
transito con catene chains required
transito con catene o pneumatici da neve use chains or snow tyres
treno train
trotta harness racing
tuffo deep water diving
tutte le operazioni all transactions

U
ufficio cambi bureau de change
ufficio informazioni information office
ufficio postale post office
ufficio prenotazioni ticket reservations
ultima novità brand new
ultima stazione di servizio per ... chilometri last gas station for ... kilometers
ultima vista alle ore ... last entry at ...
una bibite inclusa includes 1 complimentary drink
uomini men only; men (toilets)
usare con cautela take care when using
uscita exit, way out; gate
uscita autostrada freeway/motorway exit

uscita camions truck/lorry exit
uscita d'emergenza emergency/fire exit
uso della cucina cooking facilities

 V **vaccinazioni ecografie** vaccinations

vaglia postali/telegrafici drafts and transfers
vagone letto sleeper (train)
validità del passaporto passport expiration date
validità della carta di credito credit card expiration date
valido per (75 minuti) valid for (75 minutes)
valido per le fasce ... valid for zones
veicoli lenti slow vehicles
veicoli pesanti heavy vehicles
vela sailing
veleno(so) poison(ous)
velocità massima ... km/ora maximum speed
vendere entro il ... sell by ...
vendiamo a ... currency sold at...
venerdì Friday
venti forti strong winds
venti moderati light winds
verdura vegetables
vernice fresco wet paint
vero genuine
vetro glass
vetro riciclato recycled glass
via street
viaggi/viaggiare travel
viale avenue, boulevard
vicino al mare within easy reach of the sea
vicolo alley
vicolo cieco dead end
videogiochi video games
vietato forbidden
vietato a veicoli con peso superiore a ...... closed to heavy vehicles
vietato accendere il fuoco no fires
vietato ai minori di ... anni no children under ...
vietato ai pedoni no thoroughfare for pedestrians

vietato avvicinarsi alle macchine durante la traversata no access to car decks during crossing
vietato di sosta no waiting
vietato fermarsi fino a ... no stopping (between ... and ...)
vietato fotografare no photography
vietato fumare no smoking
vietato gettare rifiuti don't dump rubbish
vietato giocare con la palla no ball games
vietato l'ingresso no entry
vietato l'ingresso dopo l'inizio dello spettacolo no entry once the performance has begun
vietato pescare no fishing
vietato pescare senza autorizzazione fishing by permit only
vietato salire no entry
vietato scendere no exit
vietato sporgersi dalla finestra do not lean out of windows
vietato suonare il clacson use of horn prohibited
vigili del fuoco fire brigade
vigili di fuoco fire station
vigneti vineyards
visite guidate guided tours
vivaio garden center
voi siete qui you are here
voli internazionali international flights
voli nazionali domestic flights
volo numero ... flight number
... volte al giorno ... times a day

 WX YZ **zona a parcheggio limitato giorni feriali** limited parking zone on weekdays

zona non fumatore no smoking
zona pedonale pedestrian zone/precinct
zona riservata a carico e scarico loading bay
zone fumatore smoking
zucchero sugar

Numbers Numeri

GRAMMAR

Larger numbers are built up using the components below: e.g.

3.456.789 **tremillioniquattrocentocinquantaseimila
e settecentoottantanove**

Mille, **milione** and **miliardo** have plural forms (**mila**, **milioni**, **miliardi**).
Note that **e** can be used to break larger numbers up.

0	**zero** *dzehro*	18	**diciotto** *deechotto*
1	**uno** *oono*	19	**diciannove**
2	**due** *doo-ay*		*deechanovay*
3	**tre** *tray*	20	**venti** *vayntee*
4	**quattro** *kwattro*	21	**ventuno** *vayntoono*
5	**cinque** *cheengkweh*	22	**ventidue**
6	**sei** *sayee*		*vaynteedoo-ay*
7	**sette** *sehttay*	23	**ventitre** *vaynteetray*
8	**otto** *otto*	24	**ventiquattro**
9	**nove** *novay*		*vaynteekwattro*
10	**dieci** *dee-ehchee*	25	**venticinque**
11	**undici** *oondeechee*		*vaynteecheengkweh*
12	**dodici** *dodeechee*	26	**ventisei** *vaynteesayee*
13	**tredici** *traydeechee*	27	**ventisette**
14	**quattordici**		*vaynteesehttay*
	kwattordeechee	28	**ventotto** *vayntotto*
15	**quindici**	29	**ventinove**
	kooeendeechee		*vaynteenovay*
16	**sedici** *saydeechee*	30	**trenta** *traynta*
17	**diciassette**		
	deechassehttay		

31	**trentuno**		third	**terzo**
	trayntoono			*tayrtso*
32	**trentadue**		fourth	**quarto**
	trayntadoo-ay			*kwarto*
40	**quaranta**		fifth	**quinto**
	kwaranta			*kooeento*
50	**cinquanta**		once	**una volta**
	cheengkwanta			*oona volta*
60	**sessanta**		twice	**due volte**
	sayssanta			*doo-ay voltay*
70	**settanta**		three times	**tre volte**
	sayttantta			*tray voltay*
80	**ottanta**		a half	**mezzo**
	ottanta			*maytso*
90	**novanta**		half a(n)	**mezz'ora**
	novanta		hour	*maytsora*
100	**cento**		half a tank	**mezzo serbatoio**
	chaynto			*maytso*
101	**centouno**			*sayrbatoeeo*
	chaynto-oono		half eaten	**mezzo mangiato**
102	**centodue**			*maytso manjaato*
	chayntodoo-ay		a quarter	**un quarto**
200	**duecento**			*oon kwarto*
	doo-aychaynto		a third	**un terzo**
500	**cinquecento**			*oon tayrtso*
	cheenkwehchaynto		a pair of ...	**un paio di ...**
1,000	**mille** *meellay*			*oon paa-eeoo dee*
10,000	**diecimila**		a dozen ...	**una dozzina ...**
	deeaycheemeela			*oona dotseena*
35,750	**trentacinquemilasette**		1997	**millenovecento-**
	centocinquanta			**novantasette**
	trayntacheengkweh			*meellaynovay-*
	meelasehttaychayn			*chayntonovanta-*
	to cheengkoo-anta			*sehttay*
1,000,000	**un milione**		2001	**duemilauno**
	oon meelyonay			*doo-aymeela-oono*
first	**primo**		the 1990s	**gli anni novanta**
	preemo			*lyee annee*
second	**secondo**			*novanta*
	saykondo			

217

Days Giorni

	Monday	**lunedì** *loonaydee*
	Tuesday	**martedì** *martaydee*
	Wednesday	**mercoledì** *mayrkolaydee*
	Thursday	**giovedì** *jovaydee*
Friday		**venerdì** *vaynayrdee*
Saturday		**sabato** *sabato*
Sunday		**domenica** *domayneeka*

Months Mesi

January	**gennaio** *jaynnaaeeo*
February	**febbraio** *faybbraaeeo*
March	**marzo** *martso*
April	**aprile** *apreelay*
May	**maggio** *madjo*
June	**giugno** *jooño*
July	**luglio** *loolyo*
August	**agosto** *agosto*
September	**settembre** *sehttehmbray*
October	**ottobre** *ottobray*
November	**novembre** *novehmbray*
December	**dicembre** *deechehmbray*

Dates Date

It's …	**È …** *eh*
July 10	**il dieci luglio** *eel dee-ehchee loolyo*
Tuesday, March 1	**martedì, primo marzo** *martaydee preemo martso*
yesterday	**ieri** *ee-ehree*
today	**oggi** *odjee*
tomorrow	**domani** *domaanee*
this/last …	**questo(-a)/l'ultimo(-a) …** *kwaysto(-a)/loolteemo(-a)*
next week	**la prossima settimana** *la prosseema saytteemaana*
every month/year	**ogni mese/anno** *oñee maysee/anno*
at the weekend	**al fine settimana** *al feenay sayteemaana*

Seasons Stagioni

spring	**la primavera** *la preemav<u>a</u>yra*
summer	**l'estate** *layst<u>aa</u>tay*
fall/autumn	**l'autunno** *lowt<u>oo</u>nno*
winter	**l'inverno** *leenv<u>ay</u>rno*
in spring	**in primavera** *een preemav<u>ay</u>ra*
during the summer	**durante l'estate** *door<u>a</u>ntay layst<u>aa</u>tay*

Greetings Saluti

Happy birthday!	**Buon compleanno!** *bwon komplay<u>a</u>nno*
Merry Christmas!	**Buon Natale!** *bwon nat<u>aa</u>lay*
Happy New Year!	**Felice Anno Nuovo! Buon anno!** *fayl<u>ee</u>chay <u>a</u>nno noo-<u>o</u>vo/bwon <u>a</u>nno*
Happy Easter!	**Buona Pasqua!** *bw<u>o</u>na p<u>a</u>skwa*
Best wishes!	**I migliori auguri!** *ee meely<u>o</u>ree owg<u>oo</u>ree*
Congratulations!	**Felicitazioni!/Congratulazioni!** *fayleecheetatsee<u>o</u>nee/kongraatoolatsee<u>o</u>nee*
Good luck!/All the best!	**Buona fortuna!** *bw<u>o</u>na fort<u>oo</u>na*
Have a good trip!	**Buon viaggio!** *bwon vee<u>a</u>djo*
Give my regards to ...	**Saluti ... da parte mia.** *sal<u>oo</u>tee ... da partay m<u>ee</u>a*

Public holidays Giorni festivi

There are a number of regional holidays observed in Italy, such as **Festa del patrono** (the local patron saint's day); this sees Rome close down for St. Peter and Paul on June 29. National holidays are listed below.

January 1	**Capodanno or Primo dell'Anno**	New Year's Day
January 6	**Epifania/Befana**	Epiphany
April 25	**Anniversario della Liberazione (1945)**	Liberation Day
May 1	**Festa del Lavoro**	Labor Day
August 15	**Ferragosto**	Assumption Day
November 1	**Ognissanti**	All Saints' Day
December 8	**L'Immacolata Concezione**	Immaculate Conception
December 25	**Natale**	Christmas
December 26	**Santo Stefano**	St Stephen's Day
Movable dates:	**Lunedì di Pasqua/Pasquetta**	Easter Monday

Except for April 25, all Italian holidays are celebrated in the **Ticino** (Italian-speaking Switzerland), as well as: March 19 (**San Giuseppe**), August 1st (National Holiday), and the holidays of **Ascensione** (Ascension Day) and **Corpus Domini**.

Time Ora

The official time system uses the 24-hour clock. However, in ordinary conversation, time is generally expressed as shown below, often with the addition of **di mattina** (morning), **di pomeriggio** (afternoon) or **di sera** (evening).

Excuse me. Can you tell me the time?	**Scusi, può dirmi che ora è?** *skoozee pwo deermee kay ora eh*
It's five past one.	**È l'una e cinque.** *eh loona ay cheenkway*
It's ...	**Sono le ...** *sono lay*
ten past two	**due e dieci** *doo-ay ay dee-ehchee*
a quarter past three	**tre e un quarto** *tray ay oon kwarto*
twenty past four	**quattro e venti** *kwattro ay vayntee*
twenty-five past five	**cinque e venticinque** *cheenkway ay vaynteecheenkway*
half past six	**sei e trenta** *seh-ee ay traynta*
twenty-five to seven	**sette meno venticinque** *sehttay mayno vaynteecheenkway*
twenty to eight	**otto meno venti** *otto mayno vayntee*
a quarter to nine	**nove meno un quarto** *novay mayno oon kwarto*
ten to ten	**dieci meno dieci** *dee-ehchee mayno dee-ehchee*
five to eleven	**undici meno cinque** *oondeechee mayno cheenkway*
It's twelve o'clock (noon/midnight).	**È mezzogiorno/mezzanotte.** *eh maytsojorno/maytsanottay*

at dawn	**all'alba** *all<u>a</u>lba*
in the morning	**al mattino**
	al matt<u>ee</u>no
during the day	**durante il giorno**
	door<u>a</u>ntay eel j<u>o</u>rno
before lunch	**prima di pranzo**
	pr<u>ee</u>ma dee pr<u>a</u>ndzo
after lunch	**dopo pranzo** *d<u>o</u>po pr<u>a</u>ndzo*
in the afternoon	**nel pomeriggio** *nayl pomayr<u>ee</u>djo*
in the evening	**di sera** *dee s<u>a</u>yra*
at night	**di notte** *dee n<u>o</u>ttay*
I'll be ready in five minutes.	**Sarò pronto(-a) fra cinque minuti.**
	sar<u>o</u> pr<u>o</u>nto(-a) fra ch<u>ee</u>nkway meen<u>oo</u>tee
He'll be back in a quarter of an hour.	**Ritorna fra un quarto d'ora.**
	reet<u>o</u>rno fra oon kw<u>a</u>rto d<u>o</u>ra
She arrived half an hour ago.	**È arrivata mezz'ora fa.**
	eh arreev<u>aa</u>ta mayts<u>o</u>ra fa
The train leaves at …	**il treno parte …** *eel tr<u>a</u>yno p<u>a</u>rtay*
13:04	**alle tredici e zero quattro**
	<u>a</u>llay tr<u>a</u>ydeechee ay dz<u>a</u>yro kw<u>a</u>ttro
0:40	**alle zero e quaranta**
	<u>a</u>llay dz<u>a</u>yro ay kwar<u>aa</u>nta
10 minutes late/early	**con dieci minuti di ritardo/di anticipo**
	kon dee-<u>e</u>hchee meen<u>oo</u>tee dee reet<u>aa</u>rdo/dee anteech<u>ee</u>po
5 minutes fast/slow	**cinque minuti avanti/indietro**
	ch<u>ee</u>nkway meen<u>oo</u>tee av<u>aa</u>ntee/ eendee<u>ay</u>tro
from 9:00 to 5:00	**dalle nove alle cinque**
	d<u>a</u>llay n<u>o</u>vay <u>a</u>llay ch<u>ee</u>nkway
between 8:00 and 2:00	**fra le otto e le due**
	fra lay <u>o</u>tto ay lay d<u>oo</u>-ay
I'll be leaving by …	**Partirò entro …** *part<u>ee</u>ro <u>a</u>yntro*
Will you be back before …?	**Ritornerà prima di …?**
	reetornayr<u>a</u> pr<u>ee</u>ma dee
We'll be here until …	**Saremo qui fino alle …**
	sar<u>a</u>ymo kwee f<u>ee</u>no <u>a</u>llay